CHALLENGE
❖
NUMBER TWO

Ten Further Years of Mathematical Challenges

2006 to 2016

The United Kingdom Mathematics Trust

Ten Further Years of Mathematical Challenges

© 2016 United Kingdom Mathematics Trust

All rights reserved. No part of this publication may be reproduced or transmitted in any form or by any means, electronic or mechanical, including photocopy, recording, or any information storage and retrieval system, without permission in writing from the publisher.

Published by The United Kingdom Mathematics Trust.
Maths Challenges Office, School of Mathematics, University of Leeds,
Leeds, LS2 9JT, United Kingdom
http://www.ukmt.org.uk

First published 2016

ISBN 978-1-906001-27-8

Printed in the UK for the UKMT by The Charlesworth Press, Wakefield.
http://www.charlesworth.com

Typographic design by Andrew Jobbings of Arbelos.
http://www.arbelos.co.uk

Typeset with LaTeX.

The books published by the United Kingdom Mathematics Trust are grouped into series.

The EXCURSIONS IN MATHEMATICS series consists of monographs which focus on a particular topic of interest and investigate it in some detail, using a wide range of ideas and techniques. They are aimed at high school students, undergraduates and others who are prepared to pursue a subject in some depth, but do not require specialised knowledge.
1. *The Backbone of Pascal's Triangle*, Martin Griffiths
2. *A Prime Puzzle*, Martin Griffiths

The HANDBOOKS series is aimed particularly at students at secondary school who are interested in acquiring the knowledge and skills which are useful for tackling challenging problems, such as those posed in the competitions administered by the UKMT and similar organisations.
1. *Plane Euclidean Geometry: Theory and Problems*, A D Gardiner and C J Bradley
2. *Introduction to Inequalities*, C J Bradley
3. *A Mathematical Olympiad Primer*, Geoff C Smith
4. *Introduction to Number Theory*, C J Bradley
5. *A Problem Solver's Handbook*, Andrew Jobbings
6. *Introduction to Combinatorics*, Gerry Leversha and Dominic Rowland
7. *First Steps for Problem Solvers*, Mary Teresa Fyfe and Andrew Jobbings
8. *A Mathematical Olympiad Companion*, Geoff C Smith

The PATHWAYS series aims to provide classroom teaching material for use in secondary schools. Each title develops a subject in more depth and in more detail than is normally required by public examinations or national curricula.
1. *Crossing the Bridge*, Gerry Leversha
2. *The Geometry of the Triangle*, Gerry Leversha

❖

The PROBLEMS series consists of collections of high-quality and original problems of Olympiad standard.
1. *New Problems in Euclidean Geometry*, David Monk

The CHALLENGES series is aimed at students at secondary school who are interested in tackling stimulating problems, such as those posed in the Mathematical Challenges administered by the UKMT and similar organisations.

1. *Ten Years of Mathematical Challenges: 1997 to 2006*
2. *Ten Further Years of Mathematical Challenges: 2006 to 2016*
3. *Intermediate Problems*, Andrew Jobbings

The YEARBOOKS series documents all the UKMT activities, including details of all the challenge papers and solutions, lists of high scorers, accounts of the IMO and Olympiad training camps, and other information about the Trust's work during each year.

Contents

Series Editor's Foreword	ix
Preface	xi
Question papers	**1**
Junior Challenge 2007 paper	3
Junior Challenge 2008 paper	7
Junior Challenge 2009 paper	11
Junior Challenge 2010 paper	15
Junior Challenge 2011 paper	19
Junior Challenge 2012 paper	23
Junior Challenge 2013 paper	27
Junior Challenge 2014 paper	31
Junior Challenge 2015 paper	35
Junior Challenge 2016 paper	39
Intermediate Challenge 2007 paper	43
Intermediate Challenge 2008 paper	47

Intermediate Challenge 2009 paper	51
Intermediate Challenge 2010 paper	55
Intermediate Challenge 2011 paper	59
Intermediate Challenge 2012 paper	63
Intermediate Challenge 2013 paper	67
Intermediate Challenge 2014 paper	71
Intermediate Challenge 2015 paper	75
Intermediate Challenge 2016 paper	79
Senior Challenge 2006 paper	83
Senior Challenge 2007 paper	87
Senior Challenge 2008 paper	91
Senior Challenge 2009 paper	95
Senior Challenge 2010 paper	99
Senior Challenge 2011 paper	103
Senior Challenge 2012 paper	107
Senior Challenge 2013 paper	111
Senior Challenge 2014 paper	115
Senior Challenge 2015 paper	119
Answers and solutions	**123**
Junior Challenge 2007 solutions	125
Junior Challenge 2008 solutions	129

Junior Challenge 2009 solutions	133
Junior Challenge 2010 solutions	137
Junior Challenge 2011 solutions	141
Junior Challenge 2012 solutions	145
Junior Challenge 2013 solutions	149
Junior Challenge 2014 solutions	153
Junior Challenge 2015 solutions	157
Junior Challenge 2016 solutions	161
Intermediate Challenge 2007 solutions	165
Intermediate Challenge 2008 solutions	169
Intermediate Challenge 2009 solutions	173
Intermediate Challenge 2010 solutions	177
Intermediate Challenge 2011 solutions	181
Intermediate Challenge 2012 solutions	185
Intermediate Challenge 2013 solutions	189
Intermediate Challenge 2014 solutions	193
Intermediate Challenge 2015 solutions	197
Intermediate Challenge 2016 solutions	201
Senior Challenge 2006 solutions	205
Senior Challenge 2007 solutions	209
Senior Challenge 2008 solutions	213
Senior Challenge 2009 solutions	217

Senior Challenge 2010 solutions	**221**
Senior Challenge 2011 solutions	**225**
Senior Challenge 2012 solutions	**229**
Senior Challenge 2013 solutions	**233**
Senior Challenge 2014 solutions	**237**
Senior Challenge 2015 solutions	**241**

Series Editor's Foreword

This book is part of a series whose aim is to help young mathematicians prepare for competitions at secondary school level. Here the focus is on the questions from the Mathematical Challenge papers. Like other volumes in the Challenges series, it provides cheap and ready access to directly relevant material.

I hope that every secondary school will have these books in its library. The prices have been set low so that many students will wish to purchase their own copies. Schools wishing to give out large numbers of copies of these books, perhaps as prizes, should note that discounts may be negotiated with the UKMT office.

London, UK   GERRY LEVERSHA

Preface

The book includes all thirty of the Mathematical Challenge papers set between autumn 2006 and summer 2016, and their solutions, as they appeared in the booklets sent to schools:

Senior	2006–2015
Intermediate	2007–2016
Junior	2007–2016

Since 2011, extended solutions have also been produced with the aim of providing full solutions with all steps explained. In addition, sometimes alternative solutions are given, as well as exercises for further investigation. These extended solutions are not given in the book, but are available to download after each Challenge from

ukmt.org.uk

Acknowledgements

The quality of the problems used in the Mathematical Challenges is a direct consequence of the hard work and enthusiasm of the members of our excellent Problems Groups. During the period covered by this book, these were most ably chaired by:

JMC	Howard Groves	2007–2016
IMC	Howard Groves	2007–2016
SMC	Howard Groves	2006–2008
	Dean Bunnell	2009–2010
	Howard Groves	2011–2013
	Karen Fogden	2014–2015

It is not possible to give credit to all of the individuals involved in the creation and production of the Challenges, however, this book is dedicated to this amazing team of volunteers.

Leeds, UK

RACHEL GREENHALGH,
UKMT DIRECTOR

Question papers

Junior Challenge 2007 paper

1. What is the value of 0.1 + 0.2 + 0.3 × 0.4?

   A 0.24   B 0.312   C 0.42   D 1.0   E 1.5

2. My train was scheduled to leave at 17:40 and to arrive at 18:20. However, it started five minutes late and the journey then took 42 minutes. At what time did I arrive?

   A 18:21   B 18:23   C 18:25   D 18:27   E 18:29

3. What is the remainder when 354972 is divided by 7 ?

   A 1   B 2   C 3   D 4   E 5

4. Which of the following numbers is three less than a multiple of 5 and three more than a multiple of 6?

   A 12   B 17   C 21   D 22   E 27

5. In the diagram, the small squares are all the same size. What fraction of the large square is shaded?

   A $\frac{9}{20}$ B $\frac{9}{16}$ C $\frac{3}{7}$ D $\frac{3}{5}$ E $\frac{1}{2}$

6. When the following fractions are put in their correct places on the number line, which fraction is in the middle?

   A $-\frac{1}{7}$ B $\frac{1}{6}$ C $-\frac{1}{5}$ D $\frac{1}{4}$ E $-\frac{1}{3}$

7. The equilateral triangle XYZ is fixed in position. Two of the four small triangles are to be painted black and the other two are to be painted white. In how many different ways can this be done?

   A 3   B 4   C 5   D 6   E more than 6

   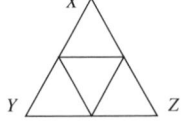

8. Amy, Ben and Chris are standing in a row. If Amy is to the left of Ben and Chris is to the right of Amy, which of these statements must be true?

   A Ben is furthest to the left   B Chris is furthest to the right   C Amy is in the middle
   D Amy is furthest to the left   E None of statements A, B, C, D is true

9. In the diagram on the right, ST is parallel to UV. What is the value of x ?

   A 46   B 48   C 86   D 92   E 94

   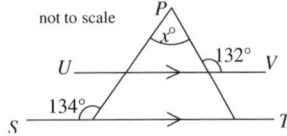

10. Which of the following has the largest value?

   A $\frac{1}{2} + \frac{1}{4}$ B $\frac{1}{2} - \frac{1}{4}$ C $\frac{1}{2} \times \frac{1}{4}$ D $\frac{1}{2} \div \frac{1}{4}$ E $\frac{1}{4} \div \frac{1}{2}$

11. A station clock shows each digit by illuminating up to seven bars in a display. For example, the displays for 1, 6, 4 and 9 are shown. When all the digits from 0 to 9 are shown in turn, which bar is used least?

    A   B   C   D   E

12. The six-member squad for the Ladybirds five-a-side team consists of a 2-spot ladybird, a 10-spot, a 14-spot, an 18-spot, a 24-spot and a pine ladybird (on the bench). The average number of spots for members of the squad is 12. How many spots has the pine ladybird?

    A 4   B 5   C 6   D 7   E 8

13. Points P and Q have coordinates $(1, 4)$ and $(1, -2)$ respectively. For which of the following possible coordinates of point R would triangle PQR **not** be isosceles?

    A $(-5, 4)$ B $(7, 1)$ C $(-6, 1)$ D $(-6, -2)$ E $(7, -2)$

14. If the line on the right were 0.2 mm thick, how many metres long would the line need to be to cover an area of one square metre?

    A 0.5   B 5   C 50   D 500   E 5000

15. I choose three numbers from this number square, including one number from each row and one number from each column. I then multiply the three numbers together. What is the largest possible product?

    A 72   B 96   C 105   D 162   E 504

1	2	3
4	5	6
7	8	9

16. What is the sum of the six marked angles?

    A 1080°   B 1440°   C 1620°   D 1800°   E more information needed

17. Just William's cousin, Sweet William, has a rectangular block of fudge measuring 2 inches by 3 inches by 6 inches. He wants to cut the block up into cubes whose side lengths are whole numbers of inches. What is the smallest number of cubes he can obtain?

    A 3   B 8   C 15   D 29   E 36

18. The letters *J, M, C* represent three different non-zero digits.
    What is the value of *J* + *M* + *C* ?

    A 19   B 18   C 17   D 16   E 15

    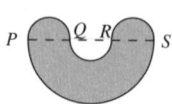

19. The points *P, Q, R, S* lie in order along a straight line, with
    PQ = *QR* = *RS* = 2 cm. Semicircles with diameters *PQ, QR, RS*
    and *SP* join to make the shape shown on the right. What, in cm², is the
    area of the shape?

    A 5π   B 9π/2   C 4π   D 7π/2   E 3π

20. At halftime, Boarwarts Academy had scored all of the points so far in their annual match
    against Range Hill School. In the second half, each side scored three points. At the end of the
    match, Boarwarts Academy had scored 90% of the points. What fraction of the points in the
    match was scored in the second half?

    A $\frac{3}{100}$ B $\frac{3}{50}$ C $\frac{1}{10}$ D $\frac{9}{50}$ E $\frac{1}{5}$

21. A list of ten numbers contains two of each of the numbers 0, 1, 2, 3, 4. The two 0s are next to
    each other, the two 1s are separated by one number, the two 2s by two numbers, the two 3s by
    three numbers and the two 4s by four numbers. The list starts 3, 4, ... What is the last
    number?

    A 0   B 1   C 2   D 3   E 4

22. Only one choice of the digit *d* gives a prime number for each of the three-digit
    numbers read across and downwards in the diagram on the right. Which digit is *d* ?

    A 4   B 5   C 6   D 7   E 8

23. The diagram shows a square with sides of length *y* divided into a
    square with sides of length *x* and four congruent rectangles.
    What is the length of the longer side of each rectangle?

    A $\frac{y-x}{2}$ B $\frac{y+2x}{3}$ C *y* − *x*   D $\frac{2y}{3}$ E $\frac{y+x}{2}$

    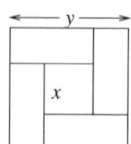

24. The pages of a book are numbered 1, 2, 3, ... In total, it takes 852 digits to number all the
    pages of the book. What is the number of the last page?

    A 215   B 314   C 320   D 329   E 422

25. A piece of paper in the shape of a polygon is folded in half along a line of symmetry. The
    resulting shape is also folded in half, again along a line of symmetry. The final shape is a
    triangle. How many possibilities are there for the number of sides of the original polygon?

    A 3   B 4   C 5   D 6   E 7

Junior Challenge 2008 paper

1. Which of these calculations produces a multiple of 5?

   A 1 × 2 + 3 + 4   B 1 + 2 × 3 + 4   C 1 × 2 + 3 × 4   D 1 + 2 × 3 × 4   E 1 × 2 × 3 × 4

2. Which of these diagrams could be drawn without taking the pen off the page and without drawing along a line already drawn?

3. All of the Forty Thieves were light-fingered, but only two of them were caught red-handed. What percentage is that?

   A 2   B 5   C 10   D 20   E 50

4. In this diagram, what is the value of x?

   A 16   B 36   C 64   D 100   E 144

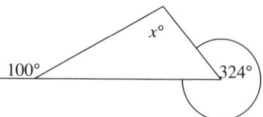

5. At Spuds-R-Us, a 2.5kg bag of potatoes costs £1.25. How much would one tonne of potatoes cost?

   A £5   B £20   C £50   D £200   E £500

6. The diagram shows a single floor tile in which the outer square has side 8cm and the inner square has side 6cm. If Adam Ant walks once around the perimeter of the inner square and Annabel Ant walks once around the perimeter of the outer square, how much further does Annabel walk than Adam?

   A 2 cm   B 4 cm   C 6 cm   D 8 cm   E 16 cm

7. King Harry's arm is twice as long as his forearm, which is twice as long as his hand, which is twice as long as his middle finger, which is twice as long as his thumb. His new bed is as long as four arms. How many thumbs length is that?

   A 16   B 32   C 64   D 128   E 256

8. The shape on the right is made up of three rectangles, each measuring 3cm by 1cm. What is the perimeter of the shape?

   A 16 cm   B 18 cm   C 20 cm   D 24 cm   E More information needed

9. Which of the following has the smallest value?

   A $\dfrac{1}{2} - \dfrac{1}{3}$ B $\dfrac{1}{3} - \dfrac{1}{4}$ C $\dfrac{1}{4} - \dfrac{1}{5}$ D $\dfrac{1}{5} - \dfrac{1}{6}$ E $\dfrac{1}{6} - \dfrac{1}{7}$

Junior Challenge 2008 paper

10. The faces of a cube are painted so that any two faces which have an edge in common are painted different colours. What is the smallest number of colours required?

   A 2   B 3   C 4   D 5   E 6

11. In 1833 a ship arrived in Calcutta with 120 tons remaining of its cargo of ice. One third of the original cargo was lost because it had melted on the voyage. How many tons of ice was the ship carrying when it set sail?

   A 40   B 80   C 120   D 150   E 180

12. The sculpture 'Cubo Vazado' [Emptied Cube] by the Brazilian artist Franz Weissmann is formed by removing cubical blocks from a solid cube to leave the symmetrical shape shown.
   If all the edges have length 1, 2 or 3, what is the volume of the sculpture?

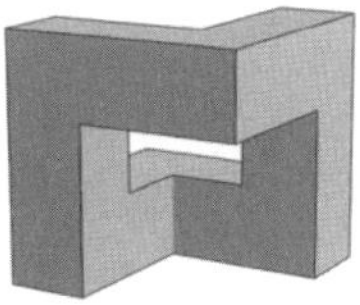

   A 9   B 11   C 12   D 14   E 18

13. A rectangle *PQRS* is cut into two pieces along *PX*, where *PX* = *XR* and *PS* = *SX* as shown. The two pieces are reassembled without turning either piece over, by matching two edges of equal length. Not counting the original rectangle, how many different shapes are possible?

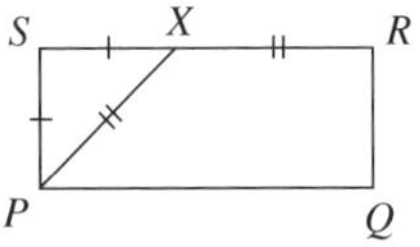

   A 1   B 2   C 3   D 4   E 5

14. A solid wooden cube is painted blue on the outside. The cube is then cut into eight smaller cubes of equal size. What fraction of the total surface area of these new cubes is blue?

   A $\dfrac{1}{8}$ B $\dfrac{1}{3}$ C $\dfrac{3}{8}$ D $\dfrac{1}{2}$ E $\dfrac{3}{4}$

15. An active sphagnum bog deposits a depth of about 1 metre of peat per 1000 years. Roughly how many millimetres is that per day?

   A 0.0003   B 0.003   C 0.03   D 0.3   E 3

16. The figures below are all drawn to scale. Which figure would result from repeatedly following the instructions in the box on the right?

   Move forward 2 units.
   Turn right.
   Move forward 15 units.
   Turn right.
   Move forward 20 units.
   Turn right.

   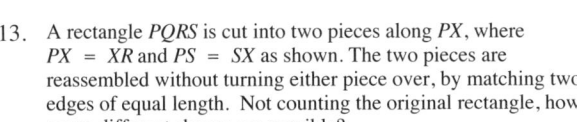

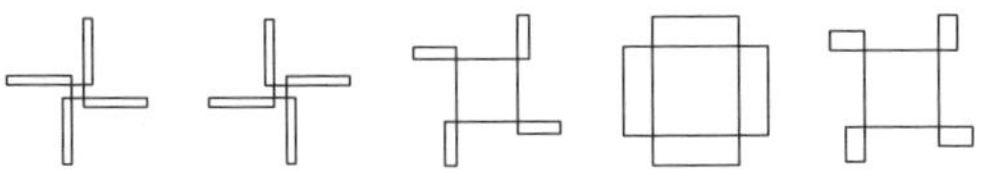

   A   B   C   D   E

17. In this *Multiplication Magic Square*, the **product** of the three numbers in each row, each column and each of the diagonals is 1. What is the value of *r* + *s*?

p	q	r
s	1	t
u	4	$\frac{1}{8}$

   A $\dfrac{1}{2}$ B $\dfrac{9}{16}$ C $\dfrac{5}{4}$ D $\dfrac{33}{16}$ E 24

18. Granny swears that she is getting younger. She has calculated that she is four times as old as I am now, but remembers that 5 years ago she was five times as old as I was at that time. What is the sum of our ages now?

    A 95   B 100   C 105   D 110   E 115

19. In the diagram on the right, $PT = QT = TS$, $QS = SR$, $\angle PQT = 20°$. What is the value of x?

    A 20   B 25   C 30   D 35   E 40

    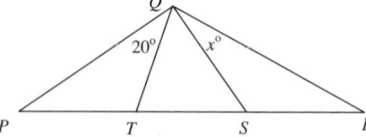

20. If all the whole numbers from 1 to 1000 inclusive are written down, which digit appears the smallest number of times?

    A 0   B 2   C 5   D 9   E none: no single digit appears fewer times than all the others

21. What is the value of ♥ if each row and each column has the total given?

			Total
♥	☼	♪	12
♪	♥	♥	11
☼	☼	♪	13
Total 12	11	13	

    A 3   B 4   C 5   D 6   E more information needed

22. On a digital clock displaying hours, minutes and seconds, how many times in each 24-hour period do all six digits change simultaneously?

    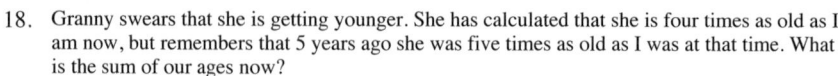

    A 0   B 1   C 2   D 3   E 24

23. In a 7-digit numerical code each group of four adjacent digits adds to 16 and each group of five adjacent digits adds to 19. What is the sum of all seven digits?

    A 21   B 25   C 28   D 32   E 35

24. The list 2, 1; 3, 2; 2, 3; 1, 4; describes itself, since there are two 1s, three 2s, two 3s and one 4. There is exactly one other list of eight numbers containing only the numbers 1, 2, 3, and 4 that, in the same way, describes the numbers of 1s, 2s, 3s and 4s in that order. What is the total number of 1s and 3s in this other list?

    A 2   B 3   C 4   D 5   E 6

25. A large square is divided into adjacent pairs of smaller squares with integer sides, as shown in the diagram (which is not drawn to scale). Each size of smaller square occurs only twice. The shaded square has sides of length 10. What is the area of the large square?

    A 1024   B 1089   C 1156   D 1296   E 1444

    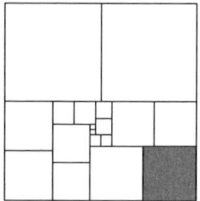

Junior Challenge 2009 paper

1. What is the value of 9002 − 2009?

   A 9336   B 6993   C 6339   D 3996   E 3669

2. How many of the six faces of a die (shown below) have fewer than three lines of symmetry?

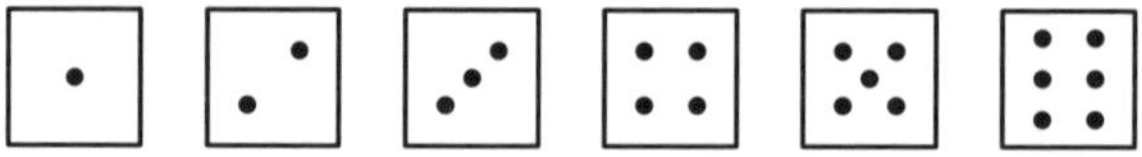

   A 2   B 3   C 4   D 5   E 6

3. Which of the following is correct?

   A 0 × 9 + 9 × 0 = 9   B 1 × 8 + 8 × 1 = 18   C 2 × 7 + 7 × 2 = 27
   D 3 × 6 + 6 × 3 = 36   E 4 × 5 + 5 × 4 = 45

4. Which of the following points is *not* at a distance of 1 unit from the origin?

   A (0, 1)   B (1, 0)   C (0, −1)   D (−1, 0)   E (1, 1)

5. Which of the following numbers is divisible by 7?

   A 111   B 1111   C 11 111   D 111 111   E 1 111 111

6. Each square in the figure is 1 unit by 1 unit. What is the area of triangle *ABM* (in square units)?

   A 4   B 4.5   C 5   D 5.5   E 6

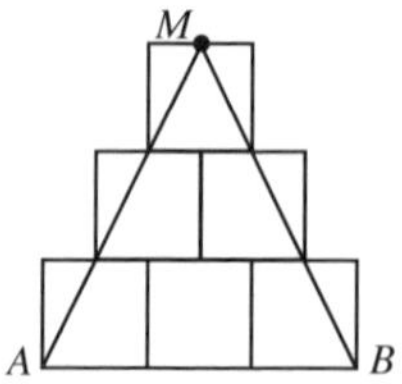

7. How many minutes are there from 11:11 until 23:23 on the same day?

   A 12   B 720   C 732   D 1212   E 7212

8. The figure on the right shows an arrangement of ten square tiles. Which labelled tile could be removed, but still leave the length of the perimeter unchanged?

   A   B   C   D   E

   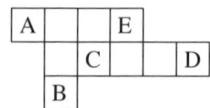

9. How many different digits appear when $\frac{20}{11}$ is written as a recurring decimal?

   A 2   B 3   C 4   D 5   E 6

Junior Challenge 2009 paper

10. The diagram shows three squares of the same size. What is the value of x?

    A 105   B 120   C 135   D 150   E 165

11. In a sequence of numbers, each term after the first three terms is the sum of the previous three terms. The first three terms are $-3, 0, 2$. Which is the first term to exceed 100?

    A 11th term   B 12th term   C 13th term   D 14th term   E 15th term

12. Gill is 21 this year. At the famous visit to the clinic in 1988, her weight was calculated to be 5kg, but she now weighs 50kg. What has been the percentage increase in Gill's weight from 1988 to 2009?

    A 900%   B 1000%   C 5000%   D 9000%   E 10 000%

13. The sum of ten consecutive integers is 5. What is the largest of these integers?

    A 2   B 3   C 4   D 5   E more information needed

14. Karen was given a mark of 72 for Mayhematics. Her average mark for Mayhematics and Mathemagics was 78. What was her mark for Mathemagics?

    A 66   B 75   C 78   D 82   E 84

15. In Matt's pocket there are 8 watermelon jellybeans, 4 vanilla jellybeans and 4 butter popcorn jellybeans. What is the smallest number of jellybeans he must take out of his pocket to be certain that he takes at least one of each flavour?

    A 3   B 4   C 8   D 9   E 13

16. The kettle in Keith's kitchen is 80% full. After 20% of the water in it has been poured out, there are 1152 ml of water left. What volume of water does Keith's kitchen kettle hold when it is full?

    A 1400 ml   B 1600 ml   C 1700 ml   D 1800 ml   E 2000 ml

17. The tiling pattern shown uses two sizes of square, with sides of length 1 and 4. A very large number of these squares is used to tile an enormous floor in this pattern. Which of the following is closest to the ratio of the number of grey tiles on the floor to the number of white tiles?

    A 1:1   B 4:3   C 3:2   D 2:1   E 4:1

18. Six friends are having dinner together in their local restaurant. The first eats there every day, the second eats there every other day, the third eats there every third day, the fourth eats there every fourth day, the fifth eats there every fifth day and the sixth eats there every sixth day. They agree to have a party the next time they all eat together there. In how many days' time is the party?

    A 30 days   B 60 days   C 90 days   D 120 days   E 360 days

19. The diagram on the right shows a rhombus *FGHI* and an isosceles triangle *FGJ* in which *GF* = *GJ*. Angle *FJI* = 111°.
    What is the size of angle *JFI* ?

    A 27°   B 29°   C 31°   D 33°   E 34½°

20. In the diagram on the right, the number in each box is obtained by adding the numbers in the two boxes immediately underneath. What is the value of *x*?

    A 300   B 320   C 340
    D 360   E more information needed

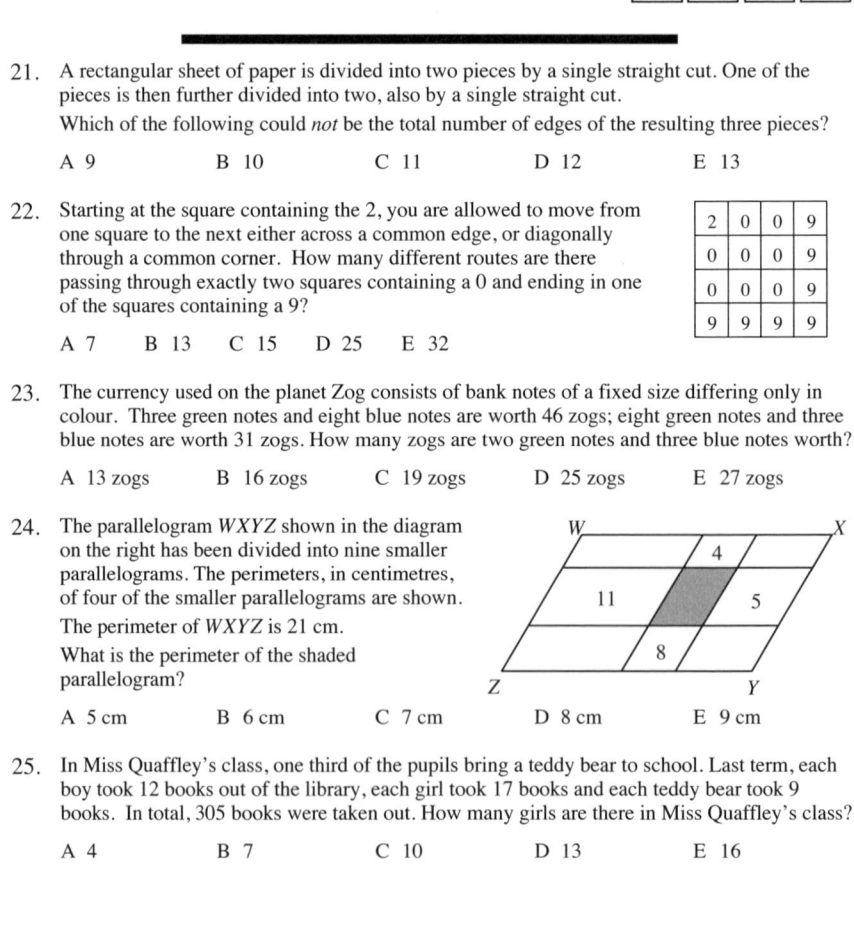

21. A rectangular sheet of paper is divided into two pieces by a single straight cut. One of the pieces is then further divided into two, also by a single straight cut.
    Which of the following could *not* be the total number of edges of the resulting three pieces?

    A 9   B 10   C 11   D 12   E 13

22. Starting at the square containing the 2, you are allowed to move from one square to the next either across a common edge, or diagonally through a common corner. How many different routes are there passing through exactly two squares containing a 0 and ending in one of the squares containing a 9?

    A 7   B 13   C 15   D 25   E 32

23. The currency used on the planet Zog consists of bank notes of a fixed size differing only in colour. Three green notes and eight blue notes are worth 46 zogs; eight green notes and three blue notes are worth 31 zogs. How many zogs are two green notes and three blue notes worth?

    A 13 zogs   B 16 zogs   C 19 zogs   D 25 zogs   E 27 zogs

24. The parallelogram *WXYZ* shown in the diagram on the right has been divided into nine smaller parallelograms. The perimeters, in centimetres, of four of the smaller parallelograms are shown. The perimeter of *WXYZ* is 21 cm.
    What is the perimeter of the shaded parallelogram?

    A 5 cm   B 6 cm   C 7 cm   D 8 cm   E 9 cm

25. In Miss Quaffley's class, one third of the pupils bring a teddy bear to school. Last term, each boy took 12 books out of the library, each girl took 17 books and each teddy bear took 9 books. In total, 305 books were taken out. How many girls are there in Miss Quaffley's class?

    A 4   B 7   C 10   D 13   E 16

Junior Challenge 2010 paper

1. What is 2010 + (+2010) + (−2010) − (+2010) − (−2010) ?

   A 0   B 2010   C 4020   D 6030   E 8040

2. Each letter in the abbreviation shown is rotated through 90° clockwise. **U K M T**
   Which of the following could be the result?

   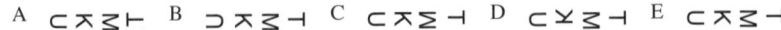

3. Which of the following could have a length of 2010 mm?

   A a table   B an oil tanker   C a teaspoon   D a school hall   E a hen's egg

4. If the net shown is folded to make a cube, which letter is opposite X?

   A   B   C   D   E

5. The diagram shows a pattern of 16 circles inside a square. The central circle passes through the points where the other circles touch.
   The circles divide the square into regions. How many regions are there?

   A 17   B 26   C 30   D 32   E 38

   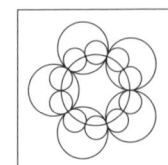

6. Which of the following has the largest value?

   A $6 \div \frac{1}{2}$ B $5 \div \frac{1}{3}$ C $4 \div \frac{1}{4}$ D $3 \div \frac{1}{5}$ E $2 \div \frac{1}{6}$

7. Mr Owens wants to keep the students quiet during a Mathematics lesson. He asks them to multiply all the numbers from 1 to 99 together and then tell him the last-but-one digit of the result. What is the correct answer?

   A 0   B 1   C 2   D 8   E 9

8. In a triangle with angles $x°$, $y°$, $z°$ the mean of y and z is x.
   What is the value of x?

   A 90   B 80   C 70   D 60   E 50

   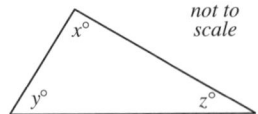

9. Which of the following is the longest period of time?

   A 3002 hours   B 125 days   C $17\frac{1}{2}$ weeks   D 4 months   E $\frac{1}{3}$ of a year

10. At the Marldon Apple-Pie-Fayre bake-off, prize money is awarded for 1st, 2nd and 3rd places in the ratio 3 : 2 : 1. Last year Mrs Keat and Mr Jewell shared third prize equally. What fraction of the total prize money did Mrs Keat receive?

    A $\frac{1}{4}$ B $\frac{1}{5}$ C $\frac{1}{6}$ D $\frac{1}{10}$ E $\frac{1}{12}$

Junior Challenge 2010 paper

11. In the diagram shown, all the angles are right angles and all the sides are of length 1 unit, 2 units or 3 units.
What, in square units, is the area of the shaded region?

    A 22   B 24   C 26   D 28   E 30

12. Sir Lance has a lot of tables and chairs in his house. Each rectangular table seats eight people and each round table seats five people. What is the smallest number of tables he will need to use to seat 35 guests and himself, without any of the seating around these tables remaining unoccupied?

    A 4   B 5   C 6   D 7   E 8

13. The diagram shows a Lusona, a sand picture of the Tshokwe people from the West Central Bantu area of Africa. To draw a Lusona the artist uses a stick to draw a single line in the sand, starting and ending in the same place without lifting the stick in between. At which point could this Lusona have started?

    A   B   C   D   E

14. The Severn Bridge has carried just over 300 million vehicles since it was opened in 1966. On average, roughly how many vehicles is this per day?

    A 600   B 2 000   C 6 000   D 20 000   E 60 000

15. A 6 by 8 and a 7 by 9 rectangle overlap with one corner coinciding as shown.
What is the area (in square units) of the region *outside* the overlap?

    A 6   B 21   C 27   D 42   E 69

16. One of the examination papers for Amy's Advanced Arithmetic Award was worth 18% of the final total. The maximum possible mark on this paper was 108 marks. How many marks were available overall?

    A 420   B 480   C 540   D 560   E 600

17. The lengths, in cm, of the sides of the equilateral triangle PQR are as shown.
Which of the following could *not* be the values of x and y?

    A (18, 12)   B (15, 10)   C (12, 8)   D (10, 6)   E (3, 2)

18. Sam's 101st birthday is tomorrow. So Sam's age in years changes from a square number (100) to a prime number (101). How many times has this happened before in Sam's lifetime?

    A 1   B 2   C 3   D 4   E 5

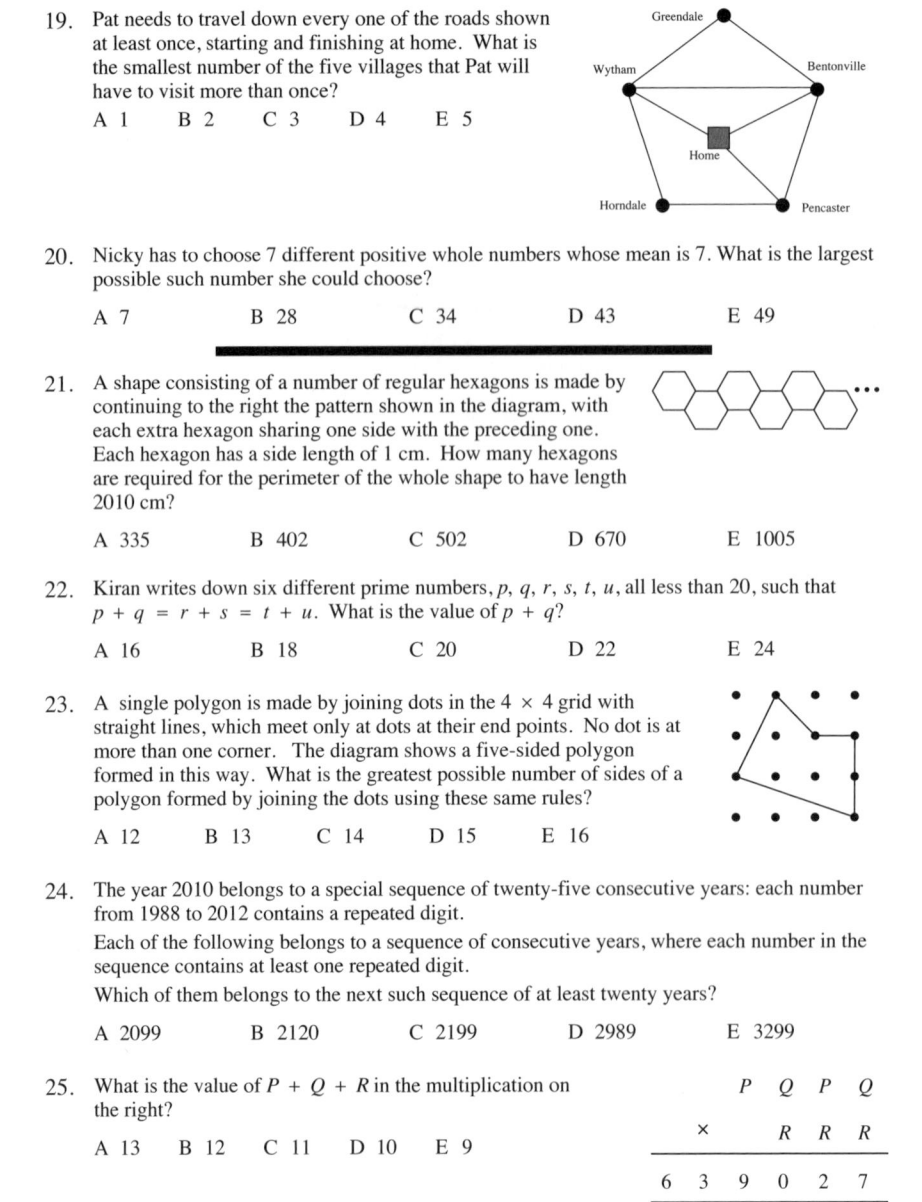

19. Pat needs to travel down every one of the roads shown at least once, starting and finishing at home. What is the smallest number of the five villages that Pat will have to visit more than once?

    A 1   B 2   C 3   D 4   E 5

20. Nicky has to choose 7 different positive whole numbers whose mean is 7. What is the largest possible such number she could choose?

    A 7   B 28   C 34   D 43   E 49

21. A shape consisting of a number of regular hexagons is made by continuing to the right the pattern shown in the diagram, with each extra hexagon sharing one side with the preceding one. Each hexagon has a side length of 1 cm. How many hexagons are required for the perimeter of the whole shape to have length 2010 cm?

    A 335   B 402   C 502   D 670   E 1005

22. Kiran writes down six different prime numbers, p, q, r, s, t, u, all less than 20, such that $p + q = r + s = t + u$. What is the value of $p + q$?

    A 16   B 18   C 20   D 22   E 24

23. A single polygon is made by joining dots in the 4 × 4 grid with straight lines, which meet only at dots at their end points. No dot is at more than one corner. The diagram shows a five-sided polygon formed in this way. What is the greatest possible number of sides of a polygon formed by joining the dots using these same rules?

    A 12   B 13   C 14   D 15   E 16

24. The year 2010 belongs to a special sequence of twenty-five consecutive years: each number from 1988 to 2012 contains a repeated digit.

    Each of the following belongs to a sequence of consecutive years, where each number in the sequence contains at least one repeated digit.

    Which of them belongs to the next such sequence of at least twenty years?

    A 2099   B 2120   C 2199   D 2989   E 3299

25. What is the value of $P + Q + R$ in the multiplication on the right?

    A 13   B 12   C 11   D 10   E 9

```
      P Q P Q
    ×       R
    ─────────
    R R 
    6 3 9 0 2 7
```

Junior Challenge 2011 paper

1. What is the value of 2 × 0 × 1 + 1 ?

   A 0   B 1   C 2   D 3   E 4

2. How many of the integers 123, 234, 345, 456, 567 are multiples of 3?

   A 1   B 2   C 3   D 4   E 5

3. A train display shows letters by lighting cells in a grid, such as the letter 'o' shown. A letter is made **bold** by also lighting any unlit cell immediately to the right of one in the normal letter. How many cells are lit in a **bold** 'o'?

   A 22   B 24   C 26   D 28   E 30

4. The world's largest coin, made by the Royal Mint of Canada, was auctioned in June 2010. The coin has mass 100 kg, whereas a standard British £1 coin has mass 10 g. What sum of money in £1 coins has the same mass as the record-breaking coin?

   A £100   B £1000   C £10 000   D £100 000   E £1 000 000

5. All old Mother Hubbard had in her cupboard was a Giant Bear chocolate bar. She gave each of her children one-twelfth of the chocolate bar. One third of the bar was left. How many children did she have?

   A 6   B 8   C 12   D 15   E 18

6. What is the sum of the marked angles in the diagram?

   A 90°   B 180°   C 240°   D 300°   E 360°

7. Peter Piper picked a peck of pickled peppers. 1 peck = $\frac{1}{4}$ bushel and 1 bushel = $\frac{1}{9}$ barrel. How many **more** pecks must Peter Piper pick to fill a barrel?

   A 12   B 13   C 34   D 35   E 36

8. A square is divided into three congruent rectangles. The middle rectangle is removed and replaced on the side of the original square to form an octagon as shown. What is the ratio of the length of the perimeter of the square to the length of the perimeter of the octagon?

   A 3:5   B 2:3   C 5:8   D 1:2   E 1:1

Junior Challenge 2011 paper   21

9. What is the smallest possible difference between two different nine-digit integers, each of which includes all of the digits 1 to 9?

   A 9   B 18   C 27   D 36   E 45

10. You want to draw the shape on the right without taking your pen off the paper and without going over any line more than once. Where should you start?

    A only at T or Q B only at P C only at S or R
    D at any point   E the task is impossible

11. The diagram shows an equilateral triangle inside a rectangle. What is the value of $x + y$?

    A 30   B 45   C 60   D 75   E 90

12. If ▲+▲=■ and ■+▲=● and ♦=●+■+▲, how many ▲s are equal to ♦?

    A 2   B 3   C 4   D 5   E 6

13. What is the mean of $\frac{2}{3}$ and $\frac{4}{9}$?

    A $\frac{1}{2}$ B $\frac{2}{9}$ C $\frac{7}{9}$ D $\frac{3}{4}$ E $\frac{5}{9}$

14. The diagram shows a cuboid in which the area of the shaded face is one-quarter of the area of each of the two visible unshaded faces. The total surface area of the cuboid is 72 cm². What, in cm², is the area of one of the visible unshaded faces of the cuboid?

    A 16   B 28.8   C 32   D 36   E 48

15. What is the smallest number of *additional* squares which must be shaded so that this figure has at least one line of symmetry *and* rotational symmetry of order 2?

    A 3   B 5   C 7   D 9   E more than 9

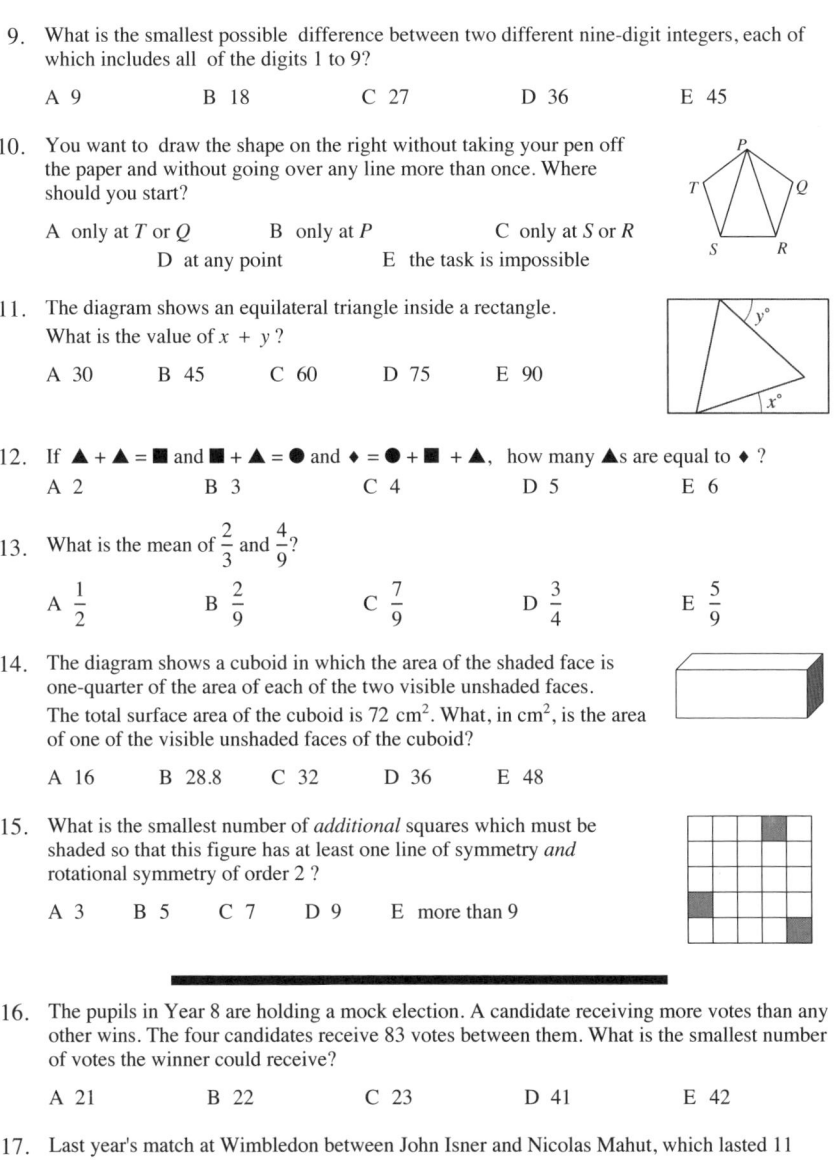

16. The pupils in Year 8 are holding a mock election. A candidate receiving more votes than any other wins. The four candidates receive 83 votes between them. What is the smallest number of votes the winner could receive?

    A 21   B 22   C 23   D 41   E 42

17. Last year's match at Wimbledon between John Isner and Nicolas Mahut, which lasted 11 hours and 5 minutes, set a record for the longest match in tennis history. The fifth set of the match lasted 8 hours and 11 minutes.
    Approximately what fraction of the whole match was taken up by the fifth set?

    A $\frac{1}{5}$ B $\frac{2}{5}$ C $\frac{3}{5}$ D $\frac{3}{4}$ E $\frac{9}{10}$

18. Peri the winkle leaves on Monday to go and visit Granny, 90m away. Except for rest days, Peri travels 1m each day (24-hour period) at a constant rate and without pause. However, Peri stops for a 24-hour rest every tenth day, that is, after every nine days' travelling. On which day of the week does Peri arrive at Granny's?

    A Sunday   B Monday   C Tuesday   D Wednesday   E Thursday

19. A list is made of every digit that is the units digit of at least one prime number. How many of the following numbers appear in the list?

    A 1   B 2   C 3   D 4   E 5

20. One cube has each of its faces covered by one face of an identical cube, making a solid as shown. The volume of the solid is 875 cm^3. What, in cm^2, is the surface area of the solid?

    A 750   B 800   C 875   D 900   E 1050

21. Gill leaves Lille by train at 09:00. The train travels the first 27 km at 96 km/h. It then stops at Lens for 3 minutes before travelling the final 29 km to Lillers at 96 km/h. At what time does Gill arrive at Lillers?

    A 09:35   B 09:38   C 09:40   D 09:41   E 09:43

22. Last week Evariste and Sophie both bought some stamps for their collections. Each stamp Evariste bought cost him £1.10, whilst Sophie paid 70p for each of her stamps. Between them they spent exactly £10. How many stamps did they buy in total?

    A 9   B 10   C 11   D 12   E 13

23. The points S, T, U lie on the sides of the triangle PQR, as shown, so that $QS = QU$ and $RS = RT$. $\angle TSU = 40°$. What is the size of $\angle TPU$?

    A 60°   B 70°   C 80°   D 90°   E 100°

24. Two adults and two children wish to cross a river. They make a raft but it will carry only the weight of one adult or two children. What is the minimum number of times the raft must cross the river to get all four people to the other side? (N.B. The raft may not cross the river without at least one person on board.)

    A 3   B 5   C 7   D 9   E 11

25. The diagram shows a trapezium made from three equilateral triangles. Three copies of the trapezium are placed together, without gaps or overlaps and so that only complete edges coincide, to form a polygon with N sides.
    How many different values of N are possible?

    A 4   B 5   C 6   D 7   E 8

Junior Challenge 2012 paper

1. What is the smallest four-digit positive integer which has four different digits?

   A 1032   B 2012   C 1021   D 1234   E 1023

2. What is half of 1.01?

   A 5.5   B 0.55   C 0.505   D 0.5005   E 0.055

3. Which of the following has exactly one factor other than 1 and itself?

   A 6   B 8   C 13   D 19   E 25

4. Beatrix looks at the word JUNIOR in a mirror.
   How many of the reflected letters never look the same as the original, no matter how Beatrix holds the mirror?

   A 1   B 2   C 3   D 4   E 5

5. One of the mascots for the 2012 Olympic Games is called 'Wenlock' because the town of Wenlock in Shropshire first held the Wenlock Olympian Games in 1850. How many years ago was that?

   A 62   B 152   C 158   D 162   E 172

6. The diagrams on the right show three different views of the same cube. Which letter is on the face opposite U?

   A I   B P   C K   D M   E O

7. A small ink cartridge has enough ink to print 600 pages. Three small cartridges can print as many pages as two medium cartridges. Three medium cartridges can print as many pages as two large cartridges. How many pages can be printed using a large cartridge?

   A 1200   B 1350   C 1800   D 2400   E 5400

8. Tommy Thomas's tankard holds 480ml when it is one quarter empty. How much does it hold when it is one quarter full?

   A 120 ml   B 160 ml   C 240 ml   D 960 ml   E 1440 ml

9. The diagram on the right shows the positions of four people (each marked ×) in an Art Gallery. In the middle of the room is a stone column. Ali can see none of the other three people. Bea can see only Caz. Caz can see Bea and Dan. Dan can see only Caz.
   Who is at position *P*?

   A Ali   B Bea   C Caz
              D Dan   E More information needed

10. The diagram shows two arrows drawn on separate 4 cm × 4 cm grids. One arrow points North and the other points West.
    When the two arrows are drawn on the same 4 cm × 4 cm grid (still pointing North and West) they overlap. What is the area of overlap?

    A 4 cm²   B 4½ cm²   C 5 cm²   D 5½ cm²   E 6 cm²

11. In the following expression, each ☐ is to be replaced with either + or − in such a way that the result of the calculation is 100.

$$123 \; \square \; 45 \; \square \; 67 \; \square \; 89$$

The number of + signs used is p and the number of − signs used is m. What is the value of $p - m$?

   A −3   B −1   C 0   D 1   E 3

12. Laura wishes to cut this shape, which is made up of nine small squares, into pieces that she can then rearrange to make a 3 × 3 square.
   What is the smallest number of pieces that she needs to cut the shape into so that she can do this?

   A 2   B 3   C 4   D 5   E 6

13. In the multiplication grid on the right, the input factors (in the first row and the first column) are all missing and only some of the products within the table have been given.
   What is the value of $A + B + C + D + E$?

   A 132   B 145   C 161   D 178   E 193

×				
	A	10		20
	15	B	40	
	18		C	60
		20		D	24
			56		E

14. A pattern that repeats every six symbols starts as shown below:

   ♥ ♣ ♥ ♦ ♥ ♠ ♥ ♣ ♥ ♦ ♥ ♠ ...

   Which are the 100th and 101st symbols, in that order, in the pattern?

   A ♦ ♥   B ♥ ♦   C ♥ ♣   D ♠ ♥   E ♣ ♥

15. Talulah plants 60 tulip bulbs. When they flower, she notes that half are yellow; one third of those which are not yellow are red; and one quarter of those which are neither yellow nor red are pink. The remainder are white. What fraction of the tulips are white?

   A $\frac{1}{24}$ B $\frac{1}{12}$ C $\frac{1}{6}$ D $\frac{1}{5}$ E $\frac{1}{4}$

16. Beth, Carolyn and George love reading their favourite bedtime story together. They take it in turns to read a page, always in the order Beth, then Carolyn, then George. All twenty pages of the story are read on each occasion. One evening, Beth is staying at Grandma's house but Carolyn and George still read the same bedtime story and take it in turns to read a page with Carolyn reading the first page.
   In total, how many pages are read by the person who usually reads that page?

   A 1   B 2   C 4   D 6   E 7

17. There are six more girls than boys in Miss Spelling's class of 24 pupils. What is the ratio of girls to boys in this class?

   A 5:3   B 4:1   C 3:1   D 1:4   E 3:5

18. The numbers 2, 3, 4, 5, 6, 7, 8 are to be placed, one per square, in the diagram shown such that the four numbers in the horizontal row add up to 21 and the four numbers in the vertical column also add up to 21. Which number should replace x?

    A 2   B 3   C 5   D 7   E 8

19. In rectangle *PQRS*, the ratio of $\angle PSQ$ to $\angle PQS$ is 1:5. What is the size of $\angle QSR$?

    A $15°$ B $18°$ C $45°$ D $72°$ E $75°$

20. Aroon says his age is 50 years, 50 months, 50 weeks and 50 days old. What age will he be on his next birthday?

    A 56   B 55   C 54   D 53   E 51

21. Dominic wants to place the six dominoes above in a hexagonal ring so that, for every pair of adjacent dominoes, the numbers of pips match. The ring on the right indicates how one adjacent pair match.
    In a completed ring, how many of the other five dominoes can he definitely *not* place adjacent to [·|∴] ?

    A 1   B 2   C 3   D 4   E 5

22. The diagram shows a design formed by drawing six lines in a regular hexagon. The lines divide each edge of the hexagon into three equal parts.
    What fraction of the hexagon is shaded?

    A $\dfrac{1}{5}$ B $\dfrac{2}{9}$ C $\dfrac{1}{4}$ D $\dfrac{3}{10}$ E $\dfrac{5}{16}$

23. Peter wrote a list of all the numbers that could be produced by changing one digit of the number 200. How many of the numbers on Peter's list are prime?

    A 0   B 1   C 2   D 3   E 4

24. After playing 500 games, my success rate at Spider Solitaire is 49%. Assuming I win every game from now on, how many extra games do I need to play in order that my success rate increases to 50%?

    A 1   B 2   C 5   D 10   E 50

25. The interior angles of a triangle are $(5x + 3y)°$, $(3x + 20)°$ and $(10y + 30)°$ where x, y are positive integers.
    What is the value of $x + y$?

    A 15   B 14   C 13   D 12   E 11

Junior Challenge 2013 paper

1. Which of the following has the largest value?

   A 1 − 0.1   B 1 − 0.01   C 1 − 0.001   D 1 − 0.0001   E 1 − 0.00001

2. Heidi is 2.1 m tall, while Lola is only 1.4 m tall. What is their average height?

   A 1.525 m   B 1.6 m   C 1.7 m   D 1.725 m   E 1.75 m

3. What is the value of x?

   A 25   B 35   C 40   D 65   E 155

4. Gill went for a five-hour walk. Her average speed was between 3 km/h and 4 km/h. Which of the following could be the distance she walked?

   A 12 km   B 14 km   C 19 km   D 24 km   E 35 km

5. The diagram shows a weaver's design for a *rihlèlò*, a winnowing tray from Mozambique.
   How many lines of symmetry does the design have?

   A 0   B 1   C 2   D 4   E 8

6. What is the value of $((1-1)-1)-(1-(1-1))$?

   A −2   B −1   C 0   D 1   E 2

7. After tennis training, Andy collects twice as many balls as Roger and five more than Maria. They collect 35 balls in total. How many balls does Andy collect?

   A 20   B 19   C 18   D 16   E 8

8. Two identical rulers are placed together, as shown (not to scale).
   Each ruler is exactly 10 cm long and is marked in centimetres from 0 to 10. The 3 cm mark on each ruler is aligned with the 4 cm mark on the other.

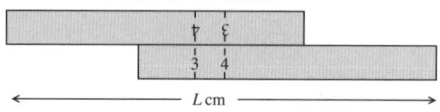

   The overall length is L cm. What is the value of L?

   A 13   B 14   C 15   D 16   E 17

9. Peter has three times as many sisters as brothers. His sister Louise has twice as many sisters as brothers. How many children are there in the family?

   A 15   B 13   C 11   D 9   E 5

10. On standard dice the total number of pips on each pair of opposite faces is 7. Two standard dice are placed in a stack, as shown, so that the total number of pips on the two touching faces is 5. What is the total number of pips on the top and bottom faces of the stack?

    A 5   B 6   C 7   D 8   E 9

11. Usain runs twice as fast as his mum. His mum runs five times as fast as his pet tortoise, Turbo. They all set off together for a run down the same straight path. When Usain has run 100 m, how far apart are his mum and Turbo the tortoise?

    A 5 m   B 10 m   C 40 m   D 50 m   E 55 m

12. How many hexagons are there in the diagram?

    A 4   B 6   C 8   D 10   E 12

13. When painting the lounge, I used half of a 3 litre can to complete the first coat of paint. I then used two thirds of what was left to complete the second coat. How much paint was left after both coats were complete?

    A 150 ml   B 200 ml   C 250 ml   D 500 ml   E 600 ml

14. Each side of an isosceles triangle is a whole number of centimetres. Its perimeter has length 20 cm. How many possibilities are there for the lengths of its sides?

    A 3   B 4   C 5   D 6   E 7

15. The Grand Old Duke of York had 10 000 men. He lost 10% of them on the way to the top of the hill, and he lost 15% of the rest as he marched them back down the hill. What percentage of the 10 000 men were still there when they reached the bottom of the hill?

    A $76\frac{1}{2}\%$ B 75%   C $73\frac{1}{2}\%$ D $66\frac{2}{3}\%$ E 25%

16. Ulysses, Kim, Mei and Tanika have their 12th, 14th, 15th and 15th birthdays today. In what year will their ages first total 100?

    A 2023   B 2024   C 2025   D 2057   E 2113

17. A 5 cm × 5 cm square is cut into five pieces, as shown. Each cut is a sequence of identical copies of the same shape but pointing up, down, left or right. Which piece has the longest perimeter?

    A   B   C   D   E

18. Weighing the baby at the clinic was a problem. The baby would not keep still and caused the scales to wobble. So I held the baby and stood on the scales while the nurse read off 78 kg. Then the nurse held the baby while I read off 69 kg. Finally I held the nurse while the baby read off 137 kg. What was the combined weight of all three ?

    A 142 kg   B 147 kg   C 206 kg   D 215 kg   E 284 kg

    (*This problem appeared in the first Schools' Mathematical Challenge in 1988 – 25 years ago.*)

19. A swimming club has three categories of members: junior, senior, veteran. The ratio of junior to senior members is 3 : 2 and the ratio of senior members to veterans is 5 : 2.
    Which of the following could be the total number of members in the swimming club?

    A 30   B 35   C 48   D 58   E 60

20. A 'long knight' moves on a square grid. A single move, as shown, consists of moving three squares in one direction (horizontally or vertically) and then one square at right angles to the first direction. What is the smallest number of moves a long knight requires to go from one corner of an 8 × 8 square board to the diagonally opposite corner?

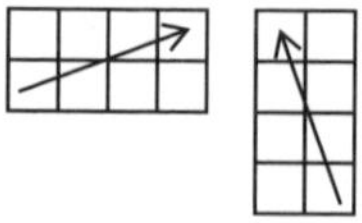

    A 4   B 5   C 6   D 7   E 8

21. The 5 × 4 grid is divided into blocks. Each block is a square or a rectangle and contains the number of cells indicated by the integer within it. Which integer will be in the same block as the shaded cell?

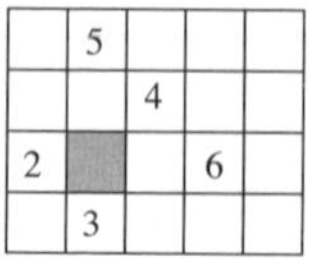

    A 2   B 3   C 4   D 5   E 6

22. Two numbers in the 4 × 4 grid can be swapped to create a Magic Square (in which all rows, all columns and both main diagonals add to the same total).
    What is the sum of these two numbers?

    A 12   B 15   C 22   D 26   E 28

23. In our school netball league a team gains a certain whole number of points if it wins a game, a lower whole number of points if it draws a game and no points if it loses a game. After 10 games my team has won 7 games, drawn 3 and gained 44 points. My sister's team has won 5 games, drawn 2 and lost 3. How many points has her team gained?

    A 28   B 29   C 30   D 31   E 32

24. Three congruent squares overlap as shown. The areas of the three overlapping sections are 2 cm^2, 5 cm^2 and 8 cm^2 respectively. The total area of the non-overlapping parts of the squares is 117 cm^2.
    What is the side-length of each square?

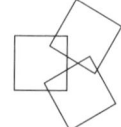

    A 6 cm   B 7 cm   C 8 cm   D 9 cm   E 10 cm

25. For Beatrix's latest art installation, she has fixed a 2 × 2 square sheet of steel to a wall. She has two 1 × 2 magnetic tiles, both of which she attaches to the steel sheet, in any orientation, so that none of the sheet is visible and the line separating the two tiles cannot be seen. As shown alongside, one tile has one black cell and one grey cell; the other tile has one black cell and one spotted cell.
    How many different looking 2 × 2 installations can Beatrix obtain?

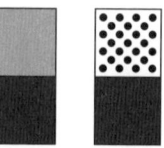

    A 4   B 8   C 12   D 14   E 24

Junior Challenge 2014 paper

1. What is (999 − 99 + 9) ÷ 9 ?

   A 91   B 99   C 100   D 101   E 109

2. How many minutes are there in $\frac{1}{12}$ of a day?

   A 240   B 120   C 60   D 30   E 15

3. In my row in the theatre the seats are numbered consecutively from T1 to T50. I am sitting in seat T17 and you are sitting in seat T39. How many seats are there between us?

   A 23   B 22   C 21   D 20   E 19

4. The number 987 654 321 is multiplied by 9. How many times does the digit 8 occur in the result?

   A 1   B 2   C 3   D 4   E 9

5. What is the difference between the smallest 4-digit number and the largest 3-digit number?

   A 1   B 10   C 100   D 1000   E 9899

6. The diagram shows a square divided into strips of equal width. Three strips are black and two are grey. What fraction of the perimeter of the square is grey?

   A $\frac{1}{5}$ B $\frac{1}{4}$ C $\frac{4}{25}$ D $\frac{1}{3}$ E $\frac{2}{5}$

7. What is 2014 − 4102 ?

   A −2012   B −2088   C −2092   D −2098   E −2112

8. How many prime numbers are there in the list

   1, 12, 123, 1234, 12 345, 123 456 ?

   A 0   B 1   C 2   D 3   E 4

9. Triangles XYZ and PQR are drawn on a square grid. What fraction of the area of triangle XYZ is the area of triangle PQR?

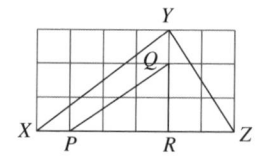

   A $\frac{1}{4}$ B $\frac{7}{18}$ C $\frac{1}{2}$ D $\frac{5}{18}$ E $\frac{1}{3}$

10. An equilateral triangle is surrounded by three squares, as shown. What is the value of x?

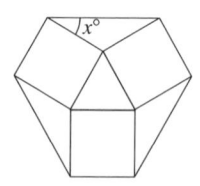

    A 15   B 18   C 24   D 30   E 36

11. The first two terms of a sequence are 1 and 2. Each of the following terms in the sequence is the sum of all the terms which come before it in the sequence.
    Which of these is *not* a term in the sequence?

    A 6   B 24   C 48   D 72   E 96

12. In this subtraction, P, Q, R, S and T represent single digits.

    What is the value of $P + Q + R + S + T$?

    ```
      7  Q  2  S  T
    - P  3  R  9  6
      ─────────────
      2  2  2  2  2
    ```

    A 30   B 29   C 28   D 27   E 26

13. A rectangle is split into triangles by drawing in its diagonals.
    What is the ratio of the area of triangle P to the area of triangle Q?

    A 1 : 1   B 1 : 2   C 2 : 1   D 2 : 3

    E the ratio depends on the lengths of the sides of the rectangle

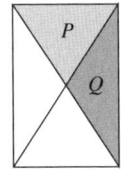

14. Which of these is equal to one million millimetres?

    A 1 metre   B 10 metres   C 100 metres   D 1 kilometre   E 10 kilometres

15. The diagram shows a rectangular envelope made by folding (and gluing) a single piece of paper.
    What could the original unfolded piece of paper look like?
    (The dashed lines are the fold lines.)

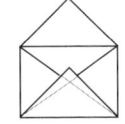

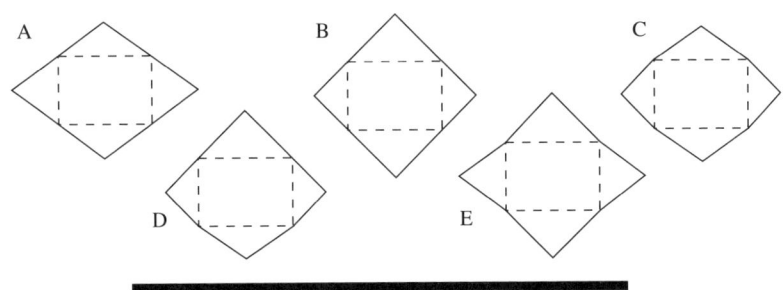

16. Only one of the following statements is true. Which one?

    A 'B is true'   B 'E is false'   C 'Statements A to E are true'
    D 'Statements A to E are false'   E 'A is false'

17. The diagram is a 'map' of Jo's local rail network, where the dots represent stations and the lines are routes. Jo wants to visit all the stations, travelling only by train, starting at any station and ending at any station, with no restrictions on which routes are taken.
    What is the smallest number of stations that Jo must go to more than once?

    A 1   B 2   C 3   D 4   E 5

18. Which of these statements is true?

    A $15\,614 = 1 + 5^6 - 1 \times 4$ B $15\,615 = 1 + 5^6 - 1 \times 5$ C $15\,616 = 1 + 5^6 - 1 \times 6$
    D $15\,617 = 1 + 5^6 - 1 \times 7$ E $15\,618 = 1 + 5^6 - 1 \times 8$

19. Jack and Jill played a game for two people. In each game, the winner was awarded 2 points and the loser 1 point. No games were drawn. Jack won exactly 4 games and Jill had a final score of 10 points. How many games did they play?

    A 5   B 6   C 7   D 8   E impossible to determine

20. Box P has p chocolates and box Q has q chocolates, where p and q are both odd and $p > q$. What is the smallest number of chocolates which would have to be moved from box P to box Q so that box Q has more chocolates than box P?

    A $\dfrac{q-p+2}{2}$ B $\dfrac{p-q+2}{2}$ C $\dfrac{q+p-2}{2}$ D $\dfrac{p-q-2}{2}$ E $\dfrac{q+p+2}{2}$

21. Pablo's teacher has given him 27 identical white cubes. She asks him to paint some of the faces of these cubes grey and then stack the cubes so that they appear as shown. What is the largest possible number of the individual white cubes which Pablo can leave with no faces painted grey?

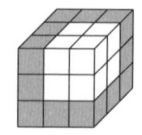

    A 8   B 12   C 14   D 15   E 16

22. In the division calculation $952\,473 \div 18$, which two adjacent digits should be swapped in order to increase the result by 100?

    A 9 and 5   B 5 and 2   C 2 and 4   D 4 and 7   E 7 and 3

23. Sam wants to complete the diagram so that each of the nine circles contains one of the digits from 1 to 9 inclusive and each contains a different digit. Also, the digits in each of the three lines of four circles must have the same total. What is this total?

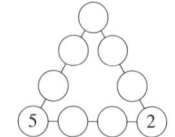

    A 17   B 18   C 19   D 20   E 21

24. The diagram shows a regular octagon with sides of length 1. The octagon is divided into regions by four diagonals.
    What is the difference between the area of the hatched region and the area of the region shaded grey?

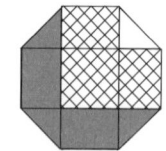

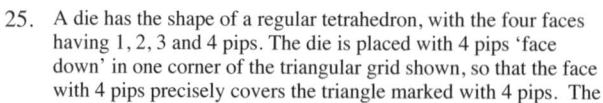

    A 0   B $\dfrac{1}{8}$ C $\dfrac{1}{4}$ D $\dfrac{1}{2}$ E 1

25. A die has the shape of a regular tetrahedron, with the four faces having 1, 2, 3 and 4 pips. The die is placed with 4 pips 'face down' in one corner of the triangular grid shown, so that the face with 4 pips precisely covers the triangle marked with 4 pips. The die is now 'rolled', by rotating about an edge without slipping, so that 1 pip is face down. It is rolled again, so that 2 pips are face down, as indicated. The rolling continues until the die rests on the shaded triangle in the opposite corner of the grid. How many pips are now face down?

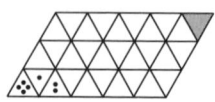

    A 1   B 2   C 3   D 4   E it depends on the route taken

Junior Challenge 2015 paper

1. Which of the following calculations gives the largest answer?

   A 1 − 2 + 3 + 4   B 1 + 2 − 3 + 4   C 1 + 2 + 3 − 4   D 1 + 2 − 3 − 4   E 1 − 2 − 3 + 4

2. It has just turned 22:22. How many minutes are there until midnight?

   A 178   B 138   C 128   D 108   E 98

3. What is the value of $\dfrac{12\,345}{1 + 2 + 3 + 4 + 5}$?

   A 1   B 8   C 678   D 823   E 12 359

4. In this partly completed pyramid, each rectangle is to be filled with the sum of the two numbers in the rectangles immediately below it.

   What number should replace x?

   A 3   B 4   C 5   D 7   E 12

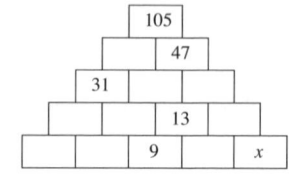

5. The difference between $\dfrac{1}{3}$ of a certain number and $\dfrac{1}{4}$ of the same number is 3. What is that number?

   A 24   B 36   C 48   D 60   E 72

6. What is the value of x in this triangle?

   A 45   B 50   C 55   D 60   E 65

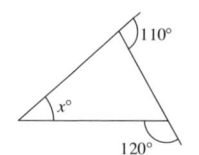

7. The result of the calculation 123 456 789 × 8 is almost the same as 987 654 321 except that two of the digits are in a different order. What is the sum of these two digits?

   A 3   B 7   C 9   D 15   E 17

8. Which of the following has the same remainder when it is divided by 2 as when it is divided by 3?

   A 3   B 5   C 7   D 9   E 11

9. According to a newspaper report, "A 63-year-old man has rowed around the world without leaving his living room." He clocked up 25 048 miles on a rowing machine that he received for his 50th birthday.

   Roughly how many miles per year has he rowed since he was given the machine?

   A 200   B 500   C 1000   D 2000   E 4000

10. In the expression 1 □ 2 □ 3 □ 4   each □ is to be replaced by either + or ×. What is the largest value of all the expressions that can be obtained in this way?

    A 10   B 14   C 15   D 24   E 25

Junior Challenge 2015 paper

11. What is the smallest prime number that is the sum of three different prime numbers?

   A 11   B 15   C 17   D 19   E 23

12. A fish weighs the total of 2 kg plus a third of its own weight. What is the weight of the fish in kg?

   A $2\frac{1}{3}$ B 3   C 4   D 6   E 8

13. In the figure shown, each line joining two numbers is to be labelled with the sum of the two numbers that are at its end points.

   How many of these labels are multiples of 3?

   A 10   B 9   C 8   D 7   E 6

14. Digits on a calculator are represented by a number of horizontal and vertical illuminated bars. The digits and the bars which represent them are shown in the diagram.
   How many digits are both prime and represented by a prime number of illuminated bars?

   A 0   B 1   C 2   D 3   E 4

15. Which of the following is divisible by all of the integers from 1 to 10 inclusive?

   A 23×34 B 34×45 C 45×56 D 56×67 E 67×78

16. The diagram shows a square inside an equilateral triangle. What is the value of $x + y$?

   A 105   B 120   C 135   D 150   E 165

17. Knave of Hearts: "I stole the tarts."
   Knave of Clubs: "The Knave of Hearts is lying."
   Knave of Diamonds: "The Knave of Clubs is lying."
   Knave of Spades: "The Knave of Diamonds is lying."

   How many of the four Knaves were telling the truth?

   A 1   B 2   C 3   D 4   E more information needed

18. Each of the fractions $\frac{2637}{18\,459}$ and $\frac{5274}{36\,918}$ uses the digits 1 to 9 exactly once. The first fraction simplifies to $\frac{1}{7}$. What is the simplified form of the second fraction?

   A $\frac{1}{8}$ B $\frac{1}{7}$ C $\frac{5}{34}$ D $\frac{9}{61}$ E $\frac{2}{7}$

19. One of the following cubes is the smallest cube that can be written as the sum of three positive cubes. Which is it?

   A 27   B 64   C 125   D 216   E 512

20. The diagram shows a pyramid made up of 30 cubes, each measuring $1\,\text{m} \times 1\,\text{m} \times 1\,\text{m}$.
   What is the total surface area of the whole pyramid (including its base)?

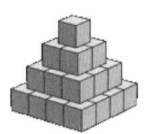

   A $30\,\text{m}^2$ B $62\,\text{m}^2$ C $72\,\text{m}^2$ D $152\,\text{m}^2$ E $180\,\text{m}^2$

21. Gill is now 27 and has moved into a new flat. She has four pictures to hang in a horizontal row on a wall which is 4800 mm wide. The pictures are identical in size and are 420 mm wide. Gill hangs the first two pictures so that one is on the extreme left of the wall and one is on the extreme right of the wall. She wants to hang the remaining two pictures so that all four pictures are equally spaced. How far should Gill place the centre of each of the two remaining pictures from a vertical line down the centre of the wall?

   A 210 mm   B 520 mm   C 730 mm   D 840 mm   E 1040 mm

22. The diagram shows a shaded region inside a regular hexagon.
   The shaded region is divided into equilateral triangles.
   What fraction of the area of the hexagon is shaded?

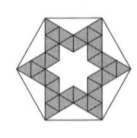

   A $\dfrac{3}{8}$ B $\dfrac{2}{5}$ C $\dfrac{3}{7}$ D $\dfrac{5}{12}$ E $\dfrac{1}{2}$

23. The diagram shows four shaded glass squares, with areas 1 cm², 4 cm², 9 cm² and 16 cm², placed in the corners of a rectangle. The largest square overlaps two others. The area of the region inside the rectangle but not covered by any square (shown unshaded) is 1.5 cm².
   What is the area of the region where squares overlap (shown dark grey)?

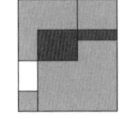

   A $2.5\,\text{cm}^2$ B $3\,\text{cm}^2$ C $3.5\,\text{cm}^2$ D $4\,\text{cm}^2$ E $4.5\,\text{cm}^2$

24. A *palindromic number* is a number that reads the same when the order of its digits is reversed. What is the difference between the largest and smallest five-digit palindromic numbers that are both multiples of 45?

   A 9180   B 9090   C 9000   D 8910   E 8190

25. The four straight lines in the diagram are such that $VU = VW$. The sizes of $\angle UXZ$, $\angle VYZ$ and $\angle VZX$ are $x°, y°$ and $z°$.
   Which of the following equations gives x in terms of y and z?

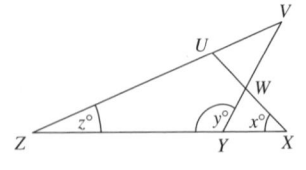

   A $x = y - z$ B $x = 180 - y - z$ C $x = y - \dfrac{z}{2}$

   D $x = y + z - 90$ E $x = \dfrac{y - z}{2}$

Junior Challenge 2016 paper

1. Which of the following is closest to zero?

   A 6 + 5 + 4   B 6 + 5 − 4   C 6 + 5 × 4   D 6 − 5 × 4   E 6 × 5 ÷ 4

2. What number is twenty-one less than sixty thousand?

   A 59 979   B 59 981   C 57 900   D 40 001   E 39 000

3. One lap of a standard running track is 400 m.
   How many laps does each athlete run in a 5000 m race?

   A 4   B 5   C 8   D 10   E $12\frac{1}{2}$

4. In January 1859, an eight-year-old boy dropped a newly-hatched eel into a well in Sweden (apparently in order to keep the water free of insects). The eel, named Åle, finally died in August 2014.
   How many years old was Åle when it died?

   A 135   B 145   C 155   D 165   E 175

5. What is the value of $\frac{1}{25}$ + 0.25?

   A 0.29   B 0.3   C 0.35   D 0.50   E 0.65

6. Gill is now 28 years old and is a teacher of Mathematics at a school which has 600 pupils. There are 30 more girls than boys at the school.
   How many girls are at Gill's school?

   A 270   B 300   C 315   D 330   E 345

7. A distance of 8 km is approximately 5 miles.
   Which of the following is closest to 1.2 km?

   A 0.75 miles   B 1 mile   C 1.2 miles   D 1.6 miles   E 1.9 miles

8. What is the value of $\dfrac{2 + 4 + 6 + 8 + 10 + 12 + 14 + 16 + 18 + 20}{1 + 2 + 3 + 4 + 5 + 6 + 7 + 8 + 9 + 10}$?

   A 2   B 10   C 20   D 40   E 1024

9. One of the three symbols +, −, × is inserted somewhere between the digits of 2016 to give a new number. For example, 20 − 16 gives 4.
   How many of the following four numbers can be obtained in this way?

   $$36 \quad 195 \quad 207 \quad 320$$

   A 0   B 1   C 2   D 3   E 4

10. A square is folded exactly in half and then in half again.
    Which of the following could not be the resulting shape?

Junior Challenge 2016 paper　　　　41

11. Which of the following statements is false?

    A 12 is a multiple of 2　　　B 123 is a multiple of 3　　　C 1234 is a multiple of 4
    D 12 345 is a multiple of 5　　　　　　E 123 456 is a multiple of 6

12. The musical *Rent* contains a song that starts 'Five hundred and twenty five thousand six hundred minutes'.
    Which of the following is closest to this length of time?

    A a week　　B a year　　C a decade　　D a century　　E a millennium

13. The diagram shows five circles placed at the corners of a pentagon. The numbers 1, 2, 3, 4, 5 are placed in the circles shown, one in each, so that the numbers in adjacent circles always differ by more than 1.
    What is the sum of the numbers in the two circles adjacent to the circle which contains the number 5?

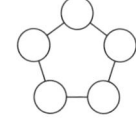

    A 3　　B 4　　C 5　　D 6　　E 7

14. In the diagram, $AB = AC$ and D is a point on AC such that $BD = BC$. Angle BAC is 40°.
    What is angle ABD?

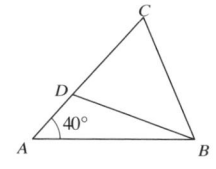

    A 15°　　B 20°　　C 25°　　D 30°　　E 35°

15. How many of these four expressions are perfect squares?

    $1^3 + 2^3$　　　$1^3 + 2^3 + 3^3$　　　$1^3 + 2^3 + 3^3 + 4^3$　　　$1^3 + 2^3 + 3^3 + 4^3 + 5^3$

    A 0　　B 1　　C 2　　D 3　　E 4

16. Each of the nine small squares in this grid can be coloured completely black or completely white.
    What is the largest number of squares that can be coloured black so that the design created has rotational symmetry of order 2, but no lines of symmetry?

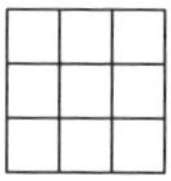

    A 4　　B 5　　C 6　　D 7　　E 8

17. In a group of 48 children, the ratio of boys to girls is 3 : 5.
    How many boys must join the group to make the ratio of boys to girls 5 : 3?

    A 48　　B 40　　C 32　　D 24　　E 8

18. In the addition sum shown, each letter represents a different non-zero digit.
    What digit does X represent?

    A 1　　B 3　　C 5　　D 7　　E 9

    ```
      S E E
    + S E E
    ─────
    A X E S
    ```

19. Three boxes under my stairs contain apples or pears or both. Each box contains the same number of pieces of fruit. The first box contains all twelve of the apples and one-ninth of the pears.
    How many pieces of fruit are there in each box?

    A 14　　B 16　　C 18　　D 20　　E 36

20. A cyclic quadrilateral has all four vertices on the circumference of a circle. Brahmagupta (598–670AD) gave the following formula for the area, A, of a cyclic quadrilateral whose edges have lengths a, b, c, d :
$A = \sqrt{(s - a)(s - b)(s - c)(s - d)}$, where s is half of the perimeter of the quadrilateral.
What is the area of the cyclic quadrilateral with sides of length 4 cm, 5 cm, 7 cm and 10 cm?

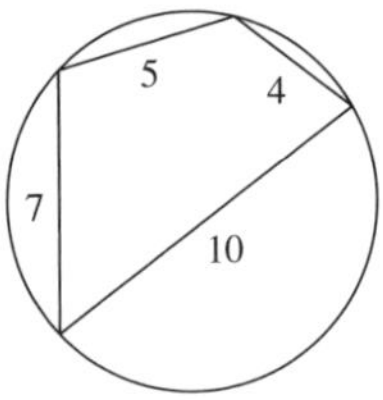

A 6 cm^2 B 13 cm^2 C 26 cm^2 D 30 cm^2 E 36 cm^2

21. The diagram shows a pentagon drawn on a square grid. All vertices of the pentagon and triangle are grid points.
What fraction of the area of the pentagon is shaded?

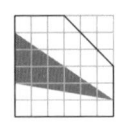

A $\frac{2}{7}$ B $\frac{1}{3}$ C $\frac{2}{5}$ D $\frac{1}{4}$ E $\frac{2}{9}$

22. Four copies of the triangle shown are joined together, without gaps or overlaps, to make a parallelogram.
What is the largest possible perimeter of the parallelogram?

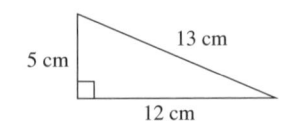

A 46 cm   B 52 cm   C 58 cm   D 62 cm   E 76 cm

23. The diagram shows the first few squares of a 'spiral' sequence of squares. All but the first three squares have been numbered. After the first six squares, the sequence is continued by placing the next square alongside three existing squares – the largest existing square and two others.
The three smallest squares have sides of length 1. What is the side length of the 12th square?

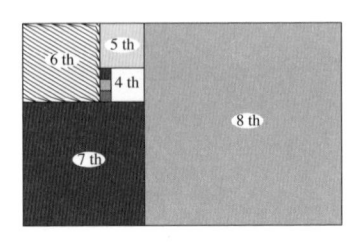

A 153   B 123   C 83   D 53   E 13

24. Part of a wall is to be decorated with a row of four square tiles. Three different colours of tiles are available and there are at least two tiles of each colour available. Tiles of all three colours must be used.
In how many ways can the row of four tiles be chosen?

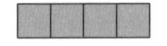

A 12   B 18   C 24   D 36   E 48

25. Beatrix places dominoes on a 5 × 5 board, either horizontally or vertically, so that each domino covers two small squares. She stops when she cannot place another domino, as in the example shown in the diagram.
When Beatrix stops, what is the largest possible number of squares that may still be uncovered?

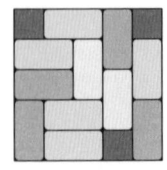

A 4   B 5   C 6   D 7   E 8

Intermediate Challenge 2007 paper

1. At midnight on 15 December 2005, the moon reached its highest point in the sky, an event which occurs every 18.6 years. In which year will it next occur?

   A 2007   B 2008   C 2023   D 2024   E 2191

2. The information display on a train shows letters by illuminating dots in a rectangular 5 × 8 array. In the letter 't' shown, what fraction of the dots in the array is illuminated?

   A $\dfrac{9}{20}$ B $\dfrac{19}{40}$ C $\dfrac{1}{2}$ D $\dfrac{21}{40}$ E $\dfrac{11}{20}$

3. In how many ways can a square be cut in half using a single straight line cut?

   A 1   B 2   C 4   D 8   E Infinitely many

4. Between them, Ginger and Victoria eat two thirds of a cake. If Ginger eats one quarter of the cake, what fraction of the cake does Victoria eat?

   A $\dfrac{1}{2}$ B $\dfrac{2}{5}$ C $\dfrac{3}{8}$ D $\dfrac{4}{9}$ E $\dfrac{5}{12}$

5. What is the value of (12340 + 12·34) ÷ 1234 ?

   A 100.01   B 100.1   C 10.001   D 10.01   E 10.1

6. The sum of 9 consecutive positive whole numbers is 2007. What is the difference between the largest and smallest of these numbers?

   A 8   B 9   C 10   D 18   E 223

7. If the numbers 1, 2, 3, 4, 5, 6, 7, 8, 9, 10 are all multiplied together, how many zeros are at the end of the answer?

   A 1   B 2   C 3   D 4   E 10

8. The mean of three numbers x, y and z is x. What is the mean of y and z ?

   A $\tfrac{1}{2}x$ B x C $2x$ D $3x$ E $4x$

9. A male punky fish has 9 stripes and a female punky fish has 8 stripes. I count 86 stripes on the fish in my tank. What is the ratio of male fish to female fish?

   A 2 : 3   B 3 : 2   C 4 : 1   D 4 : 7   E 7 : 4

10. The diagram shows three squares drawn on the sides of a triangle. What is the sum of the three marked angles?

    A 180°   B 270°   C 360°
    D 450°   E It depends on the shape of the triangle

Intermediate Challenge 2007 paper 45

11. The numbers 72, 8, 24, 10, 5, 45, 36, 15 are grouped in pairs so that the product of each pair is the same. Which number is paired with 10?

    A 36 B 45 C 24 D 15 E 72

12. Which of the following could be the graph showing the circumference C of a circle in terms of its diameter d?

13. A 30 cm × 40 cm page of a book includes a 2 cm margin on each side, as shown.
    What percentage of the page is occupied by the margins?

    A 14% B 16% C 18% D 20% E 22%

14. If p is a positive integer and q is a negative integer, which of the following is greatest?

    A $p - q$ B $q - p$ C $p + q$ D $-p - q$ E More information needed

15. The diagram shows a regular pentagon $PQRST$. The lines QS and RT meet at U. What is the size of angle PUR?

    A 108° B 112° C 116° D 126° E 132°

16. A wooden cube with edge length 12 cm is cut into cubes with edge length 1 cm. What is the total length of all the edges of all these centimetre cubes?

    A 12 cm B 12^2 cm C 12^3 cm D 12^4 cm E 12^5 cm

17. Grannie's watch gains 30 minutes every hour, whilst Grandpa's watch loses 30 minutes every hour. At midnight, they both set their watches to the correct time of 12 o'clock. What is the correct time when their two watches next agree?

    Grannie's watch: Grandpa's watch:

    A 6 am B 9 am C 12 noon D 3 pm E 6 pm

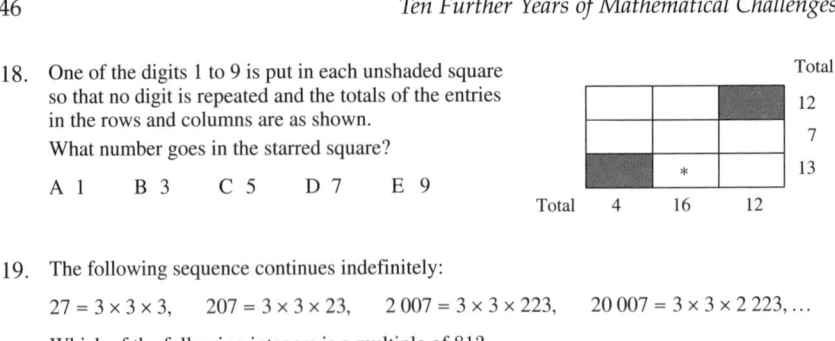

18. One of the digits 1 to 9 is put in each unshaded square so that no digit is repeated and the totals of the entries in the rows and columns are as shown.
    What number goes in the starred square?

    A 1   B 3   C 5   D 7   E 9

19. The following sequence continues indefinitely:

    $27 = 3 \times 3 \times 3$, $207 = 3 \times 3 \times 23$, $2\,007 = 3 \times 3 \times 223$, $20\,007 = 3 \times 3 \times 2\,223, \ldots$

    Which of the following integers is a multiple of 81?

    A 200 007   B 20 000 007   C 2 000 000 007   D 200 000 000 007   E 20 000 000 000 007

20. P, Q, R are points on the circumference of a circle of radius 4 cm. $\angle PQR = 45°$. What is the length of chord PR?

    A 4 cm   B $3\sqrt{3}$ cm   C $4\sqrt{2}$ cm   D 5 cm   E 6 cm

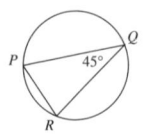

21. The diagram shows two circles and four equal semi-circular arcs. The area of the inner shaded circle is 1.
    What is the area of the outer circle?

    A $\sqrt{2}$ B 2   C $1 + \sqrt{2}$ D $\dfrac{\pi}{2}$ E $\dfrac{9}{4}$

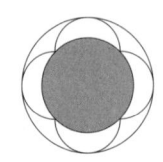

22. The diagram shows an ordinary die in which the scores on opposite faces always total 7. It is placed on a horizontal table with the '1' face facing East. The die is moved four times, rotating it each time through 90° about an edge. The faces in contact with the table are first 1, then 2, then 3, then 5. In which direction is the '1' face facing after this sequence of moves?

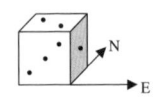

    A West   B East   C North   D South   E Up

23. As n takes each positive integer value in turn (that is, $n = 1$, $n = 2$, $n = 3$, and so on) how many different values are obtained for the remainder when n^2 is divided by $n + 4$?

    A 1   B 8   C 9   D 16   E Infinitely many

24. In the diagram on the right, how many squares, of any size, are there whose entries add up to an even total?

    A 12   B 20   C 32   D 36   E 45

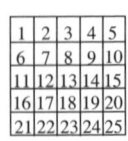

25. The diagram shows a semi-circle and an isosceles triangle which have equal areas. What is the value of $\tan x°$?

    A 1   B $\dfrac{\sqrt{3}}{2}$ C $\dfrac{\pi}{\sqrt{3}}$ D $\dfrac{2}{\pi}$ E $\dfrac{\pi}{2}$

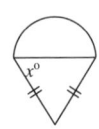

Intermediate Challenge
2008 paper

1. How many hours are there in this week?

   A 24 B 70 C 84 D 148 E 168

2. Which is the largest prime number that divides exactly into the number equal to $2 + 3 + 5 \times 7$?

   A 2 B 3 C 5 D 7 E 11

3. What is the value of $0.75 \div \frac{3}{4}$?

   A 0.5 B 1 C 1.5 D 2 E 2.5

4. What percentage of the large 5 × 5 square is shaded?

   A 40% B 60% C $66\frac{2}{3}$% D 75% E 80%

5. Which of the following is *not* equal to a whole number?

   A $\dfrac{594}{5+9+4}$ B $\dfrac{684}{6+8+4}$ C $\dfrac{756}{7+5+6}$ D $\dfrac{873}{8+7+3}$ E $\dfrac{972}{9+7+2}$

6. Four of these shapes can be placed together to make a cube. Which is the odd one out?

   A   B   C   D   E

7. The square of a non-zero number is equal to 70% of the original number. What is the original number?

   A 700 B 70 C 7 D 0.7 E 0.07

8. In a certain year, there were exactly four Tuesdays and exactly four Fridays in October. On what day of the week did Halloween, October 31st, fall that year?

   A Monday B Wednesday C Thursday D Saturday E Sunday

9. A solid wooden cube is painted blue on the outside. The cube is then cut into 27 smaller cubes of equal size. What fraction of the total surface area of these new cubes is blue?

   A $\dfrac{1}{6}$ B $\dfrac{1}{5}$ C $\dfrac{1}{4}$ D $\dfrac{1}{3}$ E $\dfrac{1}{2}$

10. Two sides of a triangle have lengths 6 cm and 5 cm. Perry suggests the following possible values for the perimeter of the triangle: (i) 11 cm (ii) 15 cm (iii) 24 cm. Which of Perry's suggestions could be correct?

    A (i) only B (i) or (ii) C (ii) only D (ii) or (iii) E (iii) only

Intermediate Challenge 2008 paper 49

11. | S is 25% of 60 | | 60 is 80% of U | | 80 is M% of 25 |

    What is $S + U + M$?

    A 100   B 103   C 165   D 330   E 410

12. The sculpture 'Cubo Vazado' [Emptied Cube] by the Brazilian artist Franz Weissmann is formed by removing cubical blocks from a solid cube to leave the symmetrical shape shown. If all the edges have length 1, 2 or 3 units, what is the surface area of the sculpture in square units?

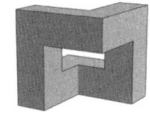

    A 36   B 42   C 48   D 54   E 60

13. The mean of a sequence of 64 numbers is 64. The mean of the first 36 numbers is 36. What is the mean of the last 28 numbers?

    A 28   B 44   C 72   D 100   E 108

14. Sam is holding two lengths of rope by their mid-points. Pat chooses two of the loose ends at random and ties them together.

    What is the probability that Sam now holds one untied length of rope and one tied loop of rope?

    A $\frac{1}{2}$ B $\frac{1}{3}$ C $\frac{1}{4}$ D $\frac{1}{5}$ E $\frac{1}{6}$

15. A designer wishes to use two copies of the logo shown on the right to create a pattern, without any of the dots overlapping. Which one of the following could be made?

    A   B   C   D   E

16. The first two terms of a sequence are $\frac{2}{3}$ and $\frac{4}{5}$. Each term after the second term is the average (mean) of the two previous terms. What is the fifth term in the sequence?

    A $\frac{5}{34}$ B $\frac{1}{2}$ C $\frac{10}{13}$ D $\frac{3}{4}$ E $\frac{10}{11}$

17. The shaded region is bounded by eight equal circles with centres at the corners and midpoints of the sides of a square.

    The perimeter of the square has length 8. What is length of the perimeter of the shaded region?

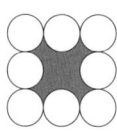

    A π B 2π C 8   D 3π E 4π

18. In the calculation $1003 \div 4995 = 0.2\dot{0}0\dot{8}$, the number $0.2\dot{0}0\dot{8}$ represents the recurring decimal fraction 0.2008008008.... When the answers to the following calculations are arranged in numerical order, which one is in the middle?

    A $226 \div 1125 = 0.200\dot{8}$ B $251 \div 1250 = 0.2008$ C $497 \div 2475 = 0.20\dot{0}\dot{8}$
    D $1003 \div 4995 = 0.2\dot{0}0\dot{8}$ E $2008 \div 9999 = 0.\dot{2}00\dot{8}$

19. Which of the following is equal to $(1 + x + y)^2 - (1 - x - y)^2$ for all values of x and y?

    A $4x$ 　　B $2(x^2 + y^2)$ 　　C 0 　　D $4xy$ 　　E $4(x + y)$

20. What, in cm², is the area of this quadrilateral?

    A 48 　B 50 　C 52 　D 54 　E 56

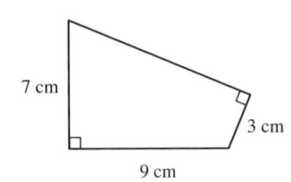

    7 cm　　3 cm　　9 cm

21. In triangle PQR, $\angle QPR = \alpha°$ and $\angle PQR = \beta°$, where $\alpha < \beta$. The line RM bisects $\angle PRQ$ and RN is the perpendicular from R to the line PQ. What is the size, in degrees, of $\angle MRN$?

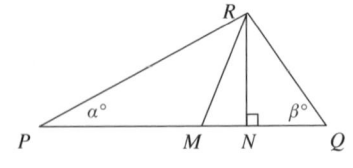

    A $\dfrac{180 - (\alpha + \beta)}{2}$ 　B $\dfrac{\beta - \alpha}{2}$ 　C $\dfrac{\alpha + 2\beta}{2}$ 　D $\dfrac{360 - \alpha - 2\beta}{2}$ 　E $\dfrac{\alpha + \beta}{2}$

22. At a cinema, a child's ticket costs £4.20 and an adult's ticket costs £7.70. When a group of adults and children went to see a film, the total cost was £C. Which of the following is a possible value of C?

    A 91 　　B 92 　　C 93 　　D 94 　　E 95

23. Beatrix has a 24-hour digital clock on a glass table-top next to her desk. When she looked at the clock at 13:08, she noticed that the reflected display also read 13:08, as shown.

    How many times in a 24-hour period do the display and its reflection give the same time?

    A 12 　　B 36 　　C 48 　　D 72 　　E 96

24. The diagram has order 4 rotational symmetry about D. If angle ABC is $15°$ and the area of $ABEF$ is 24 cm², what, in cm, is the length of CD?

    A 1 　　B $\sqrt{3}$ 　　C 2 　　D $\sqrt{5}$ 　　E $2\sqrt{3} - 1$

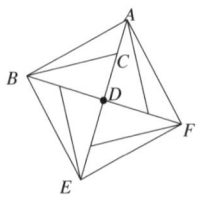

25. A garden has the shape of a right-angled triangle with sides of length 30, 40 and 50. A straight fence goes from the corner with the right-angle to a point on the opposite side, dividing the garden into two sections which have the same perimeter. How long is the fence?

    A 25 　　B $8\sqrt{3}$ 　　C $5\sqrt{11}$ 　　D $5\sqrt{39}$ 　　E $12\sqrt{5}$

Intermediate Challenge 2009 paper

1. What is the value of $1 + 2^3 + 4 \times 5$?

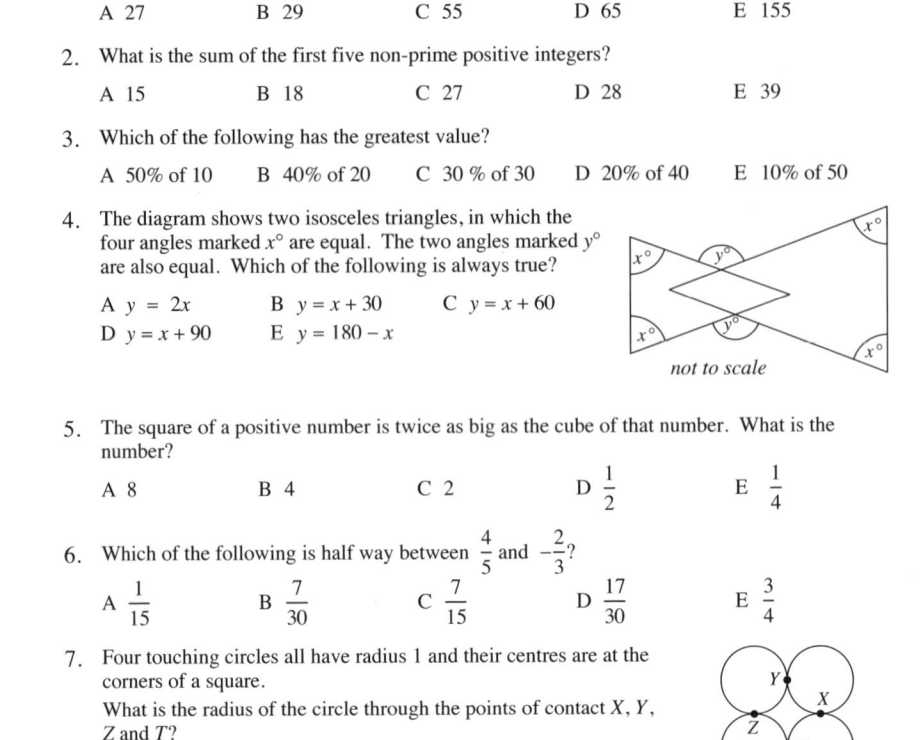

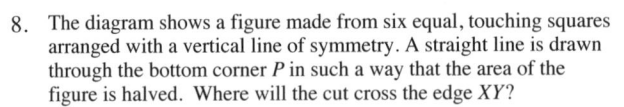

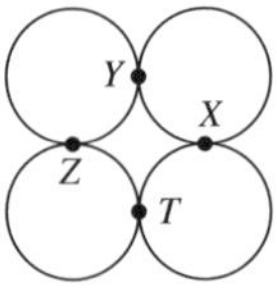

   A 27   B 29   C 55   D 65   E 155

2. What is the sum of the first five non-prime positive integers?

   A 15   B 18   C 27   D 28   E 39

3. Which of the following has the greatest value?

   A 50% of 10   B 40% of 20   C 30% of 30   D 20% of 40   E 10% of 50

4. The diagram shows two isosceles triangles, in which the four angles marked $x°$ are equal. The two angles marked $y°$ are also equal. Which of the following is always true?

   A $y = 2x$ B $y = x + 30$ C $y = x + 60$
   D $y = x + 90$ E $y = 180 - x$

   not to scale

5. The square of a positive number is twice as big as the cube of that number. What is the number?

   A 8   B 4   C 2   D $\dfrac{1}{2}$ E $\dfrac{1}{4}$

6. Which of the following is half way between $\dfrac{4}{5}$ and $-\dfrac{2}{3}$?

   A $\dfrac{1}{15}$ B $\dfrac{7}{30}$ C $\dfrac{7}{15}$ D $\dfrac{17}{30}$ E $\dfrac{3}{4}$

7. Four touching circles all have radius 1 and their centres are at the corners of a square.
   What is the radius of the circle through the points of contact X, Y, Z and T?

   A $\dfrac{1}{2}$ B $\dfrac{1}{2}\sqrt{2}$ C 1   D $\sqrt{2}$ E 2

8. The diagram shows a figure made from six equal, touching squares arranged with a vertical line of symmetry. A straight line is drawn through the bottom corner P in such a way that the area of the figure is halved. Where will the cut cross the edge XY?

   A at X B one quarter the way down XY
   C half way down XY D three-quarters the way down XY
   E at Y

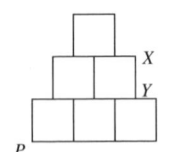

9. Joseph's flock has 55% more sheep than goats. What is the ratio of goats to sheep in the flock?

   A 9:11   B 20:31   C 11:20   D 5:9   E 9:20

10. Fussy Fiona wants to buy a new house but she doesn't like house numbers that are divisible by 3 or by 5. If all the houses numbered between 100 and 150 inclusive are for sale, how many houses can she choose from?

    A 24   B 25   C 26   D 27   E 28

Intermediate Challenge 2009 paper

11. The diagram below shows a pattern which repeats every 12 dots.

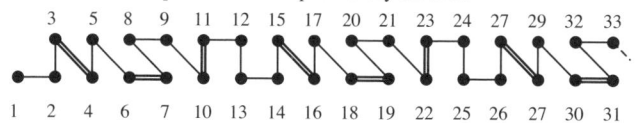

    Which of the following does the piece between 2007 and 2011 look like?

    A 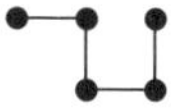   B    C    D 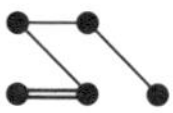   E

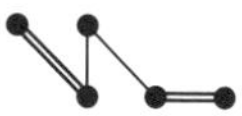

12. The diagram shows a square inside a regular hexagon. What is the size of the marked angle at *X*?

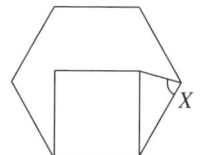

    A 45°   B 50°   C 60°   D 75°   E 80°

13. The diagram on the right shows a rectangle with sides of length 5 cm and 4 cm. All the arcs are quarter-circles of radius 2 cm. What is the total shaded area in cm^2?

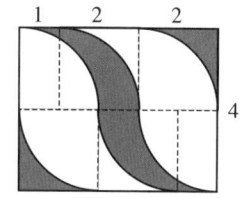

    A $12 - 2\pi$ B 8   C $8 + 2\pi$
    D 10   E $20 - 4\pi$

14. Catherine's computer correctly calculates $\dfrac{66^{66}}{2}$. What is the units digit of its answer?

    A 1   B 2   C 3   D 6   E 8

15. What is the value of $\dfrac{1}{x+2}$, given that $\dfrac{1}{x} = 3.5$?

    A $\dfrac{7}{9}$ B $\dfrac{7}{16}$ C $\dfrac{9}{7}$ D $\dfrac{7}{4}$ E $\dfrac{16}{7}$

16. How many different positive integers *n* are there for which *n* and $n^3 + 3$ are both prime numbers?

    A 0   B 1   C 2   D 3   E infinitely many

17. *PQR* is a triangle and *S* is a point on *QR*.
    QP = *QR* = 9 cm and *PR* = *PS* = 6 cm.
    What is the length of *SR*?

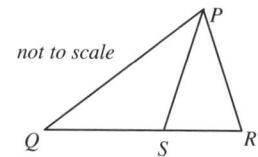

    A 1cm   B 2cm   C 3cm   D 4cm   E 5cm

    not to scale

18. If p, q are distinct primes less than 7, what is the largest possible value of the highest common factor of $2p^2q$ and $3pq^2$?

    A 60   B 45   C 36   D 20   E 15

19. Driving to Birmingham airport, Mary cruised at 55 miles per hour for the first two hours and then flew along at 70 miles per hour for the remainder of the journey. Her average speed for the entire journey was 60 miles per hour. How long did Mary's journey to Birmingham Airport take?

    A 6 hours   B $4\frac{1}{2}$ hours   C 4 hours   D $3\frac{1}{2}$ hours   E 3 hours

20. A square, of side two units, is folded in half to form a triangle. A second fold is made, parallel to the first, so that the apex of this triangle folds onto a point on its base, thereby forming an isosceles trapezium. What is the perimeter of this trapezium?

    A $4 + \sqrt{2}$ B $4 + 2\sqrt{2}$ C $3 + 2\sqrt{2}$ D $2 + 3\sqrt{2}$ E 5

21. There are lots of ways of choosing three dots from this 4 by 4 array. How many triples of points are there where all three lie on a straight line (not necessarily equally spaced)?

    A 8   B 16   C 20   D 40   E 44

22. A square is divided into eight congruent triangles, as shown. Two of these triangles are selected at random and shaded black. What is the probability that the resulting figure has at least one axis of symmetry?

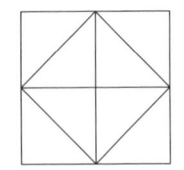

    A $\dfrac{1}{4}$ B $\dfrac{4}{7}$ C $\dfrac{1}{2}$ D $\dfrac{5}{7}$ E 1

23. The diagram shows part of a tiling pattern which is made from two types of individual tiles: 8 by 6 rectangular white tiles and square black tiles. If the pattern is extended to cover an infinite plane, what fraction is coloured black?

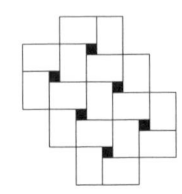

    A $\dfrac{1}{12}$ B $\dfrac{1}{13}$ C $\dfrac{1}{25}$ D $\dfrac{1}{37}$ E $\dfrac{1}{40}$

24. What is the largest number of the following statements that can be true at the same time?

    $0 < x^2 < 1$, $x^2 > 1$, $-1 < x < 0$, $0 < x < 1$, $0 < x - x^2 < 1$

    A 1   B 2   C 3   D 4   E 5

25. One coin among N identical-looking coins is a fake and is slightly heavier than the others, which all have the same weight. To compare two groups of coins you are allowed to use a set of scales with two pans which balance exactly when the weight in each pan is the same. What is the largest value of N for which the fake coin can be identified using a maximum of two such comparisons?

    A 4   B 6   C 7   D 8   E 9

Intermediate Challenge
2010 paper

1. What is the value of 10 + 10 × 10 × (10 + 10) ?

   A 21 000   B 20 100   C 2100   D 2010   E 210

2. Three of the interior angles of a given quadrilateral are each 80°. What is the fourth angle of this quadrilateral?

   A 120°   B 110°   C 100°   D 90°   E 80°

3. Exactly one of the following is a prime number. Which is it?

   A 2345   B 23 456   C 234 567   D 2 345 678   E 23 456 789

4. A radio advertisement claimed that using a particular brand of artificial sweetener every day would 'save 7 000 calories in a year'. Approximately how many calories is this per day?

   A 20   B 40   C 70   D 100   E 140

5. Which of the following has the greatest value?

   A one half of $\frac{1}{25}$ B one third of $\frac{1}{20}$ C one quarter of $\frac{1}{15}$

   D one fifth of $\frac{1}{10}$ E one sixth of $\frac{1}{5}$

6. In triangle PQR, S is a point on QR such that $QS = SP = PR$ and $\angle QPS = 20°$. What is the size of $\angle PRS$?

   A 20°   B 35°   C 40°   D 55°   E 60°

7. The Three Choirs Festival is held annually. Its venue rotates in a three-year cycle among Hereford, Gloucester and Worcester. In 2009, it was held in Hereford, in 2010 it will be held in Gloucester, next year it will be held in Worcester.

   Assuming that this three-year cycle continues, in which one of the following years will the Festival *not* be held in Worcester?

   A 2020   B 2032   C 2047   D 2054   E 2077

8. On my clock's display, the time has just changed to 02:31. How many minutes will it be until all the digits 0, 1, 2, 3 next appear together again?

   A 1   B 41   C 50   D 60   E 61

9. The perimeters of the three shapes shown are made up of straight lines and semi-circular arcs of diameter 2. They will fit snugly together as in a jigsaw.
   What is the difference between the total perimeter of the three separate pieces and the perimeter of the shape formed when the three pieces fit together?

   A 0   B $2 + 2\pi$ C $8 + 4\pi$ D $22 + 2\pi$ E $30 + 6\pi$

Intermediate Challenge 2010 paper 57

10. One year in the 1990s, January 1st fell on a Monday. Eleven years later, January 1st was also a Monday. How many times did February 29th occur during those eleven years?

   A 1   B 2   C 3   D 4   E 5

11. "You eat more than I do," said Tweedledee to Tweedledum.
    "That is not true," said Tweedledum to Tweedledee.
    "You are both wrong," said Alice, to them both.
    "You are right," said the White Rabbit to Alice.
    How many of the four statements were true?

   A 0   B 1   C 2   D 3   E 4

12. A cuboid is cut away from a cube of side 10 cm as shown. By what fraction does the total surface area of the solid decrease as a result?

   A $\frac{1}{4}$ B $\frac{1}{6}$ C $\frac{1}{10}$ D $\frac{1}{12}$ E $\frac{1}{18}$

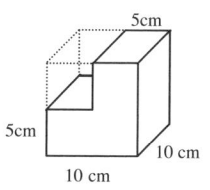

13. At Corbett's Ironmongery a fork handle and a candle cost a total of £6.10. The fork handle costs £4.60 more than the candle. What is the cost of two fork handles and four candles?

   A £14.45   B £13.70   C £12.95   D £12.20   E £8.35

14. Given that $4x - y = 5, 4y - z = 7$ and $4z - x = 18$, what is the value of $x + y + z$?

   A 8   B 9   C 10   D 11   E 12

15. Bill is trying to sketch the graph of $y = 2x + 6$ but in drawing the axes he has placed the *x*-axis up the page and the *y*-axis across the page. Which of these five graphs is a correct sketch of $y = 2x + 6$ when the axes are placed in this way?

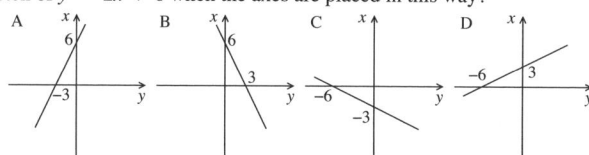

16. Albert Einstein is experimenting with two unusual clocks which both have 24-hour displays. One clock goes at twice the normal speed. The other clock goes backwards, but at the normal speed. Both clocks show the correct time at 13:00.
    What is the correct time when the displays on the clocks next agree?

   A 05:00   B 09:00   C 13:00   D 17:00   E 21:00

17. Last year Gill's cylindrical 21st birthday cake wasn't big enough to feed all her friends. This year she will double the radius and triple the height. What will be the ratio of the volume of this year's birthday cake to the volume of last year's cake?

   A 12:1   B 7:1   C 6:1   D 4:1   E 3:1

18. Supergran walks from her chalet to the top of the mountain. She knows that if she walks at a speed of 6 mph she will arrive at 1 pm, whereas if she leaves at the same time and walks at 10 mph, she will arrive at 11 am.
At what speed should she walk if she wants to arrive at 12 noon?

   A 7.5 mph   B $7\frac{1}{2}$ mph   C 7.75 mph   D $\sqrt{60}$ mph   E 8 mph

19. A snail is at one corner of the top face of a cube with side length 1 m. The snail can crawl at a speed of 1 m per hour. What proportion of the cube's surface is made up of points which the snail could reach within one hour?

   A $\dfrac{\pi}{16}$ B $\dfrac{\pi}{8}$ C $\dfrac{1}{4}$ D $\dfrac{1}{2}$ E $\dfrac{\sqrt{3}}{4}$

20. Shahbaz thinks of an integer, n, such that the difference between $\sqrt{n}$ and 7 is less than 1. How many different possibilities are there for n?

   A 13   B 14   C 26   D 27   E 28

---

21. A square maze has 9 rooms with gaps in the walls between them. Once a person has travelled through a gap in the wall it then closes behind them. How many different ways can someone travel through the maze from X to Y?

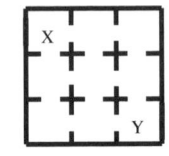

   A 8   B 10   C 12   D 14   E 16

22. Curly and Larry like to have their orange squash made to the same strength. Unfortunately, Moe has put 25 ml of squash with 175 ml of water in Curly's glass and 15 ml of squash with 185 ml of water in Larry's glass. How many millilitres of the mixture in Curly's glass must be put into Larry's glass so that they end up with drinks of the same strength?

   A 5   B 7   C 10   D 12   E it is not possible

23. The diagram shows a pattern of eight equal shaded squares inside a circle of area π square units. What is the area (in square units) of the shaded region?

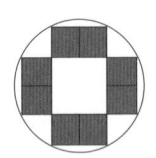

   A $1\dfrac{1}{3}$ B $1\dfrac{3}{5}$ C $1\dfrac{2}{3}$ D $1\dfrac{7}{9}$ E 2

24. A new taxi firm needs a memorable phone number. They want a number which has a maximum of two different digits. Their phone number must start with the digit 3 and be six digits long. How many such numbers are possible?

   A 288   B 280   C 279   D 226   E 225

25. Two squares, each of side length $1 + \sqrt{2}$ units, overlap. The overlapping region is a regular octagon.
What is the area (in square units) of the octagon?

   A $1 + \sqrt{2}$ B $1 + 2\sqrt{2}$ C $2 + \sqrt{2}$ D $2 + 2\sqrt{2}$ E $2 + 3\sqrt{2}$

Intermediate Challenge
2011 paper

1. What is the value of 4.5 × 5.5 + 4.5 × 4.5?

   A 36.5   B 45   C 50   D 90   E 100

2. To find the diameter in mm of a Japanese knitting needle, you multiply the size by 0.3 and add 2.1. What is the diameter in mm of a size 5 Japanese knitting needle?

   A 3.6   B 7.4   C 10.8   D 12   E 17.1

3. The consecutive digits 1, 2, 3, 4 in that order can be arranged to make the correct division, 12 ÷ 3 = 4. One *other* sequence of four consecutive digits p, q, r, s makes a correct division, 'pq' ÷ $r = s$. What is the value of s in this case?

   A 4   B 5   C 6   D 7   E 8

4. The angles of a triangle are in the ratio 2:3:5. What is the difference between the largest angle and the smallest angle?

   A 9°   B 18°   C 36°   D 45°   E 54°

5. The diagram shows a rectangle placed on a grid of 1 cm × 1 cm squares. What is the area of the rectangle in cm^2?

   A 15   B $22\frac{1}{2}$ C 30   D 36   E 45

6. When I glanced at my car milometer it showed 24942, a palindromic number. Two days later, I noticed that it showed the next palindromic number. How many miles did my car travel in those two days?

   A 100   B 110   C 200   D 220   E 1010

7. What is the value of x in this diagram?

   A 30   B 35   C 40   D 45   E 50

8. A square piece of card has a square of side 2 cm cut out from each of its corners. The remaining card is then folded along the dotted lines shown to form an open box whose total internal surface area is 180 cm^2.

   What is the volume of the open box in cm^3?

   A 100   B 128   C 162   D 180   E 200

9. In the diagram, XY is a straight line. What is the value of x?

   A 170   B 160   C 150
   D 140   E 130

10. Merlin magically transforms a 6 tonne monster into mice with the same total mass. Each mouse has a mass of 20g. How many mice does Merlin make?

    A 30　　　B 300　　　C 3000　　　D 30 000　　　E 300 000

11. What is the value of $19\frac{1}{2} \times 20\frac{1}{2}$?

    A 250　　　B $380\frac{1}{4}$　　　C $390\frac{1}{4}$　　　D 395　　　E $399\frac{3}{4}$

12. What is the sum of the first 2011 digits when $20 \div 11$ is written as a decimal?

    A 6013　　　B 7024　　　C 8035　　　D 9046　　　E 10057

13. The three blind mice stole a piece of cheese. In the night, the first mouse ate $\frac{1}{3}$ of the cheese. Later, the second mouse ate $\frac{1}{3}$ of the remaining cheese. Finally, the third mouse ate $\frac{1}{3}$ of what was then left of the cheese.
    Between them, what fraction of the cheese did they eat?

    A $\frac{16}{27}$　　　B $\frac{17}{27}$　　　C $\frac{2}{3}$　　　D $\frac{19}{27}$　　　E $\frac{20}{27}$

14. The number 6 lies exactly halfway between 3 and 3^2. Which of the following is not halfway between a positive integer and its square?

    A 3　　　B 10　　　C 15　　　D 21　　　E 30

15. The equilateral triangle ABC has sides of length 1 and AB lies on the line XY. The triangle is rotated clockwise around B until BC lies on the line XY. It is then rotated similarly around C and then about A as shown in the diagram.
    What is the length of the path traced out by point C during this sequence of rotations?

    A $\frac{4\pi}{3}$　　　B $2\sqrt{3}$　　　C $\frac{8\pi}{3}$　　　D 3　　　E $\frac{2\pi}{3}$

16. The diagram shows an L-shape divided into 1×1 squares. Gwyn cuts the shape along some of the lines shown to make two pieces, neither of which is a square. She then uses the pieces to form a 2×6 rectangle.
    What is the difference between the areas of the two pieces?

    A 0　　B 1　　C 2　　D 3　　E 4

17. A shop advertised "Everything half price in our sale", but also now advertises that there is "An additional 15% off sale prices". Overall, this is equivalent to what reduction on the original prices?

    A 7.5%　　　B 35%　　　C 57.5%　　　D 65%　　　E 80%

18. The diagram contains six equilateral triangles with sides of length 2 and a regular hexagon with sides of length 1.

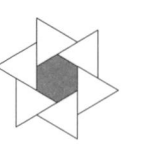

    What fraction of the whole shape is shaded?

    A $\frac{1}{8}$ B $\frac{1}{7}$ C $\frac{1}{6}$ D $\frac{1}{5}$ E $\frac{1}{4}$

19. Harrogate is 23km due north of Leeds, York is 30km due east of Harrogate, Doncaster is 48km due south of York, and Manchester is 70km due west of Doncaster. To the nearest kilometre, how far is it from Leeds to Manchester, as the crow flies?

    A 38km   B 47km   C 56km   D 65km   E 74km

20. Max and his dog Molly set out for a walk. Max walked up the road and then back down again, completing a six mile round trip. Molly, being an old dog, walked at half Max's speed. When Max reached the end of the road, he turned around and walked back to the starting point, at his original speed. Part way back he met Molly, who then turned around and followed Max home, still maintaining her original speed. How far did Molly walk?

    A 1 mile   B 2 miles   C 3 miles   D 4 miles   E 5 miles

---

21. A regular octagon is placed inside a square, as shown. The shaded square connects the midpoints of four sides of the octagon.

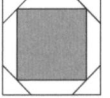

    What fraction of the outer square is shaded?

    A $\sqrt{2}-1$ B $\frac{1}{2}$ C $\frac{\sqrt{2}+1}{4}$ D $\frac{\sqrt{2}+2}{5}$ E $\frac{3}{4}$

22. You are given that $5^p = 9$, $9^q = 12$, $12^r = 16$, $16^s = 20$ and $20^t = 25$. What is the value of $pqrst$?

    A 1   B 2   C 3   D 4   E 5

23. A window frame in Salt's Mill consists of two equal semicircles and a circle inside a large semicircle with each touching the other three as shown. The width of the frame is 4m.

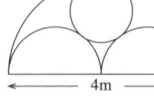

    What is the radius of the circle, in metres?

    A $\frac{2}{3}$ B $\frac{\sqrt{2}}{2}$ C $\frac{3}{4}$ D $2\sqrt{2}-1$ E 1

24. Given any positive integer n, Paul adds together the distinct factors of n, other than n itself. Which of these numbers can never be Paul's answer?

    A 1   B 3   C 5   D 7   E 9

25. The diagram shows a square, a diagonal and a line joining a vertex to the midpoint of a side. What is the ratio of area P to area Q?

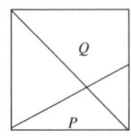

    A $1:\sqrt{2}$ B $2:3$ C $1:2$ D $2:5$ E $1:3$

Intermediate Challenge 2012 paper

1. How many of the following four numbers are prime?

           3   33   333   3333

   A 0   B 1   C 2   D 3   E 4

2. Three positive integers are all different. Their sum is 7. What is their product?

   A 12   B 10   C 9   D 8   E 5

3. An equilateral triangle, a square and a pentagon all have the same side length. The triangle is drawn on and above the top edge of the square and the pentagon is drawn on and below the bottom edge of the square. What is the sum of the interior angles of the resulting polygon?

   A $10 \times 180°$ B $9 \times 180°$ C $8 \times 180°$ D $7 \times 180°$ E $6 \times 180°$

4. All four digits of two 2-digit numbers are different. What is the largest possible sum of two such numbers?

   A 169   B 174   C 183   D 190   E 197

5. How many minutes will elapse between 20:12 today and 21:02 tomorrow?

   A 50   B 770   C 1250   D 1490   E 2450

6. Triangle QRS is isosceles and right-angled.
   Beatrix reflects the P-shape in the side QR to get an image.
   She reflects the first image in the side QS to get a second image.
   Finally, she reflects the second image in the side RS to get a third image.
   What does the third image look like?

       A   B   C   D   E

7. The prime numbers p and q are the smallest primes that differ by 6. What is the sum of p and q?

   A 12   B 14   C 16   D 20   E 28

8. Seb has been challenged to place the numbers 1 to 9 inclusive in the nine regions formed by the Olympic rings so that there is exactly one number in each region and the sum of the numbers in each ring is 11. The diagram shows part of his solution. What number goes in the region marked * ?

   A 6   B 4   C 3   D 2   E 1

9. Auntie Fi's dog Itchy has a million fleas. His anti-flea shampoo claims to leave no more than 1% of the original number of fleas after use. What is the least number of fleas that will be eradicated by the treatment?

   A 900 000   B 990 000   C 999 000   D 999 990   E 999 999

Intermediate Challenge 2012 paper

10. An 'abundant' number is a positive integer N, such that the sum of the factors of N (excluding N itself) is greater than N. What is the smallest abundant number?

    A 5   B 6   C 10   D 12   E 15

11. In the diagram, $PQRS$ is a parallelogram; $\angle QRS = 50°$; $\angle SPT = 62°$ and $PQ = PT$.
What is the size of $\angle TQR$?

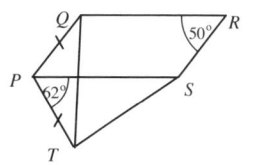

    A 84°   B 90°   C 96°   D 112°   E 124°

12. Which one of the following has a different value from the others?

    A 18% of £30   B 12% of £50   C 6% of £90   D 4% of £135   E 2% of £270

13. Alex Erlich and Paneth Farcas shared an opening rally of 2 hours and 12 minutes during their table tennis match at the 1936 World Games. Each player hit around 45 shots per minute. Which of the following is closest to the total number of shots played in the rally?

    A 200   B 2000   C 8000   D 12 000   E 20 000

14. What value of x makes the mean of the first three numbers in this list equal to the mean of the last four?

    15   5 x 7   9   17

    A 19   B 21   C 24   D 25   E 27

15. Which of the following has a value that is closest to 0?

    A $\frac{1}{2} + \frac{1}{3} \times \frac{1}{4}$ B $\frac{1}{2} + \frac{1}{3} \div \frac{1}{4}$ C $\frac{1}{2} \times \frac{1}{3} \div \frac{1}{4}$ D $\frac{1}{2} - \frac{1}{3} \div \frac{1}{4}$ E $\frac{1}{2} - \frac{1}{3} \times \frac{1}{4}$

16. The diagram shows a large equilateral triangle divided by three straight lines into seven regions. The three grey regions are equilateral triangles with sides of length 5 cm and the central black region is an equilateral triangle with sides of length 2 cm.
What is the side length of the original large triangle?

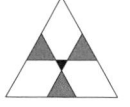

    A 18 cm   B 19 cm   C 20 cm   D 21 cm   E 22 cm

17. The first term of a sequence of positive integers is 6. The other terms in the sequence follow these rules:
    if a term is even then divide it by 2 to obtain the next term;
    if a term is odd then multiply it by 5 and subtract 1 to obtain the next term.
For which values of n is the nth term equal to n?

    A 10 only   B 13 only   C 16 only   D 10 and 13 only   E 13 and 16 only

18. Peri the winkle starts at the origin and slithers anticlockwise around a semicircle with centre $(4, 0)$. Peri then slides anticlockwise around a second semicircle with centre $(6, 0)$, and finally clockwise around a third semicircle with centre $(3, 0)$.
Where does Peri end this expedition?

    A $(0, 0)$ B $(1, 0)$ C $(2, 0)$ D $(4, 0)$ E $(6, 0)$

19. The shaded region shown in the diagram is bounded by four arcs, each of the same radius as that of the surrounding circle. What fraction of the surrounding circle is shaded?

    A $\frac{4}{\pi} - 1$ B $1 - \frac{\pi}{4}$ C $\frac{1}{2}$ D $\frac{1}{3}$ E it depends on the radius of the circle

20. A rectangle with area 125 cm^2 has sides in the ratio 4:5. What is the perimeter of the rectangle?

    A 18 cm B 22.5 cm C 36 cm D 45 cm E 54 cm

21. The parallelogram $PQRS$ is formed by joining together four equilateral triangles of side 1 unit, as shown.
    What is the length of the diagonal SQ?

    A $\sqrt{7}$ B $\sqrt{8}$ C 3 D $\sqrt{6}$ E $\sqrt{5}$

22. What is the maximum possible value of the median number of cups of coffee bought per customer on a day when Sundollars Coffee Shop sells 477 cups of coffee to 190 customers, and every customer buys at least one cup of coffee?

    A 1.5 B 2 C 2.5 D 3 E 3.5

23. In triangle PQR, $PS = 2$; $SR = 1$; $\angle PRQ = 45°$; T is the foot of the perpendicular from P to QS and $\angle PST = 60°$.
    What is the size of $\angle QPR$?

    A 45° B 60° C 75° D 90° E 105°

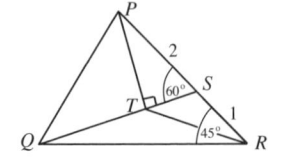

24. All the positive integers are written in the cells of a square grid. Starting from 1, the numbers spiral anticlockwise. The first part of the spiral is shown in the diagram.

    What number will be immediately below 2012?

    A 1837 B 2011 C 2013 D 2195 E 2210

25. The diagram shows a ceramic design by the Catalan architect Antoni Gaudi. It is formed by drawing eight lines connecting points which divide the edges of the outer regular octagon into three equal parts, as shown.
    What fraction of the octagon is shaded?

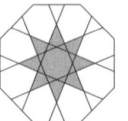

    A $\frac{1}{5}$ B $\frac{2}{9}$ C $\frac{1}{4}$ D $\frac{3}{10}$ E $\frac{5}{16}$

Intermediate Challenge
2013 paper

1. Which of the following is divisible by 6?

   A one million minus one   B one million minus two   C one million minus three
   D one million minus four   E one million minus five

2. A machine cracks open 180 000 eggs per hour. How many eggs is that per second?

   A 5   B 50   C 500   D 5000   E 50 000

3. How many quadrilaterals are there in this diagram, which is constructed using 6 straight lines?

   A 4   B 5   C 7   D 8   E 9

4. A standard pack of pumpkin seeds contains 40 seeds. A special pack contains 25% more seeds. Rachel bought a special pack and 70% of the seeds germinated. How many pumpkin plants did Rachel have?

   A 20   B 25   C 28   D 35   E 50

5. The northern wheatear is a small bird weighing less than an ounce. Some northern wheatears migrate from sub-Saharan Africa to their Arctic breeding grounds, travelling almost 15 000 km. The journey takes just over 7 weeks. Roughly how far do they travel each day, on average?

   A 1 km   B 9 km   C 30 km   D 90 km   E 300 km

6. Which of the following has the least value?

   A $1^0 - 0^1$ B $2^1 - 1^2$ C $3^2 - 2^3$ D $4^3 - 3^4$ E $5^4 - 4^5$

7. The faces of a regular octahedron are to be painted so that no two faces which have an edge in common are painted in the same colour. What is the smallest number of colours required?

   A 2   B 3   C 4   D 6   E 8

8. Jim rolled some dice and was surprised that the sum of the scores on the dice was equal to the product of the scores on the dice. One of the dice showed a score of 2, one showed 3 and one showed 5. The rest showed a score of 1. How many dice did Jim roll?

   A 10   B 13   C 17   D 23   E 30

9. Jane has 20 identical cards in the shape of an isosceles right-angled triangle. She uses the cards to make the five shapes below. Which of the shapes has the shortest perimeter?

10. $ABCDE$ is a regular pentagon and BCF is an equilateral triangle such that F is inside $ABCDE$. What is the size of $\angle FAB$?

    A 48°   B 63°   C 66°   D 69°   E 72°

11. For which of the following numbers is the sum of all its factors *not* equal to a square number?

    A 3   B 22   C 40   D 66   E 70

12. The sum   one + four = seventy
    becomes correct if we replace each word by the number of letters in it to give 3 + 4 = 7.
    Using the same convention, which of these words could be substituted for x to make the sum
                    three + five = x true?

    A eight   B nine   C twelve   D seventeen   E eighteen

13. Four congruent isosceles trapeziums are placed so that their longer
    parallel sides form the diagonals of a square $PQRS$, as shown. The point
    X divides PQ in the ratio 3:1. What fraction of the square is shaded?

    A $\dfrac{5}{16}$ B $\dfrac{3}{8}$ C $\dfrac{7}{16}$ D $\dfrac{5}{12}$ E $\dfrac{1}{2}$

14. Which of the following has the greatest value?

    A $\left(\dfrac{11}{7}\right)^3$ B $\left(\dfrac{5}{3}\right)^3$ C $\left(\dfrac{7}{4}\right)^3$ D $\left(\dfrac{9}{5}\right)^3$ E $\left(\dfrac{3}{2}\right)^3$

15. I have a bag of coins. In it, one third of the coins are gold, one fifth of them are silver, two
    sevenths are bronze and the rest are copper. My bag can hold a maximum of 200 coins. How
    many coins are in my bag?

    A 101   B 105   C 153   D 195   E more information is needed

16. Which diagram shows the graph of $y = x$ after it has been rotated 90° clockwise about the
    point (1, 1)?

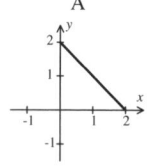

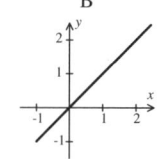

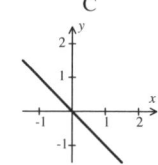

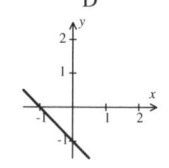

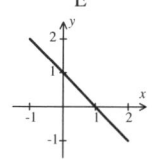

17. The diagram shows four equal discs and a square. Each disc
    touches its two neighbouring discs. Each corner of the square is
    positioned at the centre of a disc. The side length of the square is
    $2/\pi$. What is the length of the perimeter of the figure?

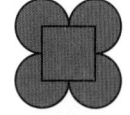

    A 3   B 4   C $\dfrac{3\pi}{2}$ D 6   E 2π

18. The triangle T has sides of length 6, 5, 5. The triangle U has sides of length 8, 5, 5.
    What is the ratio area T : area U?

    A 9 : 16   B 3 : 4   C 1 : 1   D 4 : 3   E 16 : 9

19. Which of the expressions below is equivalent to $(x \div (y \div z)) \div ((x \div y) \div z)$?

    A 1   B $\dfrac{1}{xyz}$ C x^2 D y^2 E z^2

20. Jack's teacher asked him to draw a triangle of area 7cm^2. Two sides are to be of length 6cm and 8cm. How many possibilities are there for the length of the third side of the triangle?

    A 1   B 2   C 3   D 4   E more than 4

21. The square *ABCD* has an area of 196. It contains two overlapping squares; the larger of these squares has an area 4 times that of the smaller and the area of their overlap is 1. What is the total area of the shaded regions?

    A 44   B 72   C 80   D 152
    E more information is needed

22. The diagrams show squares placed inside two identical semicircles. In the lower diagram the two squares are identical.
What is the ratio of the areas of the two shaded regions?

    A 1:2   B 2:3   C 3:4   D 4:5   E 5:6

23. Four brothers are discussing the order in which they were born. Two are lying and two are telling the truth. Which two are telling the truth?

Alfred: "Bernard is the youngest."   Horatio: "Bernard is the oldest and I am the youngest."
Inigo: "I was born last."   Bernard: "I'm neither the youngest nor the oldest."

    A Bernard and Inigo   B Horatio and Bernard   C Alfred and Horatio
                 D Alfred and Bernard   E Inigo and Horatio

24. The diagram shows a shaded shape bounded by circular arcs with the same radius. The centres of three arcs are the vertices of an equilateral triangle; the other three centres are the midpoints of the sides of the triangle. The sides of the triangle have length 2.
What is the difference between the area of the shaded shape and the area of the triangle?

    A $\dfrac{\pi}{6}$ B $\dfrac{\pi}{4}$ C $\dfrac{\pi}{3}$ D $\dfrac{\pi}{2}$ E π

25. In 1984 the engineer and prolific prime-finder Harvey Dubner found the biggest known prime each of whose digits is either a one or a zero. The prime can be expressed as $\dfrac{10^{641} \times (10^{640} - 1)}{9} + 1$. How many digits does this prime have?

    A 640   B 641   C 1280   D 1281   E 640 × 641

Intermediate Challenge
2014 paper

1. What is 25 % of $\frac{3}{4}$?

   A $\frac{3}{16}$ B $\frac{1}{4}$ C $\frac{1}{3}$ D 1   E 3

2. Which is the smallest positive integer for which all these are true?
   (i) It is odd.
   (ii) It is not prime.
   (iii) The next largest odd integer is not prime.

   A 9   B 15   C 21   D 25   E 33

3. An equilateral triangle is placed inside a larger equilateral triangle so that the diagram has three lines of symmetry. What is the value of x?

   A 100   B 110   C 120   D 130   E 150

4. You are given that m is an even integer and n is an odd integer. Which of these is an odd integer?

   A $3m + 4n$ B $5mn$ C $(m + 3n)^2$ D m^3n^3 E $5m + 6n$

5. A ship's bell is struck every half hour, starting with one bell at 0030, two bells (meaning the bell is struck twice) at 0100, three bells at 0130 until the cycle is complete with eight bells at 0400. The cycle then starts again with one bell at 0430, two bells at 0500 and so on. What is the total number of times the bell is struck between 0015 on one day and 0015 on the following day?

   A 24   B 48   C 108   D 144   E 216

6. The shape shown on the right was assembled from three identical copies of one of the smaller shapes below, without gaps or overlaps. Which smaller shape was used?

7. Just one positive integer has exactly 8 factors including 6 and 15. What is the integer?

   A 21   B 30   C 45   D 60   E 90

8. A large cube is made by stacking eight dice. The diagram shows the result, except that one of the dice is missing. Each die has faces with 1, 2, 3, 4, 5 and 6 pips and the total number of pips on each pair of opposite faces is 7. When two dice are placed face to face, the matching faces must have the same number of pips. What could the missing die look like?

9. At the age of twenty-six, Gill has passed her driving test and bought a car. Her car uses p litres of petrol per 100 km travelled. How many litres of petrol would be required for a journey of d km?

A $\dfrac{pd}{100}$ B $\dfrac{100p}{d}$ C $\dfrac{100d}{p}$ D $\dfrac{100}{pd}$ E $\dfrac{p}{100d}$

10. The diagram shows five touching semicircles, each with radius 2.

What is the length of the perimeter of the shaded shape?

A 5π B 6π C 7π D 8π E 9π

11. Not all characters in the Woodentops series tell the truth. When Mr Plod asked them, "How many people are there in the Woodentops family?", four of them replied as follows:

Jenny: "An even number."   Willie: "An odd number."   Sam: "A prime number."

Mrs Scrubitt: "A number which is the product of two integers greater than one."

How many of these four were telling the truth?

A 0 B 1 C 2 D 3 E 4

12. The diagram shows an isosceles right-angled triangle divided into strips of equal width. Four of the strips are shaded.
What fraction of the area of the triangle is shaded?

A $\dfrac{11}{32}$ B $\dfrac{3}{8}$ C $\dfrac{13}{32}$ D $\dfrac{7}{16}$ E $\dfrac{15}{32}$

13. How many numbers can be written as a sum of two different positive integers each at most 100?

A 100 B 197 C 198 D 199 E 200

14. This year the *Tour de France* starts in Leeds on 5 July. Last year, the total length of the *Tour* was 3404 km and the winner, Chris Froome, took a total time of 83 hours 56 minutes 40 seconds to cover this distance. Which of these is closest to his average speed over the whole event?

A 32 km/h B 40 km/h C 48 km/h D 56 km/h E 64 km/h

15. Zac halves a certain number and then adds 8 to the result. He finds that he obtains the same answer if he doubles his original number and then subtracts 8 from the result.
What is Zac's original number?

A $8\tfrac{2}{3}$ B $9\tfrac{1}{3}$ C $9\tfrac{2}{3}$ D $10\tfrac{1}{3}$ E $10\tfrac{2}{3}$

16. The base of a triangle is increased by 25% but the area of the triangle is unchanged. By what percentage is the corresponding perpendicular height decreased?

    A $12\frac{1}{2}$%   B 16%   C 20%   D 25%   E 50%

17. How many weeks are there in $8 \times 7 \times 6 \times 5 \times 4 \times 3 \times 2 \times 1$ minutes?

    A 1   B 2   C 3   D 4   E 5

18. Consider looking from the origin $(0, 0)$ towards all the points (m, n), where each of m and n is an integer. Some points are *hidden*, because they are directly in line with another nearer point. For example, $(2, 2)$ is hidden by $(1, 1)$.
    How many of the points $(6, 2), (6, 3), (6, 4), (6, 5)$ are *not* hidden points?

    A 0   B 1   C 2   D 3   E 4

19. Suppose that $8^m = 27$. What is the value of 4^m?

    A 3   B 4   C 9   D 13.5   E there is no such m

20. The diagram shows a regular pentagon and five circular arcs. The sides of the pentagon have length 4. The centre of each arc is a vertex of the pentagon, and the ends of the arc are the midpoints of the two adjacent edges.
    What is the total shaded area?

    A 8π B 10π C 12π D 14π E 16π

21. In King Arthur's jousting tournament, each of the several competing knights receives 17 points for every bout he enters. The winner of each bout receives an extra 3 points. At the end of the tournament, the Black Knight has exactly one more point than the Red Knight.
    What is the smallest number of bouts that the Black Knight could have entered?

    A 3   B 4   C 5   D 6   E 7

22. The positive integers a, b and c are all different. None of them is a square but all the products ab, ac and bc are squares. What is the least value that $a + b + c$ can take?

    A 14   B 28   C 42   D 56   E 70

23. A sector of a disc is removed by making two straight cuts from the circumference to the centre. The perimeter of the sector has the same length as the circumference of the original disc. What fraction of the area of the disc is removed?

    A $\dfrac{\pi - 1}{\pi}$ B $\dfrac{1}{\pi}$ C $\dfrac{\pi}{360}$ D $\dfrac{1}{3}$ E $\dfrac{1}{2}$

24. How many 4-digit integers (from 1000 to 9999) have at least one digit repeated?

    A 62×72 B 52×72 C 52×82 D 42×82 E 42×92

25. The diagram shows two concentric circles with radii 1 and 2 units, together with a shaded octagon, all of whose sides are equal.
    What is the length of the perimeter of the octagon?

    A $8\sqrt{2}$ B $8\sqrt{3}$ C $8\sqrt{3\pi}$
    D $2\sqrt{5} + 2\sqrt{2}$ E $8\sqrt{5 - 2\sqrt{2}}$

Intermediate Challenge 2015 paper

1. What is the value of 1 − 0.2 + 0.03 − 0.004?

   A 0.826 B 0.834 C 0.926 D 1.226 E 1.234

2. Last year, Australian Suzy Walsham won the annual women's race up the 1576 steps of the Empire State Building in New York for a record fifth time. Her winning time was 11 minutes 57 seconds. Approximately how many steps did she climb per minute?

   A 13 B 20 C 80 D 100 E 130

3. What is a half of a third, plus a third of a quarter, plus a quarter of a fifth?

   A $\dfrac{1}{1440}$ B $\dfrac{3}{38}$ C $\dfrac{1}{30}$ D $\dfrac{1}{3}$ E $\dfrac{3}{10}$

4. The diagram shows a regular pentagon inside a square.
   What is the value of x?

   A 48 B 51 C 54 D 60 E 72

5. Which of the following numbers is not a square?

   A 1^6 B 2^5 C 3^4 D 4^3 E 5^2

6. The equilateral triangle and regular hexagon shown have perimeters of the same length.
   What is the ratio of the area of the triangle to the area of the hexagon?

   A 5 : 6 B 4 : 5 C 3 : 4 D 2 : 3 E 1 : 1

7. A tetrahedron is a solid figure which has four faces, all of which are triangles.
   What is the product of the number of edges and the number of vertices of the tetrahedron?

   A 8 B 10 C 12 D 18 E 24

8. How many two-digit squares differ by 1 from a multiple of 10?

   A 1 B 2 C 3 D 4 E 5

9. What is the value of $p + q + r + s + t + u + v + w + x + y$ in the diagram?

   A 540 B 720 C 900 D 1080 E 1440

10. What is the remainder when $2^2 \times 3^3 \times 5^5 \times 7^7$ is divided by 8?

    A 2 B 3 C 4 D 5 E 7

Intermediate Challenge 2015 paper   77

11. Three different positive integers have a mean of 7. What is the largest positive integer that could be one of them?

    A 15   B 16   C 17   D 18   E 19

12. An ant is on the square marked with a black dot. The ant moves across an edge from one square to an adjacent square four times and then stops. How many of the possible finishing squares are black?

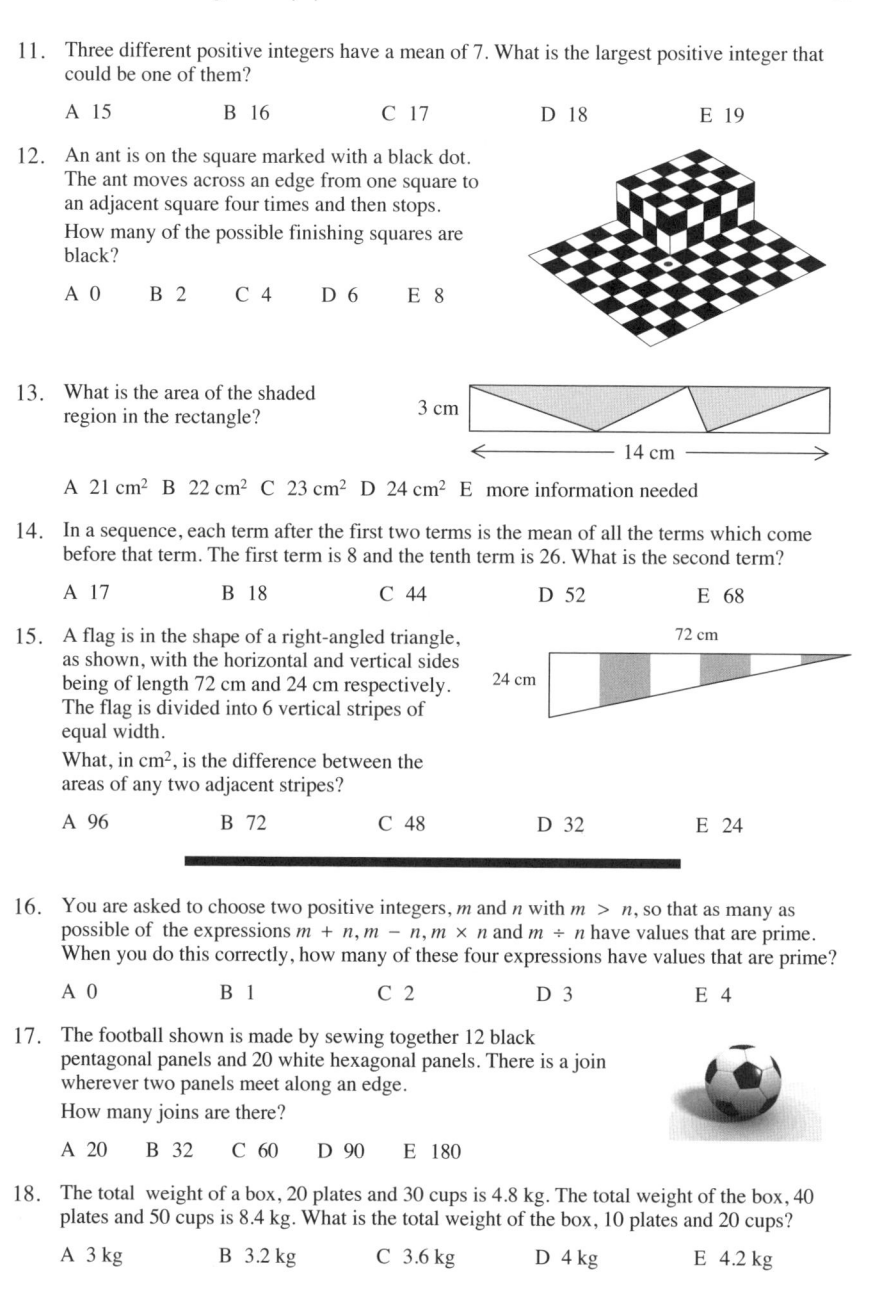

    A 0   B 2   C 4   D 6   E 8

13. What is the area of the shaded region in the rectangle?

    A 21 cm²   B 22 cm²   C 23 cm²   D 24 cm²   E more information needed

14. In a sequence, each term after the first two terms is the mean of all the terms which come before that term. The first term is 8 and the tenth term is 26. What is the second term?

    A 17   B 18   C 44   D 52   E 68

15. A flag is in the shape of a right-angled triangle, as shown, with the horizontal and vertical sides being of length 72 cm and 24 cm respectively. The flag is divided into 6 vertical stripes of equal width.
    What, in cm², is the difference between the areas of any two adjacent stripes?

    A 96   B 72   C 48   D 32   E 24

16. You are asked to choose two positive integers, m and n with $m > n$, so that as many as possible of the expressions $m + n, m - n, m \times n$ and $m \div n$ have values that are prime. When you do this correctly, how many of these four expressions have values that are prime?

    A 0   B 1   C 2   D 3   E 4

17. The football shown is made by sewing together 12 black pentagonal panels and 20 white hexagonal panels. There is a join wherever two panels meet along an edge.
    How many joins are there?

    A 20   B 32   C 60   D 90   E 180

18. The total weight of a box, 20 plates and 30 cups is 4.8 kg. The total weight of the box, 40 plates and 50 cups is 8.4 kg. What is the total weight of the box, 10 plates and 20 cups?

    A 3 kg   B 3.2 kg   C 3.6 kg   D 4 kg   E 4.2 kg

19. The figure shows four smaller squares in the corners of a large square. The smaller squares have sides of length 1 cm, 2 cm, 3 cm and 4 cm (in anticlockwise order) and the sides of the large square have length 11 cm.
    What is the area of the shaded quadrilateral?

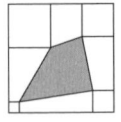

    A 35 cm²   B 36 cm²   C 37 cm²   D 38 cm²   E 39 cm²

20. A voucher code is made up of four characters. The first is a letter: V, X or P. The second and third are different digits. The fourth is the units digit of the sum of the second and third digits. How many different voucher codes like this are there?

    A 180   B 243   C 270   D 300   E 2700

21. A rectangle is placed obliquely on top of an identical rectangle, as shown.
    The area X of the overlapping region (shaded more darkly) is one eighth of the total shaded area.
    What fraction of the area of one rectangle is X ?

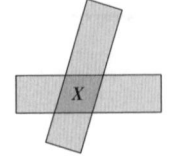

    A $\frac{1}{3}$ B $\frac{2}{7}$ C $\frac{1}{4}$ D $\frac{2}{9}$ E $\frac{1}{5}$

22. The diagram shows a shaded region inside a large square. The shaded region is divided into small squares.
    What fraction of the area of the large square is shaded?

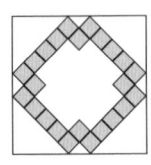

    A $\frac{3}{10}$ B $\frac{1}{3}$ C $\frac{3}{8}$ D $\frac{2}{5}$ E $\frac{3}{7}$

23. There are 120 different ways of arranging the letters, U, K, M, I and C. All of these arrangements are listed in dictionary order, starting with CIKMU. Which position in the list does UKIMC occupy?

    A 110 th   B 112 th   C 114 th   D 116 th   E 118 th

24. In square $RSTU$ a quarter-circle arc with centre S is drawn from T to R. A point P on this arc is 1 unit from TU and 8 units from RU.
    What is the length of the side of square $RSTU$?

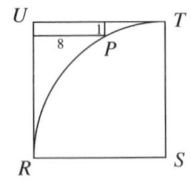

    A 9   B 10   C 11   D 12   E 13

25. A point is marked one quarter of the way along each side of a triangle, as shown.
    What fraction of the area of the triangle is shaded?

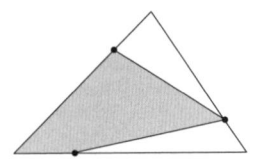

    A $\frac{7}{16}$ B $\frac{1}{2}$ C $\frac{9}{16}$ D $\frac{5}{8}$ E $\frac{11}{16}$

Intermediate Challenge
2016 paper

1. What is the value of 6102 − 2016?

   A 3994   B 4086   C 4096   D 4114   E 4994

2. Which of the following fractions is closest to 1?

   A $\dfrac{7}{8}$ B $\dfrac{8}{7}$ C $\dfrac{9}{10}$ D $\dfrac{10}{11}$ E $\dfrac{11}{10}$

3. How many of these five expressions give answers which are *not* prime numbers?

   $1^2 + 2^2$ $2^2 + 3^2$ $3^2 + 4^2$ $4^2 + 5^2$ $5^2 + 6^2$

   A 0   B 1   C 2   D 3   E 4

4. Amrita is baking a cake today. She bakes a cake every fifth day. How many days will it be before she next bakes a cake on a Thursday?

   A 5   B 7   C 14   D 25   E 35

5. When travelling from London to Edinburgh by train, you pass a sign saying 'Edinburgh 200 miles'. Then, $3\frac{1}{2}$ miles later, you pass another sign saying 'Half way between London and Edinburgh'.
   How many miles is it by train from London to Edinburgh?

   A 393   B $396\frac{1}{2}$ C 400   D $403\frac{1}{2}$ E 407

6. One third of the animals in Jacob's flock are goats, the rest are sheep. There are twelve more sheep than goats.
   How many animals are there altogether in Jacob's flock?

   A 12   B 24   C 36   D 48   E 60

7. In the diagram, what is the value of x?

   A 23   B 24   C 25   D 26   E 27

8. What is the value of $2.017 \times 2016 - 10.16 \times 201.7$?

   A 2.016   B 2.017   C 20.16   D 2016   E 2017

9. The world's fastest tortoise is acknowledged to be a leopard tortoise from County Durham called Bertie. In July 2014, Bertie sprinted along a 5.5 m long track in an astonishing 19.6 seconds.
   What was Bertie's approximate average speed in km per hour?

   A 0.1   B 0.5   C 1   D 5   E 10

10. The angles of a quadrilateral taken in order are $x°$, $5x°$, $2x°$ and $4x°$. Which of the following is the quadrilateral?

    A kite   B parallelogram   C rhombus   D arrowhead   E trapezium

Intermediate Challenge 2016 paper 81

11. The net shown consists of squares and equilateral triangles. The net is folded to form a rhombicuboctahedron, as shown.
    When the face marked P is placed face down on a table, which face will be facing up?
    A   B   C   D   E

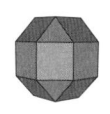

12. The sum of two numbers a and b is 7 and the difference between them is 2. What is the value of $a \times b$?
    A $8\frac{1}{4}$ B $9\frac{1}{4}$ C $10\frac{1}{4}$ D $11\frac{1}{4}$ E $12\frac{1}{4}$

13. The diagram shows a heptagon with a line of three circles on each side. Each circle is to contain exactly one number. The numbers 8 to 14 are distributed as shown and the numbers 1 to 7 are to be distributed to the remaining circles. The total of the numbers in each of the lines of three circles is to be the same.
    What is this total?
    A 18   B 19   C 20   D 21   E 22

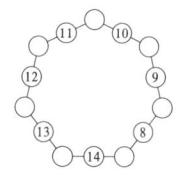

14. Tegwen has the same number of brothers as she has sisters. Each one of her brothers has 50% more sisters than brothers.
    How many children are in Tegwen's family?
    A 5   B 7   C 9   D 11   E 13

15. The circle has radius 1 cm. Two vertices of the square lie on the circle. One edge of the square goes through the centre of the circle, as shown.
    What is the area of the square?
    A $\frac{4}{5}$ cm^2 B $\frac{\pi}{5}$ cm^2 C 1 cm^2 D $\frac{\pi}{4}$ cm^2 E $\frac{5}{4}$ cm^2

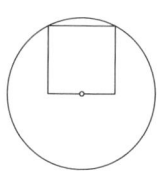

16. How many of the following positive integers are divisible by 24?
    $2^2 \times 3^2 \times 5^2 \times 7^3$ $2^2 \times 3^2 \times 5^3 \times 7^2$ $2^2 \times 3^3 \times 5^2 \times 7^2$ $2^3 \times 3^2 \times 5^2 \times 7^2$
    A 0   B 1   C 2   D 3   E 4

17. The shaded region in the diagram, bounded by two concentric circles, is called an *annulus*. The circles have radii 2 cm and 14 cm. The dashed circle divides the area of this annulus into two equal areas.
    What is its radius?
    A 9 cm   B 10 cm   C 11 cm   D 12 cm   E 13 cm

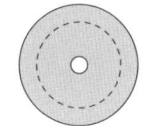

18. The sum of the areas of the squares on the sides of a right-angled isosceles triangle is 72 cm^2.
    What is the area of the triangle?
    A 6 cm^2 B 8 cm^2 C 9 cm^2 D 12 cm^2 E 18 cm^2

19. A list of positive integers has a median of 8, a mode of 9 and a mean of 10.
    What is the smallest possible number of integers in the list?
    A 5   B 6   C 7   D 8   E 9

20. Two semicircles are drawn in a rectangle as shown. What is the width of the overlap of the two semicircles?

   A 3 cm   B 4 cm   C 5 cm   D 6 cm   E 7 cm

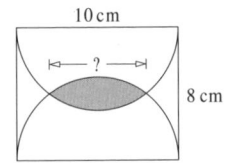

21. The diagram shows a regular octagon. What is the ratio of the area of the shaded trapezium to the area of the whole octagon?

   A 1 : 4   B 5 : 16   C 1 : 3   D $\sqrt{2}$: 2   E 3 : 8

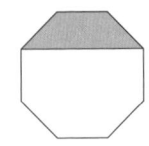

22. In a particular group of people, some always tell the truth, the rest always lie. There are 2016 in the group. One day, the group is sitting in a circle. Each person in the group says, "Both the person on my left and the person on my right are liars."
   What is the difference between the largest and smallest number of people who could be telling the truth?

   A 0   B 72   C 126   D 288   E 336

23. A Saxon silver penny, from the reign of Ethelbert II in the eighth century, was sold in 2014 for £78 000. A design on the coin depicts a circle surrounded by four equal arcs, each a quarter of a circle, as shown. The width of the design is 2 cm.
   What is the radius of the small circle, in centimetres?

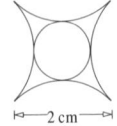

   A $\frac{1}{2}$ B $2 - \sqrt{2}$ C $\frac{1}{2}\sqrt{2}$ D $5 - 3\sqrt{2}$ E $2\sqrt{2} - 2$

24. Every day, Aimee goes up an escalator on her journey to work. If she stands still, it takes her 60 seconds to travel from the bottom to the top. One day the escalator was broken so she had to walk up it. This took her 90 seconds.
   How many seconds would it take her to travel up the escalator if she walked up at the same speed as before while it was working?

   A 30   B 32   C 36   D 45   E 75

25. The tiling pattern shown uses two types of tile, regular hexagons and equilateral triangles, with the length of each side of the equilateral triangles equal to half the length of each side of the hexagons. A large number of tiles is used to cover a floor.
   Which of the following is closest to the fraction of the floor that is shaded black?

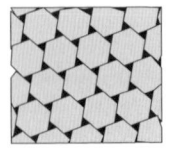

   A $\frac{1}{8}$ B $\frac{1}{10}$ C $\frac{1}{12}$ D $\frac{1}{13}$ E $\frac{1}{16}$

Senior Challenge 2006 paper

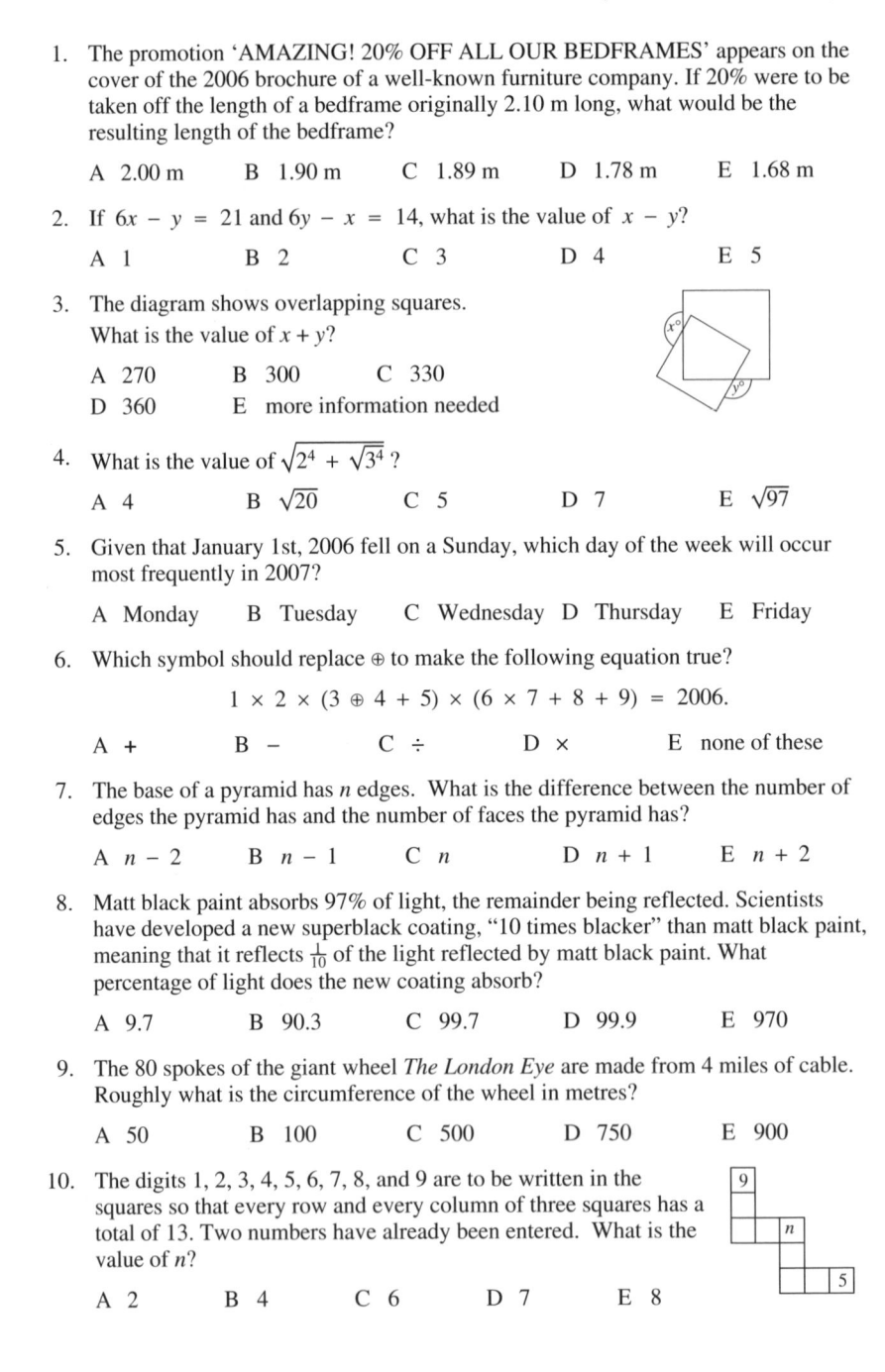

1. The promotion 'AMAZING! 20% OFF ALL OUR BEDFRAMES' appears on the cover of the 2006 brochure of a well-known furniture company. If 20% were to be taken off the length of a bedframe originally 2.10 m long, what would be the resulting length of the bedframe?

   A 2.00 m   B 1.90 m   C 1.89 m   D 1.78 m   E 1.68 m

2. If $6x - y = 21$ and $6y - x = 14$, what is the value of $x - y$?

   A 1   B 2   C 3   D 4   E 5

3. The diagram shows overlapping squares. What is the value of $x + y$?

   A 270   B 300   C 330
   D 360   E more information needed

4. What is the value of $\sqrt{2^4 + \sqrt{3^4}}$?

   A 4   B $\sqrt{20}$ C 5   D 7   E $\sqrt{97}$

5. Given that January 1st, 2006 fell on a Sunday, which day of the week will occur most frequently in 2007?

   A Monday   B Tuesday   C Wednesday   D Thursday   E Friday

6. Which symbol should replace ⊕ to make the following equation true?

   $$1 \times 2 \times (3 \oplus 4 + 5) \times (6 \times 7 + 8 + 9) = 2006.$$

   A +   B −   C ÷   D ×   E none of these

7. The base of a pyramid has n edges. What is the difference between the number of edges the pyramid has and the number of faces the pyramid has?

   A $n - 2$ B $n - 1$ C n D $n + 1$ E $n + 2$

8. Matt black paint absorbs 97% of light, the remainder being reflected. Scientists have developed a new superblack coating, "10 times blacker" than matt black paint, meaning that it reflects $\frac{1}{10}$ of the light reflected by matt black paint. What percentage of light does the new coating absorb?

   A 9.7   B 90.3   C 99.7   D 99.9   E 970

9. The 80 spokes of the giant wheel *The London Eye* are made from 4 miles of cable. Roughly what is the circumference of the wheel in metres?

   A 50   B 100   C 500   D 750   E 900

10. The digits 1, 2, 3, 4, 5, 6, 7, 8, and 9 are to be written in the squares so that every row and every column of three squares has a total of 13. Two numbers have already been entered. What is the value of n?

    A 2   B 4   C 6   D 7   E 8

Senior Challenge 2006 paper

11. Three consecutive even numbers are such that the sum of four times the smallest and twice the largest exceeds three times the second by 2006. What is the sum of the digits of the smallest number?

   A 8   B 11   C 14   D 17   E 20

12. The factorial of n, written $n!$, is defined by $n! = 1 \times 2 \times 3 \times \ldots \times (n-2) \times (n-1) \times n$. Which of the following values of n provides a counterexample to the statement:
   "If n is a prime number, then $n! + 1$ is also a prime number"?

   A 1   B 2   C 3   D 4   E 5

13. The diagram shows five discs connected by five line segments. Three colours are available to colour these discs.
   In how many different ways is it possible to colour all five discs if discs which are connected by a line segment are to have different colours?

   A 6   B 12   C 30   D 36   E 48

14. Heather and Rachel each has some pennies. Heather has more than Rachel. In fact, the number of pennies that Heather has is the square of the number that Rachel has. The total number of pennies they have between them makes a whole number of pounds. What is the smallest this total could be?

   A £1   B £6   C £57   D £99   E £101

15. $PQRS$ is a square with U and V the mid-points of the sides PS and SR respectively. Line segments PV and UR meet at T.
   What fraction of the area of the square $PQRS$ is the area of the quadrilateral $PQRT$?

   A $\frac{1}{2}$ B $\frac{5}{8}$ C $\frac{2}{3}$ D $\frac{3}{4}$ E $\frac{5}{9}$

16. If $\alpha < \beta$, how many different values are there among the following expressions?

   $\sin \alpha \sin \beta$ $\sin \alpha \cos \beta$ $\cos \alpha \sin \beta$ $\cos \alpha \cos \beta$

   A 1   B 2   C 3   D 4   E It depends on the value of α

17. A trapezium is bounded by four lines, the equations of which are $x = 0$, $x = 4$, $4y = 3x + 8$ and $y = k$, where $k < 2$.
   For which value of k is the numerical value of the perimeter of the trapezium equal to the numerical value of the area of the trapezium?

   A $\frac{3}{2}$ B 1   C $\frac{1}{2}$ D $-\frac{1}{2}$ E -1

18. What is the greatest number of the following five statements about numbers a, b which can be true at the same time?

   $\frac{1}{a} < \frac{1}{b}$ $a^2 > b^2$ $a < b$ $a < 0$ $b < 0$

   A 1   B 2   C 3   D 4   E 5

19. An engineer is directed to a faulty signal, one quarter of the way into a tunnel. Whilst there, he is warned of a train heading towards the tunnel entrance. The engineer can run at 12 mph and can either run back to the tunnel entrance or forward to the exit. In either case, the engineer and the front of the train would reach the entrance or exit together. What is the speed in mph of the train?

    A 16   B 20   C 24   D 32   E more information needed

20. A positive number $a = [a] + \{a\}$ where $[a]$ is the integer part of a and $\{a\}$ is the fractional part of a.
    Given that $x + [y] + \{z\} = 4.2$, $y + [z] + \{x\} = 3.6$, $z + [x] + \{y\} = 2.0$, and $x, y, z > 0$, what is the value of $\{y\}$?

    A 0.1   B 0.3   C 0.5   D 0.7   E 0.9

21. A toy pool table is 6 feet long and 3 feet wide. It has pockets at each of the four corners P, Q, R and S. When a ball hits a side of the table, it bounces off the side at the same angle as it hit that side. A ball, initially 1 foot to the left of pocket P, is hit from the side SP towards the side PQ as shown. 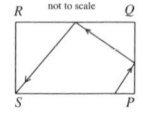
    How many feet from P does the ball hit side PQ if it lands in pocket S after two bounces?

    A 1   B $\dfrac{6}{7}$ C $\dfrac{3}{4}$ D $\dfrac{2}{3}$ E $\dfrac{3}{5}$

22. Which positive integer n satisfies the equation
    $$\frac{3}{n^3} + \frac{4}{n^3} + \frac{5}{n^3} + \ldots + \frac{n^3 - 5}{n^3} + \frac{n^3 - 4}{n^3} + \frac{n^3 - 3}{n^3} = 60 \; ?$$

    A 5   B 11   C 31   D 60   E 2006

23. In the diagram, the circle and the two semicircles have radius 1. What is the perimeter of the square?

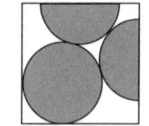

    A $6 + 4\sqrt{2}$ B $2 + 4\sqrt{2} + 2\sqrt{3}$ C $3\sqrt{2} + 4\sqrt{3}$
    D $4 + 2\sqrt{2} + 2\sqrt{6}$ E 12

24. A solid red plastic cube, volume 1 cm³, is painted white on its outside. The cube is cut by a plane passing through the midpoints of various edges, as shown.
    What, in cm², is the *total* red area exposed by the cut?

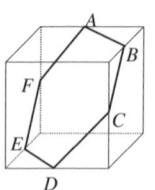

    A $\dfrac{3\sqrt{3}}{2}$ B 2   C $\dfrac{9\sqrt{2}}{5}$ D 3   E $\dfrac{3(\sqrt{3} + \sqrt{2})}{4}$

25. X is a positive integer in which each digit is 1; that is, X is of the form 11111… .
    Given that every digit of the integer $pX^2 + qX + r$ (where p, q and r are fixed integer coefficients and $p > 0$) is also 1, irrespective of the number of digits X, which of the following is a possible value of q?

    A −2   B −1   C 0   D 1   E 2

Senior Challenge 2007 paper

1. What is the value of $\frac{2007}{9} + \frac{7002}{9}$?

   A 500.5   B 545   C 1001   D 1655   E 2007

2. This morning Sam told Pat "I am getting married today, aged 30." From this information, Pat may correctly deduce that Sam was born in:

   A 1976 or 1977   B 1977   C 1978
   D 1979   E 1977 or 1978

3. What is the value of $2006 \times 2008 - 2007 \times 2007$?

   A -2007 B -1 C 0   D 1   E 4 026 042

4. The diagram shows square $PQRS$ and regular hexagon $PQTUVW$. What is the size of $\angle PSW$?

   A 10°   B 12°   C 15°   D 24°   E 30°

5. Which of the five expressions shown has a different value from the other four?

   A 2^8 B 4^4 C $8^{8/3}$ D 16^2 E $32^{6/5}$

6. Cheryl finds a bag of coins. There are 50 coins inside and the value of the contents is £1.81. Given that it contains only two-pence and five-pence coins, how many more five-pence coins are there inside the bag than two-pence coins?

   A 4   B 6   C 8   D 10   E 12

7. How many whole numbers between 1 and 2007 are divisible by 2 but not by 7?

   A 857   B 858   C 859   D 860   E 861

8. Travelling at an average speed of 100 km/hr, a train took 3 hours to travel to Birmingham. Unfortunately the train then waited just outside the station, which reduced the average speed for the whole journey to 90 km/hr. For how many minutes was the train waiting?

   A 1   B 5   C 10   D 15   E 20

9. In a sale, a shopkeeper reduced the advertised selling price of a dress by 20%. This resulted in a profit of 4% over the cost price of the dress. What percentage profit would the shopkeeper have made if the dress had been sold at the original selling price?

   A 16%   B 20%   C 24%   D 25%   E 30%

Senior Challenge 2007 paper

10. In 1954, a total of 6 527 mm of rain fell at Sprinkling Tarn and this set a UK record for annual rainfall. The tarn has a surface area of 23 450 m². Roughly how many million litres of water fell on Sprinkling Tarn in 1954?

    A 15   B 150   C 1 500   D 15 000   E 150 000

11. A $4 \times 4 \times 4$ cube has three $2 \times 2 \times 4$ holes drilled symmetrically all the way through, as shown.
    What is the surface area of the resulting solid?
    A 192   B 144   C 136   D 120   E 96

12. How many two-digit numbers N have the property that the sum of N and the number formed by reversing the digits of N is a square?

    A 2   B 5   C 6   D 7   E 8

13. Which of the following gives the exact number of seconds in the last six complete weeks of 2007?

    A 9!   B 10!   C 11!   D 12!   E 13!
    {Note that $n! = 1 \times 2 \times 3 \times \ldots \times n$.}

14. The point O is the centre of both circles and the shaded area is one-sixth of the area of the outer circle.
    What is the value of x?

    A 60   B 64   C 72   D 80   E 84

15. How many hexagons can be found in the diagram on the right if each side of a hexagon must consist of all or part of one of the straight lines in the diagram?

    A 4   B 8   C 12   D 16   E 20

16. Damien wishes to find out if 457 is a prime number. In order to do this he needs to check whether it is exactly divisible by some prime numbers. What is the smallest number of possible prime number divisors that Damien needs to check before he can be sure that 457 is a prime number?

    A 8   B 9   C 10   D 11   E 12

17. The two triangles have equal areas and the four marked lengths are equal.
    What is the value of x?

    A 30   B 45   C 60   D 75   E more information needed

18. The year 1789 (when the French Revolution started) has three and no more than three adjacent digits (7, 8 and 9) which are consecutive integers in increasing order. How many years between 1000 and 9999 have this property?

   A 130   B 142   C 151   D 169   E 180

19. The largest circle which it is possible to draw inside triangle *PQR* touches the triangle at *S*, *T* and *U*, as shown in the diagram.
   The size of ∠*STU* = 55°. What is the size of ∠*PQR*?

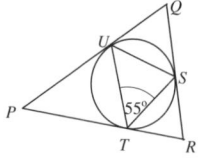

   A 55°   B 60°   C 65°   D 70°   E 75°

20. A triangle is cut from the corner of a rectangle. The resulting pentagon has sides of length 8, 10, 13, 15 and 20 units, though not necessarily in that order. What is the area of the pentagon?

   A 252.5   B 260   C 270   D 275.5   E 282.5

21. A bracelet is to be made by threading four identical red beads and four identical yellow beads onto a hoop. How many different bracelets can be made?

   A 4   B 8   C 12   D 18   E 24

22. In triangle *PQR*, *S* and *T* are the midpoints of *PR* and *PQ* respectively; *QS* is perpendicular to *RT*; *QS* = 8; *RT* = 12.
   What is the area of triangle *PQR*?

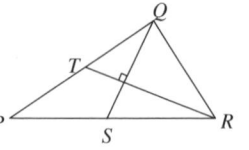

   A 24   B 32   C 48   D 64   E 96

23. The sum of the lengths of the 12 edges of a cuboid is x cm. The distance from one corner of the cuboid to the furthest corner is y cm. What, in cm^2, is the total surface area of the cuboid?

   A $\dfrac{x^2 - 2y^2}{2}$ B $x^2 + y^2$ C $\dfrac{x^2 - 4y^2}{4}$ D $\dfrac{xy}{6}$ E $\dfrac{x^2 - 16y^2}{16}$

24. A paperweight is made from a glass cube of side 2 units by first shearing off the eight tetrahedral corners which touch at the midpoints of the edges of the cube. The remaining inner core of the cube is discarded and replaced by a sphere. The eight corner pieces are now stuck onto the sphere so that they have the same positions relative to each other as they did originally. What is the diameter of the sphere?

   A $\sqrt{8} - 1$ B $\sqrt{8} + 1$ C $\tfrac{1}{3}(6 + \sqrt{3})$ D $\tfrac{4}{3}\sqrt{3}$ E $2\sqrt{3}$

25. The line with equation $y = x$ is an axis of symmetry of the curve with equation $y = \dfrac{px + q}{rx + s}$, where p, q, r, s are all non-zero. Which of the following is necessarily true?

   A $p + q = 0$ B $r + s = 0$ C $p + r = 0$ D $p + s = 0$ E $q + r = 0$

Senior Challenge 2008 paper

1. What is the value of 2 × 2008 + 2008 × 8 ?

   A 4016   B 16064   C 20080   D 64256   E 80020

2. A giant thresher shark weighing 1250 pounds, believed to be the heaviest ever caught, was landed by fisherman Roger Nowell off the Cornish coast in November 2007. The fish was sold by auction at Newlyn Fish Market for £255. Roughly, what was the cost per pound?

   A 5p   B 20p   C 50p   D £2   E £5

3. What is the value of $\sqrt{\dfrac{1}{2^6} + \dfrac{1}{6^2}}$?

   A $\dfrac{1}{10}$ B $\dfrac{1}{9}$ C $\dfrac{1}{3}$ D $\dfrac{5}{24}$ E $\dfrac{7}{24}$

4. In this subtraction, P, Q, R and S are digits. What is the value of $P + Q + R + S$?

   ```
     8 Q 0 S
   - P 0 R 2
     2 0 0 8
   ```

   A 12   B 14   C 16   D 18   E 20

5. 200 T-shirts have been bought for a Fun Run at a cost of £400 plus VAT at $17\frac{1}{2}$%. The cost of entry for the run is £5 per person. What is the minimum number of entries needed in order to cover the total cost of the T-shirts?

   A 40   B 47   C 80   D 84   E 94

6. It is required to shade at least one of the six small squares in the diagram on the right so that the resulting figure has exactly one axis of symmetry. In how many different ways can this be done?

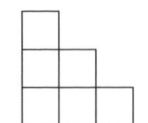

   A 6   B 9   C 10   D 12   E 15

7. A newspaper headline read 'Welsh tortoise recaptured 1.8 miles from home after 8 months on the run'. Assuming the tortoise travelled in a straight line, roughly how many minutes did the tortoise take on average to 'run' one foot?
   [1 mile = 5280 feet]

   A 3   B 9   C 16   D 36   E 60

8. In the figure shown, $AB = AF$ and ABC, AFD, BFE and CDE are all straight lines. Which of the following expressions gives z in terms of x and y?

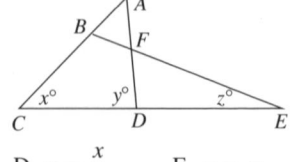

   A $\dfrac{y-x}{2}$ B $y - \dfrac{x}{2}$ C $\dfrac{y-x}{3}$ D $y - \dfrac{x}{3}$ E $y - x$

9. What is the remainder when the 2008-digit number 222 ... 22 is divided by 9?

   A 8   B 6   C 4   D 2   E 0

10. Which one of the following rational numbers *cannot* be expressed as $\frac{1}{m} + \frac{1}{n}$ where m, n are different positive integers?

   A $\frac{3}{4}$ B $\frac{3}{5}$ C $\frac{3}{6}$ D $\frac{3}{7}$ E $\frac{3}{8}$

11. The distance between two neighbouring dots in the dot lattice is 1 unit. What, in square units, is the area of the region where the two rectangles overlap?

   A 6   B $6\frac{1}{4}$ C $6\frac{1}{2}$ D 7   E $7\frac{1}{2}$

12. Mr and Mrs Stevens were married on a Saturday in July 1948. On what day of the week did their diamond wedding anniversary fall this year?

   A Monday   B Tuesday   C Thursday   D Friday   E Saturday

13. Positive integers m and n are such that $2^m + 2^n = 1280$. What is the value of $m + n$?

   A 14   B 16   C 18   D 32   E 640

14. Five touching circles each have radius 1 and their centres are at the vertices of a regular pentagon. What is the radius of the circle through the points of contact P, Q, R, S and T?

   A $\tan 18°$ B $\tan 36°$ C $\tan 45°$ D $\tan 54°$ E $\tan 72°$

15. A sequence of positive integers $t_1, t_2, t_3, t_4, \ldots$ is defined by:
    $t_1 = 13$; $t_{n+1} = \frac{1}{2} t_n$ if t_n is even; $t_{n+1} = 3 t_n + 1$ if t_n is odd.
    What is the value of t_{2008}?

   A 1   B 2   C 4   D 8   E None of these.

16. The numbers x, y and z satisfy the equations
    $$x + y + 2z = 850, \qquad x + 2y + z = 950, \qquad 2x + y + z = 1200.$$
    What is their mean?

   A 250   B $\frac{1000}{3}$ C 750   D 1000   E More information is needed.

17. Andy and his younger cousin Alice both have their birthdays today. Remarkably, Andy is now the same age as the sum of the digits of the year of his birth and the same is true of Alice. How many years older than Alice is Andy?

   A 10   B 12   C 14   D 16   E 18

18. The shaded square of the lattice shown has area 1. What is the area of the circle through the points X, Y and Z?

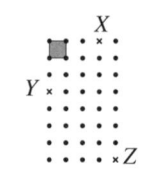

   A $\dfrac{9\pi}{2}$ B 8π C $\dfrac{25\pi}{2}$ D 25π E 50π

19. How many prime numbers p are there such that $199p + 1$ is a perfect square?

   A 0 B 1 C 2 D 4 E 8

20. The diagram shows four semicircles symmetrically placed between two circles. The shaded circle has area 4 and each semicircle has area 18. What is the area of the outer circle?

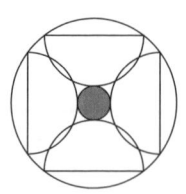

   A $72\sqrt{2}$ B 100 C 98 D 96 E $32\sqrt{3}$

21. The fraction $\dfrac{2008}{1998}$ may be written in the form $a + \dfrac{1}{b + \dfrac{1}{c + \dfrac{1}{d}}}$ where a, b, c and d are positive integers. What is the value of d?

   A 2 B 4 C 5 D 199 E 1998

22. A pentagon is made by attaching an equilateral triangle to a square with the same edge length. Four such pentagons are placed inside a rectangle, as shown.
   What is the ratio of the length of the rectangle to its width?

   A $\sqrt{3}:1$ B $2:1$ C $\sqrt{2}:1$ D $3:2$ E $4:\sqrt{3}$

23. How many pairs of real numbers (x, y) satisfy the equation $(x + y)^2 = (x + 3)(y - 3)$?

   A 0 B 1 C 2 D 4 E infinitely many

24. The length of the hypotenuse of a particular right-angled triangle is given by $\sqrt{1 + 3 + 5 + 7 + \ldots + 25}$. The lengths of the other two sides are given by $\sqrt{1 + 3 + 5 + \ldots + x}$ and $\sqrt{1 + 3 + 5 + \ldots + y}$ where x and y are positive integers. What is the value of $x + y$?

   A 12 B 17 C 24 D 28 E 32

25. What is the area of the polygon formed by all points (x, y) in the plane satisfying the inequality $||x| - 2| + ||y| - 2| \leq 4$?

   A 24 B 32 C 64 D 96 E 112

Senior Challenge 2009 paper

1. What is 20% of 30%?

   A 6%   B 10%   C 15%   D 50%   E 60%

2. Which of the following is not a multiple of 15?

   A 135   B 315   C 555   D 785   E 915

3. What is the value of $1^6 - 2^5 + 3^4 - 4^3 + 5^2 - 6^1$?

   A 1   B 2   C 3   D 4   E 5

4. Steve travelled 150 miles on a motorbike and used 10 litres of petrol. Given that 1 gallon ≈ 4.5 litres, roughly how many miles per gallon did Steve achieve on his journey?

   A 10   B 20   C 40   D 50   E 70

5. Boris Biker entered the Tour de Transylvania with an unusual bicycle whose back wheel is larger than the front. The radius of the back wheel is 40 cm, and the radius of the front wheel is 30 cm. On the first stage of the race the smaller wheel made 120000 revolutions. How many revolutions did the larger wheel make?

   A 90000   B 90000π C 160000   D $\dfrac{160000}{\pi}$ E 120000

6. A bag contains hundreds of glass marbles, each one coloured either red, orange, green or blue. There are more than 2 marbles of each colour.
   Marbles are drawn randomly from the bag, one at a time, and not replaced.
   How many marbles must be drawn from the bag in order to ensure at least three marbles of the same colour are drawn?

   A 4   B 7   C 9   D 12   E 13

7. A mini-sudoku is a 4 by 4 grid, where each row, column and 2 by 2 outlined block contains the digits 1, 2, 3 and 4 once and once only. How many different ways are there of completing the mini-sudoku shown?

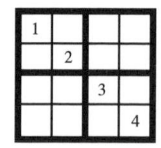

   A 1   B 2   C 4   D 8   E 12

8. The entries to the Senior Mathematical Challenge grew from 87400 in 2007 to 92690 in 2008. Approximately what percentage increase does this represent?

   A 4%   B 5%   C 6%   D 7%   E 8%

9. A square PQRS has sides of length x. T is the midpoint of QR and U is the foot of the perpendicular from T to QS. What is the length of TU?

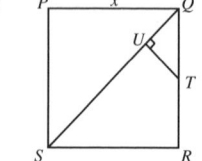

   A $\dfrac{x}{2}$ B $\dfrac{x}{3}$ C $\dfrac{x}{\sqrt{2}}$ D $\dfrac{x}{2\sqrt{2}}$ E $\dfrac{x}{4}$

10. Consider all three-digit numbers formed by using *different* digits from 0, 1, 2, 3 and 5. How many of these numbers are divisible by 6?

    A 4   B 7   C 10   D 15   E 20

11. For what value of x is $\sqrt{2} + \sqrt{2} + \sqrt{2} + \sqrt{2} = 2^x$ true?

    A $\frac{1}{2}$ B $1\frac{1}{2}$ C $2\frac{1}{2}$ D $3\frac{1}{2}$ E $4\frac{1}{2}$

12. Which of the following has the greatest value?

    A $\cos 50°$ B $\sin 50°$ C $\tan 50°$ D $\dfrac{1}{\sin 50°}$ E $\dfrac{1}{\cos 50°}$

13. Suppose that $x - \dfrac{1}{x} = y - \dfrac{1}{y}$ and $x \neq y$. What is the value of xy?

    A 4   B 1   C -1 D -4 E more information is needed

14. P, Q, R, S, T are vertices of a regular polygon. The sides PQ and TS are produced to meet at X, as shown in the diagram, and $\angle QXS = 140°$. How many sides does the polygon have?

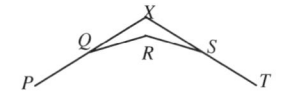

    A 9   B 18   C 24   D 27   E 40

15. For how many integers n is $\dfrac{n}{100 - n}$ also an integer?

    A 1   B 6   C 10   D 18   E 100

16. The positive numbers x and y satisfy the equations $x^4 - y^4 = 2009$ and $x^2 + y^2 = 49$. What is the value of y?

    A 1   B 2   C 3   D 4   E more information is needed

17. A solid cube is divided into two pieces by a single rectangular cut. As a result, the total surface area increases by a fraction f of the surface area of the original cube. What is the greatest possible value of f?

    A $\dfrac{1}{3}$ B $\dfrac{\sqrt{3}}{4}$ C $\dfrac{\sqrt{2}}{3}$ D $\dfrac{1}{2}$ E $\dfrac{1}{\sqrt{3}}$

18. Which of the following could be part of the graph of the curve $y^2 = x(2 - x)$?

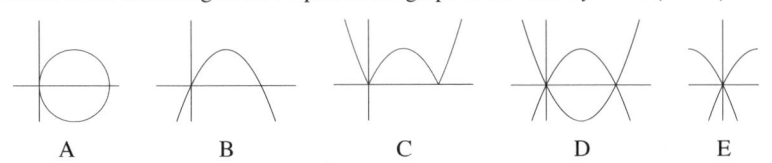

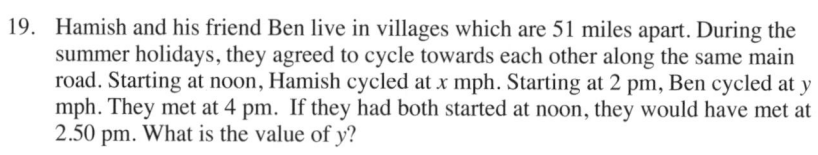

19. Hamish and his friend Ben live in villages which are 51 miles apart. During the summer holidays, they agreed to cycle towards each other along the same main road. Starting at noon, Hamish cycled at x mph. Starting at 2 pm, Ben cycled at y mph. They met at 4 pm. If they had both started at noon, they would have met at 2.50 pm. What is the value of y?

   A 7.5   B 8   C 10.5   D 12   E 12.75

20. A point P is chosen at random inside a square $QRST$. What is the probability that $\angle RPQ$ is acute?

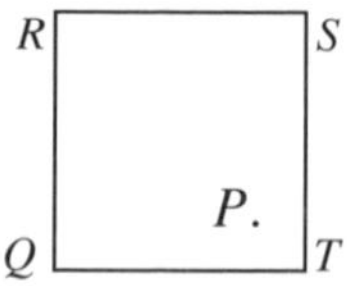

   A $\dfrac{3}{4}$ B $\sqrt{2}-1$ C $\dfrac{1}{2}$ D $\dfrac{\pi}{4}$ E $1 - \dfrac{\pi}{8}$

21. A frustum is the solid obtained by slicing a right-circular cone perpendicular to its axis and removing the small cone above the slice. This leaves a shape with two circular faces and a curved surface. The original cone has base radius 6 cm and height 8 cm, and the curved surface area of the frustum is equal to the area of the two circles. What is the height of the frustum?

   A 3 cm   B 4 cm   C 5 cm   D 6 cm   E 7 cm

22. M and N are the midpoints of sides GH and FG, respectively, of parallelogram $EFGH$. The area of triangle ENM is 12 cm^2. What is the area of the parallelogram $EFGH$?

   A 20 cm^2 B 24 cm^2 C 32 cm^2 D 48 cm^2 E more information is required

23. The net shown is folded into an icosahedron and the remaining faces are numbered such that at each vertex the numbers 1 to 5 all appear. What number must go on the face with a question mark?

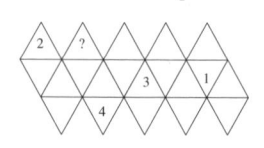

   A 1   B 2   C 3   D 4   E 5

24. A figure in the shape of a cross is made from five 1×1 squares, as shown. The cross is inscribed in a large square whose sides are parallel to the dashed square, formed by four of the vertices of the cross. What is the area of the large outer square?

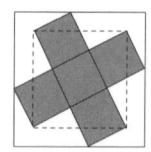

   A 9   B $\dfrac{49}{5}$ C 10   D $\dfrac{81}{8}$ E $\dfrac{32}{3}$

25. Four positive integers a, b, c and d are such that

   $abcd + abc + bcd + cda + dab + ab + bc + cd + da + ac + bd + a + b + c + d = 2009.$

   What is the value of $a + b + c + d$?

   A 73   B 75   C 77   D 79   E 81

Senior Challenge 2010 paper

1. What is the digit x in this cross-number?

   Across
   1. A cube
   3. A cube

   Down
   1. One less than a cube

1	2
3	
	x

   A 2 B 3 C 4 D 5 E 6

2. What is the smallest possible value of $20p + 10q + r$ when p, q and r are *different* positive integers?

   A 31 B 43 C 53 D 63 E 2010

3. The diagram shows an equilateral triangle touching two straight lines.
   What is the sum of the four marked angles?

   A 120° B 180° C 240° D 300° E 360°

4. The year 2010 is one in which the sum of its digits is a factor of the year itself. How many more years will it be before this is next the case?

   A 3 B 6 C 9 D 12 E 15

5. A notice on Morecambe promenade reads: 'It would take 20 million years to fill Morecambe Bay from a bath tap.' Assuming that the flow from the bath tap is 6 litres a minute, what does the notice imply is the approximate capacity of Morecambe Bay in litres?

   A 6×10^{10} B 6×10^{11} C 6×10^{12} D 6×10^{13} E 6×10^{14}

6. Dean runs up a mountain road at 8 km per hour. It takes him one hour to get to the top. He runs down the same road at 12 km per hour. How many minutes does it take him to run down the mountain?

   A 30 B 40 C 45 D 50 E 90

7. There are 120 different arrangements of the five letters in the word ANGLE. If all 120 are listed in alphabetical order starting with AEGLN and finishing with NLGEA, which position in the list does ANGLE occupy?

   A 18th B 20th C 22nd D 24th E 26th

8. Which of the following is equivalent to $(x + y + z)(x - y - z)$?

   A $x^2 - y^2 - z^2$ B $x^2 - y^2 + z^2$ C $x^2 - xy - xz - z^2$
   D $x^2 - (y+z)^2$ E $x^2 - (y-z)^2$

9. The symbol ◊ is defined by $x \lozenge y = x^y - y^x$. What is the value of $(2 \lozenge 3) \lozenge 4$?

   A -3 B $-\dfrac{3}{4}$ C 0 D $\dfrac{3}{4}$ E 3

10. A square is cut into 37 squares of which 36 have area 1 cm². What is the length of the side of the *original* square?

    A 6 cm   B 7 cm   C 8 cm   D 9 cm   E 10 cm

11. What is the median of the following numbers?

    A $9\sqrt{2}$ B $3\sqrt{19}$ C $4\sqrt{11}$ D $5\sqrt{7}$ E $6\sqrt{5}$

12. The diagram, which is not to scale, shows a square with side length 1, divided into four rectangles whose areas are equal. What is the length labelled x?

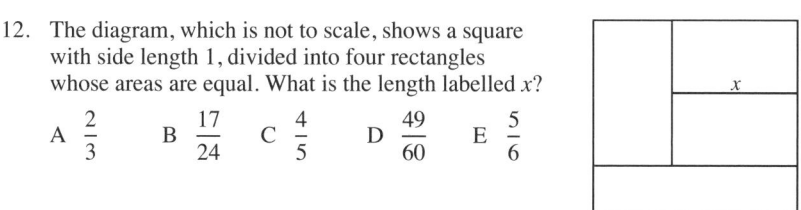

    A $\dfrac{2}{3}$ B $\dfrac{17}{24}$ C $\dfrac{4}{5}$ D $\dfrac{49}{60}$ E $\dfrac{5}{6}$

13. How many two-digit numbers have remainder 1 when divided by 3 and remainder 2 when divided by 4?

    A 8   B 7   C 6   D 5   E 4

14. The parallel sides of a trapezium have lengths $2x$ and $2y$ respectively. The diagonals are equal in length, and a diagonal makes an angle θ with the parallel sides, as shown. What is the length of each diagonal?

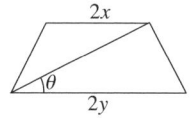

    A $x + y$ B $\dfrac{x+y}{\sin\theta}$ C $(x+y)\cos\theta$ D $(x+y)\tan\theta$ E $\dfrac{x+y}{\cos\theta}$

15. What is the smallest prime number that is equal to the sum of two prime numbers and is also equal to the sum of three different prime numbers?

    A 7   B 11   C 13   D 17   E 19

16. $PQRS$ is a quadrilateral inscribed in a circle of which PR is a diameter. The lengths of PQ, QR and RS are 60, 25 and 52 respectively. What is the length of SP?

    A $21\tfrac{2}{3}$ B $28\tfrac{11}{13}$ C 33   D 36   E 39

17. One of the following is equal to $\sqrt{9^{16x^2}}$ for all values of x. Which one?

    A 3^{4x} B 3^{4x^2} C 3^{8x^2} D 9^{4x} E 9^{8x^2}

18. A solid cube of side 2 cm is cut into two triangular prisms by a plane passing through four vertices, as shown. What is the total surface area of these two prisms?

    A $8(3 + \sqrt{2})$ B $2(8 + \sqrt{2})$ C $8(3 + 2\sqrt{2})$
    D $16(3 + \sqrt{2})$ E $8\sqrt{2}$

19. The diagrams show two different shaded rhombuses, each inside a square with sides of length 6.

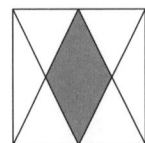

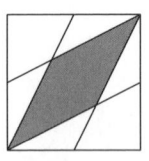

    Each rhombus is formed by joining vertices of the square to midpoints of the sides of the square. What is the difference between the shaded areas?

    A 4   B 3   C 2   D 1   E 0

20. There are 10 girls in a mixed class. If two pupils from the class are selected at random to represent the class on the School Council, then the probability that both are girls is 0.15. How many boys are in the class?

    A 10   B 12   C 15   D 18   E 20

21. The diagram shows a regular hexagon, with sides of length 1, inside a square. Two vertices of the hexagon lie on a diagonal of the square and the other four lie on the edges.

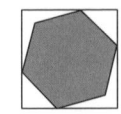

    What is the area of the square?

    A $2 + \sqrt{3}$ B 4   C $3 + \sqrt{2}$ D $1 + \dfrac{3\sqrt{3}}{2}$ E $\dfrac{7}{2}$

22. If $x^2 - px - q = 0$, where p and q are positive integers, which of the following could not equal x^3?

    A $4x + 3$ B $8x + 5$ C $8x + 7$ D $10x + 3$ E $26x + 5$

23. The diagram shows two different semicircles inside a square with sides of length 2. The common centre of the semicircles lies on a diagonal of the square.
    What is the total shaded area?

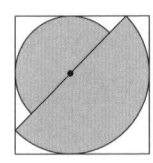

    A π B $6\pi(3 - 2\sqrt{2})$ C $\pi\sqrt{2}$ D $3\pi(2 - \sqrt{2})$ E $8\pi(2\sqrt{2} - 3)$

24. Three spheres of radius 1 are placed on a horizontal table and inside a vertical hollow cylinder of height 2 units which is just large enough to surround them. What fraction of the internal volume of the cylinder is occupied by the spheres?

    A $\dfrac{2}{7 + 4\sqrt{3}}$ B $\dfrac{2}{2 + \sqrt{3}}$ C $\dfrac{1}{3}$ D $\dfrac{3}{2 + \sqrt{3}}$ E $\dfrac{6}{7 + 4\sqrt{3}}$

25. All the digits of a number are different, the first digit is not zero, and the sum of the digits is 36. There are $N \times 7!$ such numbers. What is the value of N?

    A 72   B 97   C 104   D 107   E 128

Senior Challenge 2011 paper

1. Which of the numbers below is not a whole number?

   A $\dfrac{2011+0}{1}$ B $\dfrac{2011+1}{2}$ C $\dfrac{2011+2}{3}$ D $\dfrac{2011+3}{4}$ E $\dfrac{2011+4}{5}$

2. Jack and Jill went up the hill to fetch a pail of water. Having filled the pail to the full, Jack fell down, spilling $\frac{2}{3}$ of the water, before Jill caught the pail. She then tumbled down the hill, spilling $\frac{2}{5}$ of the remainder.

   What fraction of the pail does the remaining water fill?

   A $\dfrac{11}{15}$ B $\dfrac{1}{3}$ C $\dfrac{4}{15}$ D $\dfrac{1}{5}$ E $\dfrac{1}{15}$

3. The robot *Lumber9* moves along the number line. *Lumber9* starts at 0, takes 1 step forward (to 1), then 2 steps backward (to −1), then 3 steps forward, 4 steps backward, and so on, moving alternately forwards and backwards, one more step each time. At what number is *Lumber9* after 2011 steps?

   A 1006   B 27   C 11   D 0   E −18

4. What is the last digit of 3^{2011} ?

   A 1   B 3   C 5   D 7   E 9

5. The diagram shows a regular hexagon inside a rectangle. What is the sum of the four marked angles?

   A 90°   B 120°   C 150°   D 180°   E 210°

6. Granny and her granddaughter Gill both had their birthday yesterday. Today, Granny's age in years is an even number and 15 times that of Gill. In 4 years' time Granny's age in years will be the square of Gill's age in years. How many years older than Gill is Granny today?

   A 42   B 49   C 56   D 60   E 64

7. Two sides of a triangle have lengths 4 cm and 5 cm. The third side has length x cm, where x is a positive integer. How many different values can x have?

   A 4   B 5   C 6   D 7   E 8

8. A 2 × 3 grid of squares can be divided into 1 × 2 rectangles in three different ways.

   How many ways are there of dividing the bottom shape into 1 × 2 rectangles?

   A 1   B 4   C 6   D 7   E 8

9. Sam has a large collection of 1 × 1 × 1 cubes, each of which is either red or yellow. Sam makes a 3 × 3 × 3 block from twenty-seven cubes, so that no cubes of the same colour meet face-to-face.

   What is the difference between the largest number of red cubes that Sam can use and the smallest number?

   A 0   B 1   C 2   D 3   E 4

10. A triangle has two edges of length 5. What length should be chosen for the third side of the triangle so as to maximise the area within the triangle?

    A 5 B 6 C $5\sqrt{2}$ D 8 E $5\sqrt{3}$

11. $PQRSTU$ is a regular hexagon and V is the midpoint of PQ. What fraction of the area of $PQRSTU$ is the area of triangle STV?

    A $\dfrac{1}{4}$ B $\dfrac{2}{15}$ C $\dfrac{1}{3}$ D $\dfrac{2}{5}$ E $\dfrac{5}{12}$

12. The *primorial* of a number is the product of all of the prime numbers less than or equal to that number. For example, the primorial of 6 is $2 \times 3 \times 5 = 30$. How many different whole numbers have a primorial of 210?

    A 1 B 2 C 3 D 4 E 5

13. The diagram represents a maze. Given that you can only move horizontally and vertically and are not allowed to revisit a square, how many different routes are there through the maze?

    A 16 B 12 C 10 D 8 E 6

14. An equilateral triangle of side length 4 cm is divided into smaller equilateral triangles, all of which have side length equal to a whole number of centimetres. Which of the following cannot be the number of smaller triangles obtained?

    A 4 B 8 C 12 D 13 E 16

15. The equation $x^2 + ax + b = 0$, where a and b are different, has solutions $x = a$ and $x = b$. How many such equations are there?

    A 0 B 1 C 3 D 4 E an infinity

16. $PQRS$ is a rectangle. The area of triangle QRT is $\frac{1}{5}$ of the area of $PQRS$, and the area of triangle TSU is $\frac{1}{8}$ of the area of $PQRS$. What fraction of the area of rectangle $PQRS$ is the area of triangle QTU?

    A $\dfrac{27}{40}$ B $\dfrac{21}{40}$ C $\dfrac{1}{2}$ D $\dfrac{19}{40}$ E $\dfrac{23}{60}$

17. Jamie conducted a survey on the food preferences of pupils at a school and discovered that 70% of the pupils like pears, 75% like oranges, 80% like bananas and 85% like apples. What is the smallest possible percentage of pupils who like all four of these fruits?

    A at least 10% B at least 15% C at least 20%
    D at least 25% E at least 70%

18. Two numbers x and y are such that $x + y = 20$ and $\dfrac{1}{x} + \dfrac{1}{y} = \dfrac{1}{2}$. What is the value of $x^2y + xy^2$?

    A 80 B 200 C 400 D 640 E 800

19. The diagram shows a small regular octagram (an eight-sided star) surrounded by eight squares (dark grey) and eight kites (light grey) to make a large regular octagram. Each square has area 1. What is the area of one of the light grey kites?

    A 2
    B $\sqrt{2}+1$
    C $\dfrac{21}{8}$
    D $4\sqrt{2}-3$
    E $\dfrac{11}{4}$

20. Positive integers x and y satisfy the equation $\sqrt{x} - \sqrt{11} = \sqrt{y}$. What is the maximum possible value of $\dfrac{x}{y}$?

    A 2
    B 4
    C 8
    D 11
    E 44

21. Each of the Four Musketeers made a statement about the four of them, as follows.

    d'Artagnan: "Exactly one is lying."
    Athos: "Exactly two of us are lying."
    Porthos: "An odd number of us is lying."
    Aramis: "An even number of us is lying."

    How many of them were lying (with the others telling the truth)?

    A one
    B one or two
    C two or three
    D three
    E four

22. In the diagram, $\angle ABE = 10°$; $\angle EBC = 70°$; $\angle ACD = 50°$; $\angle DCB = 20°$; $\angle DEF = \alpha$.
    Which of the following is equal to $\tan \alpha$?

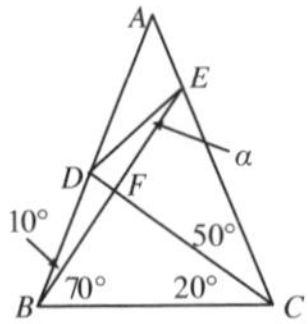

    A $\dfrac{\tan 10° \tan 20°}{\tan 50°}$
    B $\dfrac{\tan 10° \tan 20°}{\tan 70°}$
    C $\dfrac{\tan 10° \tan 50°}{\tan 70°}$
    D $\dfrac{\tan 20° \tan 50°}{\tan 70°}$
    E $\dfrac{\tan 10° \tan 70°}{\tan 50°}$

23. What is the minimum value of $x^2 + y^2 + 2xy + 6x + 6y + 4$?

    A −7
    B −5
    C −4
    D −1
    E 4

24. Three circles and the lines PQ and QR touch as shown. The distance between the centres of the smallest and the biggest circles is 16 times the radius of the smallest circle. What is the size of $\angle PQR$?

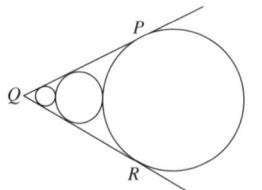

    A 45°
    B 60°
    C 75°
    D 90°
    E 135°

25. A solid sculpture consists of a $4 \times 4 \times 4$ cube with a $3 \times 3 \times 3$ cube sticking out, as shown. Three vertices of the smaller cube lie on edges of the larger cube, the same distance along each. What is the total volume of the sculpture?

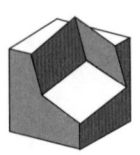

    A 79
    B 81
    C 82
    D 84
    E 85

Senior Challenge 2012 paper

1. Which of the following cannot be written as the sum of two prime numbers?

   A 5   B 7   C 9   D 10   E 11

2. The diagram shows an equilateral triangle, a square and a regular pentagon which all share a common vertex. What is the value of θ?

   A 98   B 102   C 106   D 110   E 112

3. The price of my favourite soft drink has gone up by leaps and bounds over the past ten years. In four of those years it has leapt up by 5p each year, whilst in the other six years it has bounded up by 2p each year. The drink cost 70p in 2002. How much does it cost now?

   A £0.77   B £0.90   C £0.92   D £1.02   E £1.05

4. According to one astronomer, there are one hundred thousand million galaxies in the universe, each containing one hundred thousand million stars. How many stars is that altogether?

   A 10^{13} B 10^{22} C 10^{100} D 10^{120} E 10^{121}

5. All six digits of three 2-digit numbers are different. What is the largest possible sum of three such numbers?

   A 237   B 246   C 255   D 264   E 273

6. What is the sum of the digits of the largest 4-digit palindromic number which is divisible by 15? [Palindromic numbers read the same backwards and forwards, e.g. 7227.]

   A 18   B 20   C 24   D 30   E 36

7. Given that $x + y + z = 1$, $x + y - z = 2$ and $x - y - z = 3$, what is the value of xyz?

   A -2 B $-\frac{1}{2}$ C 0   D $\frac{1}{2}$ E 2

8. The diagrams below show four types of tile, each of which is made up of one or more equilateral triangles. For how many of these types of tile can we place three identical copies of the tile together, without gaps or overlaps, to make an equilateral triangle?

   A 0   B 1   C 2   D 3   E 4

9. Pierre said, "Just one of us is telling the truth". Qadr said, "What Pierre says is not true". Ratna said, "What Qadr says is not true". Sven said, "What Ratna says is not true". Tanya said, "What Sven says is not true".
   How many of them were telling the truth?

   A 0   B 1   C 2   D 3   E 4

10. Let N be the smallest positive integer whose digits add up to 2012. What is the first digit of $N + 1$?

    A 2   B 3   C 4   D 5   E 6

Senior Challenge 2012 paper   109

11. Coco is making clown hats from a circular piece of cardboard.
    The circumference of the base of each hat equals its slant height,
    which in turn is equal to the radius of the piece of cardboard.
    What is the maximum number of hats that Coco can make from
    the piece of cardboard?

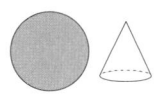

    A 3   B 4   C 5   D 6   E 7

12. The number 3 can be expressed as the sum of one or more positive integers in four
    different ways:
                    3;   1 + 2;   2 + 1;   1 + 1 + 1.
    In how many ways can the number 5 be so expressed?

    A 8   B 10   C 12   D 14   E 16

13. A cube is placed with one face on square 1 in the maze shown,
    so that it completely covers the square with no overlap. The
    upper face of the cube is covered in wet paint. The cube is then
    'rolled' around the maze, rotating about an edge each time,
    until it reaches square 25. It leaves paint on all of the squares
    on which the painted face lands, but on no others. The cube is
    removed on reaching the square 25. What is the sum of the
    numbers on the squares which are now marked with paint?

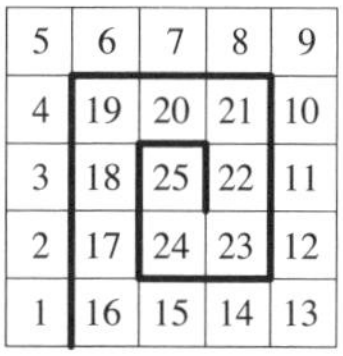

    A 78   B 80   C 82   D 169   E 625

14. Six students who share a house all speak exactly two languages. Helga speaks only
    English and German; Ina speaks only German and Spanish; Jean-Pierre speaks only
    French and Spanish; Karim speaks only German and French; Lionel speaks only French
    and English whilst Mary speaks only Spanish and English. If two of the students are
    chosen at random, what is the probability that they speak a common language?

    A $\frac{1}{2}$ B $\frac{2}{3}$ C $\frac{3}{4}$ D $\frac{4}{5}$ E $\frac{5}{6}$

15. Professor Rosseforp runs to work every day. On Thursday he ran 10% faster than
    his usual average speed. As a result, his journey time was reduced by x minutes.
    How many minutes did the journey take on Wednesday?

    A $11x$ B $10x$ C $9x$ D $8x$ E $5x$

16. The diagram shows the ellipse whose equation
    is $x^2 + y^2 - xy + x - 4y = 12$. The curve cuts the
    y-axis at points A and C and cuts the x-axis at
    points B and D. What is the area of the
    inscribed quadrilateral $ABCD$?

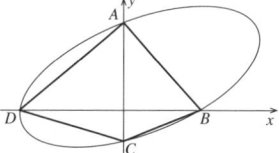

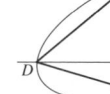

    A 28   B 36   C 42   D 48   E 56

17. The diagram shows a pattern found on a floor tile in the cathedral
    in Spoleto, Umbria. A circle of radius 1 surrounds four quarter
    circles, also of radius 1, which enclose a square. The pattern has
    four axes of symmetry. What is the side length of the square?

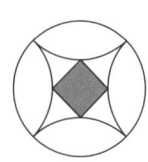

    A $\frac{1}{\sqrt{2}}$ B $2 - \sqrt{2}$ C $\frac{1}{\sqrt{3}}$ D $\frac{1}{2}$ E $\sqrt{2} - 1$

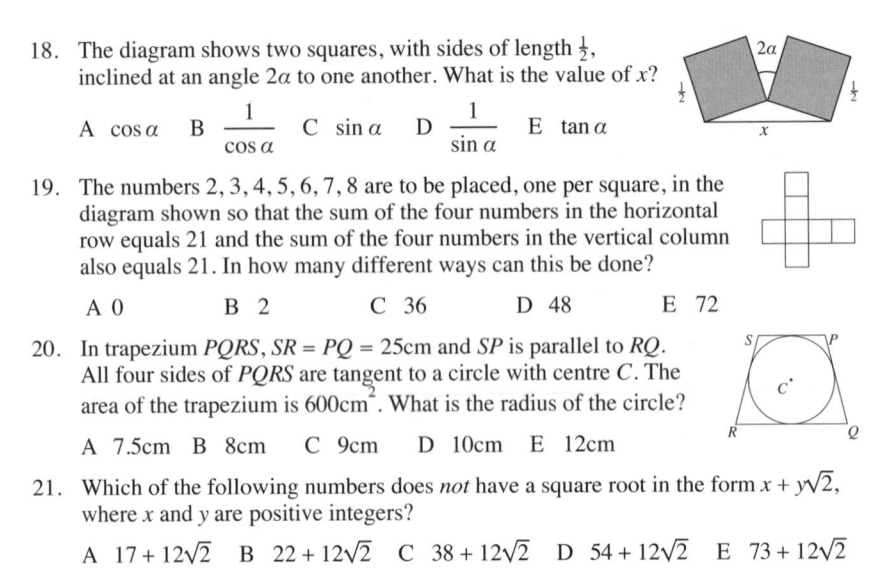

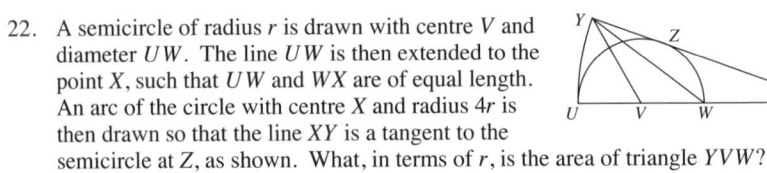

18. The diagram shows two squares, with sides of length $\frac{1}{2}$, inclined at an angle 2α to one another. What is the value of x?

   A $\cos \alpha$ B $\dfrac{1}{\cos \alpha}$ C $\sin \alpha$ D $\dfrac{1}{\sin \alpha}$ E $\tan \alpha$

19. The numbers 2, 3, 4, 5, 6, 7, 8 are to be placed, one per square, in the diagram shown so that the sum of the four numbers in the horizontal row equals 21 and the sum of the four numbers in the vertical column also equals 21. In how many different ways can this be done?

   A 0   B 2   C 36   D 48   E 72

20. In trapezium $PQRS$, $SR = PQ = 25$cm and SP is parallel to RQ. All four sides of $PQRS$ are tangent to a circle with centre C. The area of the trapezium is 600cm^2. What is the radius of the circle?

   A 7.5cm   B 8cm   C 9cm   D 10cm   E 12cm

21. Which of the following numbers does *not* have a square root in the form $x + y\sqrt{2}$, where x and y are positive integers?

   A $17 + 12\sqrt{2}$ B $22 + 12\sqrt{2}$ C $38 + 12\sqrt{2}$ D $54 + 12\sqrt{2}$ E $73 + 12\sqrt{2}$

22. A semicircle of radius r is drawn with centre V and diameter UW. The line UW is then extended to the point X, such that UW and WX are of equal length. An arc of the circle with centre X and radius $4r$ is then drawn so that the line XY is a tangent to the semicircle at Z, as shown. What, in terms of r, is the area of triangle YVW?

   A $\dfrac{4r^2}{9}$ B $\dfrac{2r^2}{3}$ C r^2 D $\dfrac{4r^2}{3}$ E $2r^2$

23. Tom and Geri have a competition. Initially, each player has one attempt at hitting a target. If one player hits the target and the other does not then the successful player wins. If both players hit the target, or if both players miss the target, then each has another attempt, with the same rules applying. If the probability of Tom hitting the target is always $\frac{4}{5}$ and the probability of Geri hitting the target is always $\frac{2}{3}$, what is the probability that Tom wins the competition?

   A $\dfrac{4}{15}$ B $\dfrac{8}{15}$ C $\dfrac{2}{3}$ D $\dfrac{4}{5}$ E $\dfrac{13}{15}$

24. The top diagram on the right shows a shape that tiles the plane, as shown in the lower diagram. The tile has nine sides, six of which have length 1. It may be divided into three congruent quadrilaterals as shown. What is the area of the tile?

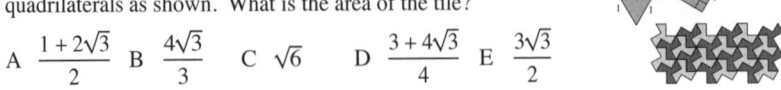

   A $\dfrac{1 + 2\sqrt{3}}{2}$ B $\dfrac{4\sqrt{3}}{3}$ C $\sqrt{6}$ D $\dfrac{3 + 4\sqrt{3}}{4}$ E $\dfrac{3\sqrt{3}}{2}$

25. How many distinct pairs (x, y) of real numbers satisfy the equation $(x + y)^2 = (x + 4)(y - 4)$?

   A 0   B 1   C 2   D 3   E 4

Senior Challenge 2013 paper

1. Which of these is the largest number?

   A $2 + 0 + 1 + 3$ B $2 \times 0 + 1 + 3$ C $2 + 0 \times 1 + 3$
   D $2 + 0 + 1 \times 3$ E $2 \times 0 \times 1 \times 3$

2. Little John claims he is 2m 8cm and 3mm tall. What is this height in metres?

   A 2.83m   B 2.803m   C 2.083m   D 2.0803m   E 2.0083m

3. What is the 'tens' digit of $2013^2 - 2013$?

   A 0   B 1   C 4   D 5   E 6

4. A route on the 3 × 3 board shown consists of a number of steps. Each step is from one square to an adjacent square of a different colour. How many different routes are there from square S to square T which pass through every other square exactly once?

   A 0   B 1   C 2   D 3   E 4

5. The numbers x and y satisfy the equations $x(y + 2) = 100$ and $y(x + 2) = 60$. What is the value of $x - y$?

   A 60   B 50   C 40   D 30   E 20

6. Rebecca went swimming yesterday. After a while she had covered one fifth of her intended distance. After swimming six more lengths of the pool, she had covered one quarter of her intended distance. How many lengths of the pool did she intend to complete?

   A 40   B 72   C 80   D 100   E 120

7. In a 'ninety nine' shop, all items cost a number of pounds and 99 pence. Susanna spent £65.76. How many items did she buy?

   A 23   B 24   C 65   D 66   E 76

8. The right-angled triangle shown has a base which is 4 times its height. Four such triangles are placed so that their hypotenuses form the boundary of a large square as shown.
   What is the side-length of the shaded square in the diagram?

   A $2x$ B $2\sqrt{2}x$ C $3x$ D $2\sqrt{3}x$ E $\sqrt{15}x$

9. According to a headline, 'Glaciers in the French Alps have lost a quarter of their area in the past 40 years'. What is the approximate percentage reduction in the length of the side of a square when it loses one quarter of its area, thereby becoming a smaller square?

   A 13%   B 25%   C 38%   D 50%   E 65%

10. Frank's teacher asks him to write down five integers such that the median is one more than the mean, and the mode is one greater than the median. Frank is also told that the median is 10. What is the smallest possible integer that he could include in his list?

    A 3   B 4   C 5   D 6   E 7

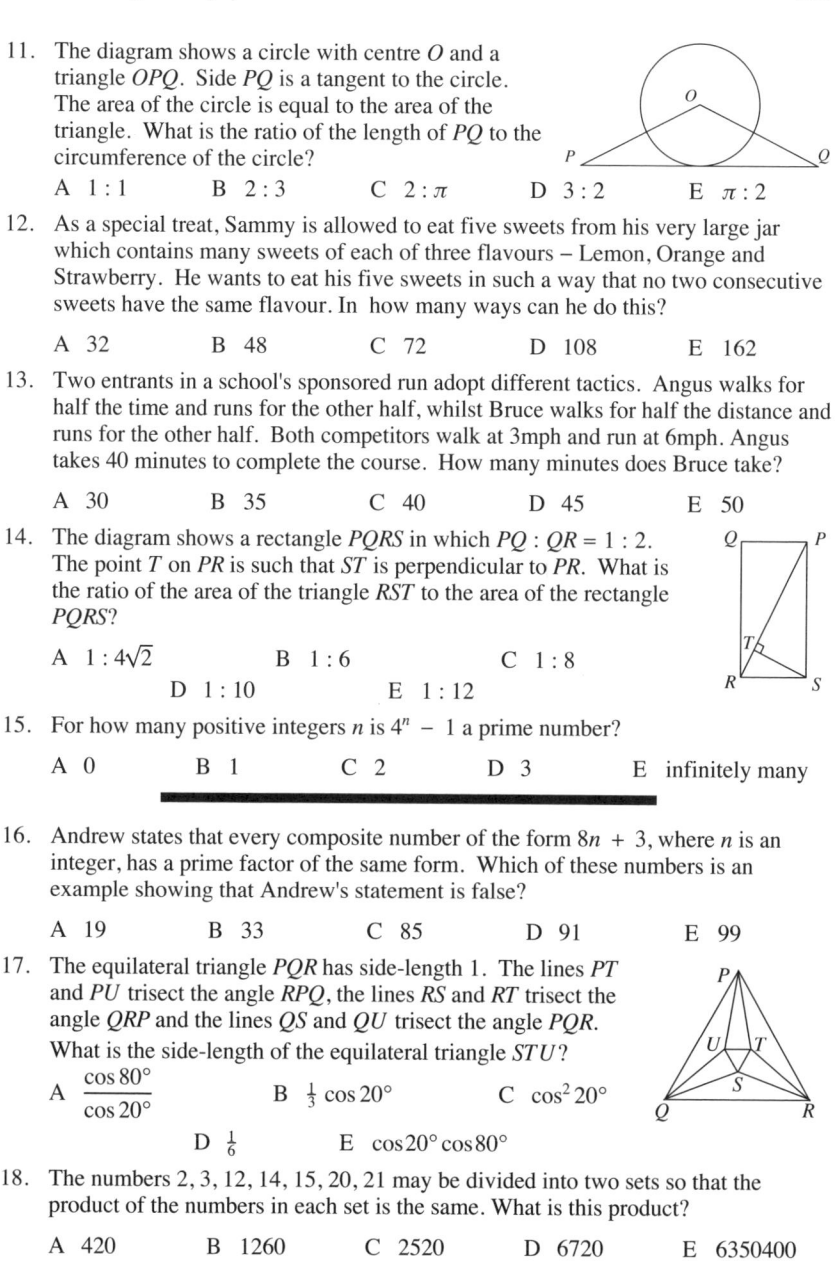

Senior Challenge 2013 paper 113

11. The diagram shows a circle with centre O and a triangle OPQ. Side PQ is a tangent to the circle. The area of the circle is equal to the area of the triangle. What is the ratio of the length of PQ to the circumference of the circle?

   A $1:1$ B $2:3$ C $2:\pi$ D $3:2$ E $\pi:2$

12. As a special treat, Sammy is allowed to eat five sweets from his very large jar which contains many sweets of each of three flavours – Lemon, Orange and Strawberry. He wants to eat his five sweets in such a way that no two consecutive sweets have the same flavour. In how many ways can he do this?

   A 32   B 48   C 72   D 108   E 162

13. Two entrants in a school's sponsored run adopt different tactics. Angus walks for half the time and runs for the other half, whilst Bruce walks for half the distance and runs for the other half. Both competitors walk at 3mph and run at 6mph. Angus takes 40 minutes to complete the course. How many minutes does Bruce take?

   A 30   B 35   C 40   D 45   E 50

14. The diagram shows a rectangle $PQRS$ in which $PQ:QR = 1:2$. The point T on PR is such that ST is perpendicular to PR. What is the ratio of the area of the triangle RST to the area of the rectangle $PQRS$?

   A $1:4\sqrt{2}$ B $1:6$ C $1:8$
   D $1:10$ E $1:12$

15. For how many positive integers n is $4^n - 1$ a prime number?

   A 0   B 1   C 2   D 3   E infinitely many

16. Andrew states that every composite number of the form $8n + 3$, where n is an integer, has a prime factor of the same form. Which of these numbers is an example showing that Andrew's statement is false?

   A 19   B 33   C 85   D 91   E 99

17. The equilateral triangle PQR has side-length 1. The lines PT and PU trisect the angle RPQ, the lines RS and RT trisect the angle QRP and the lines QS and QU trisect the angle PQR. What is the side-length of the equilateral triangle STU?

   A $\dfrac{\cos 80°}{\cos 20°}$ B $\tfrac{1}{3}\cos 20°$ C $\cos^2 20°$
   D $\tfrac{1}{6}$ E $\cos 20° \cos 80°$

18. The numbers 2, 3, 12, 14, 15, 20, 21 may be divided into two sets so that the product of the numbers in each set is the same. What is this product?

   A 420   B 1260   C 2520   D 6720   E 6350400

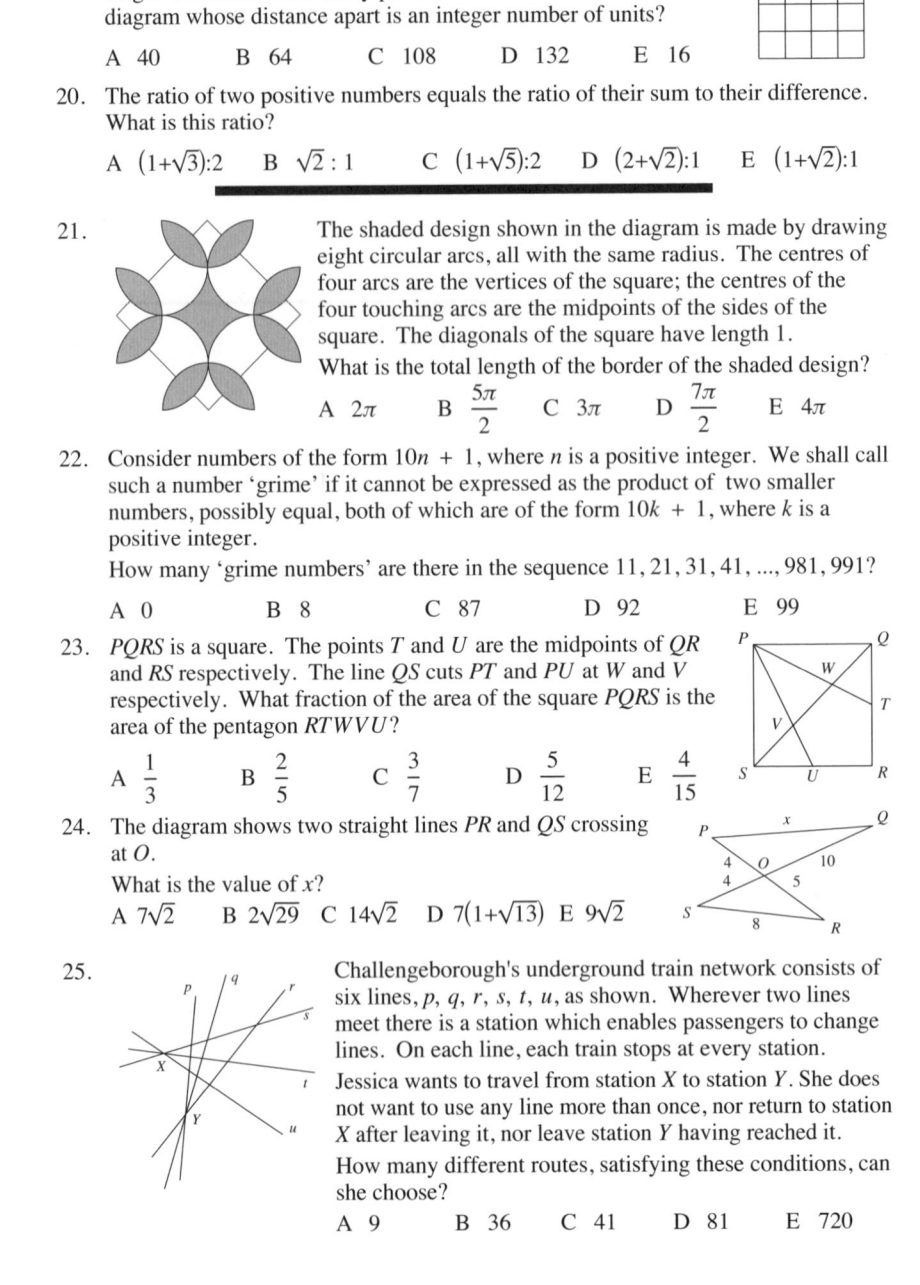

19. The 16 small squares shown in the diagram each have a side length of 1 unit. How many pairs of vertices are there in the diagram whose distance apart is an integer number of units?

   A 40   B 64   C 108   D 132   E 16

20. The ratio of two positive numbers equals the ratio of their sum to their difference. What is this ratio?

   A $(1+\sqrt{3}):2$ B $\sqrt{2}:1$ C $(1+\sqrt{5}):2$ D $(2+\sqrt{2}):1$ E $(1+\sqrt{2}):1$

21. The shaded design shown in the diagram is made by drawing eight circular arcs, all with the same radius. The centres of four arcs are the vertices of the square; the centres of the four touching arcs are the midpoints of the sides of the square. The diagonals of the square have length 1. What is the total length of the border of the shaded design?

   A 2π B $\dfrac{5\pi}{2}$ C 3π D $\dfrac{7\pi}{2}$ E 4π

22. Consider numbers of the form $10n + 1$, where n is a positive integer. We shall call such a number 'grime' if it cannot be expressed as the product of two smaller numbers, possibly equal, both of which are of the form $10k + 1$, where k is a positive integer.

    How many 'grime numbers' are there in the sequence 11, 21, 31, 41, ..., 981, 991?

    A 0   B 8   C 87   D 92   E 99

23. $PQRS$ is a square. The points T and U are the midpoints of QR and RS respectively. The line QS cuts PT and PU at W and V respectively. What fraction of the area of the square $PQRS$ is the area of the pentagon $RTWVU$?

    A $\dfrac{1}{3}$ B $\dfrac{2}{5}$ C $\dfrac{3}{7}$ D $\dfrac{5}{12}$ E $\dfrac{4}{15}$

24. The diagram shows two straight lines PR and QS crossing at O.

    What is the value of x?

    A $7\sqrt{2}$ B $2\sqrt{29}$ C $14\sqrt{2}$ D $7(1+\sqrt{13})$ E $9\sqrt{2}$

25. Challengeborough's underground train network consists of six lines, p, q, r, s, t, u, as shown. Wherever two lines meet there is a station which enables passengers to change lines. On each line, each train stops at every station.

    Jessica wants to travel from station X to station Y. She does not want to use any line more than once, nor return to station X after leaving it, nor leave station Y having reached it.

    How many different routes, satisfying these conditions, can she choose?

    A 9   B 36   C 41   D 81   E 720

Senior Challenge 2014 paper

1. What is 98 × 102?

   A 200   B 9016   C 9996   D 998   E 99 996

2. The diagram shows 6 regions. Each of the regions is to be painted a single colour, so that no two regions sharing an edge have the same colour. What is the smallest number of colours required?

   A 2   B 3   C 4   D 5   E 6

3. December 31st 1997 was a Wednesday. How many Wednesdays were there in 1997?

   A 12   B 51   C 52   D 53   E 365

4. After I had spent $\frac{1}{5}$ of my money and then spent $\frac{1}{4}$ of what was left, I had £15 remaining. How much did I start with?

   A £25   B £75   C £100   D £135   E £300

5. How many integers between 1 and 2014 are multiples of both 20 and 14?

   A 7   B 10   C 14   D 20   E 28

6. In the addition sum shown, each of the letters T, H, I and S represents a non-zero digit.
   What is $T + H + I + S$?

   ```
     T H I S
   +     I S
   ---------
     2 0 1 4
   ```

   A 34   B 22   C 15   D 9   E 7

7. According to recent research, global sea levels could rise 36.8 cm by the year 2100 as a result of melting ice. Roughly how many millimetres is that per year?

   A 10   B 4   C 1   D 0.4   E 0.1

8. The diagram shows four sets of parallel lines, containing 2, 3, 4 and 5 lines respectively.
   How many points of intersection are there?

   A 54   B 63   C 71   D 95   E 196

9. Which of the following is divisible by 9?

   A $10^{2014} + 5$ B $10^{2014} + 6$ C $10^{2014} + 7$ D $10^{2014} + 8$ E $10^{2014} + 9$

10. A rectangle has area $120 \, \text{cm}^2$ and perimeter 46 cm. Which of the following is the length of each of the diagonals?

    A 15 cm   B 16 cm   C 17 cm   D 18 cm   E 19 cm

11. A Mersenne prime is a prime of the form $2^p - 1$, where p is also a prime. One of the following is **not** a Mersenne prime. Which one is it?

    A $2^2 - 1$ B $2^3 - 1$ C $2^5 - 1$ D $2^7 - 1$ E $2^{11} - 1$

12. Karen has three times the number of cherries that Lionel has, and twice the number of cherries that Michael has. Michael has seven more cherries than Lionel. How many cherries do Karen, Lionel and Michael have altogether?

    A 12   B 42   C 60   D 77   E 84

Senior Challenge 2014 paper

13. Each of the five nets P, Q, R, S and T is made from six squares. Both sides of each square have the same colour. Net P is folded to form a cube.

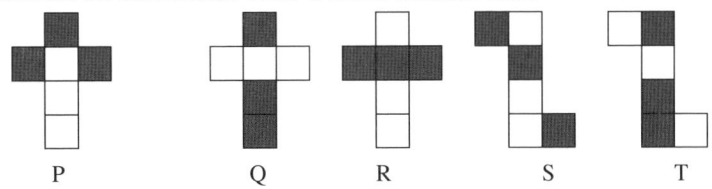

    P   Q   R   S   T

    How many of the nets Q, R, S and T can be folded to produce a cube that looks the same as that produced by P?

    A 0   B 1   C 2   D 3   E 4

14. Given that $\dfrac{3x + y}{x - 3y} = -1$, what is the value of $\dfrac{x + 3y}{3x - y}$?

    A −1   B 2   C 4   D 5   E 7

15. The figure shown alongside is made from seven small squares. Some of these squares are to be shaded so that:
    (i) at least two squares are shaded;
    (ii) two squares meeting along an edge or at a corner are not both shaded.

    How many ways are there to do this?

    A 4   B 8   C 10   D 14   E 18

16. The diagram shows a rectangle measuring 6 × 12 and a circle. The two shorter sides of the rectangle are tangents to the circle. The circle and rectangle have the same centre.
    The region that lies inside both the rectangle and the circle is shaded. What is its area?

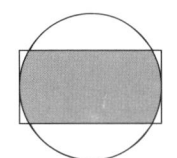

    A $12\pi + 18\sqrt{3}$ B $24\pi - 3\sqrt{3}$ C $18\pi - 8\sqrt{3}$
    D $18\pi + 12\sqrt{3}$ E $24\pi + 18\sqrt{3}$

17. An oil tanker is 100 km due north of a cruise liner. The tanker sails SE at a speed of 20 kilometres per hour and the liner sails NW at a speed of 10 kilometres per hour. What is the shortest distance between the two boats during the subsequent motion?

    A 100km   B 80km   C $50\sqrt{2}$km   D 60km   E $33\tfrac{1}{3}$km

18. Beatrix decorates the faces of a cube, whose edges have length 2. For each face, she either leaves it blank, or draws a single straight line on it. Every line drawn joins the midpoints of two edges, either opposite or adjacent, as shown.
    What is the length of the longest unbroken line that Beatrix can draw on the cube?

    A 8   B $4 + 4\sqrt{2}$ C $6 + 3\sqrt{2}$ D $8 + 2\sqrt{2}$ E 12

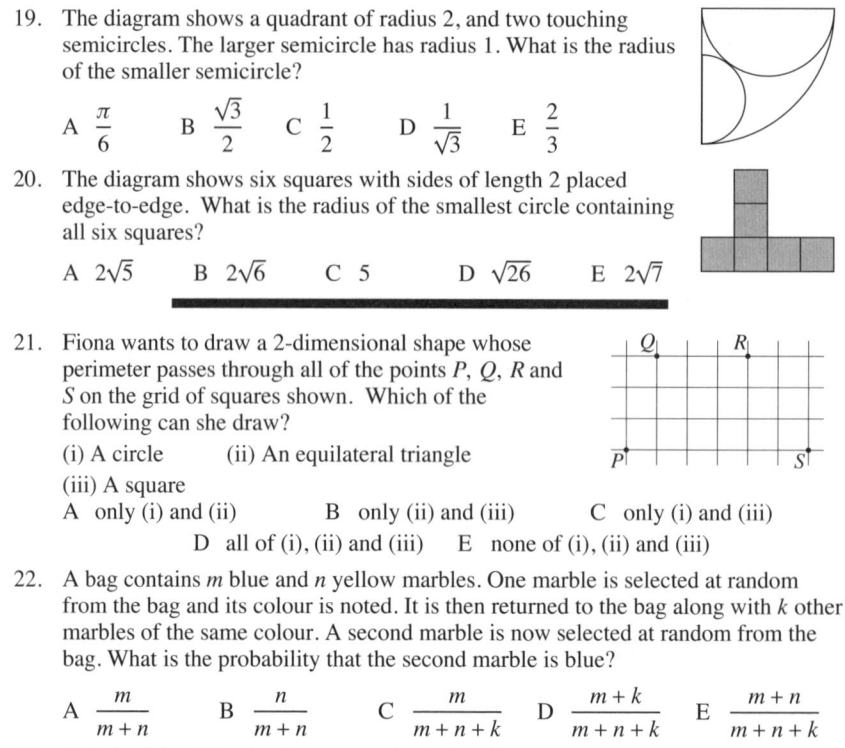

19. The diagram shows a quadrant of radius 2, and two touching semicircles. The larger semicircle has radius 1. What is the radius of the smaller semicircle?

    A $\dfrac{\pi}{6}$ B $\dfrac{\sqrt{3}}{2}$ C $\dfrac{1}{2}$ D $\dfrac{1}{\sqrt{3}}$ E $\dfrac{2}{3}$

20. The diagram shows six squares with sides of length 2 placed edge-to-edge. What is the radius of the smallest circle containing all six squares?

    A $2\sqrt{5}$ B $2\sqrt{6}$ C 5   D $\sqrt{26}$ E $2\sqrt{7}$

21. Fiona wants to draw a 2-dimensional shape whose perimeter passes through all of the points P, Q, R and S on the grid of squares shown. Which of the following can she draw?
    (i) A circle   (ii) An equilateral triangle
    (iii) A square
    A only (i) and (ii)   B only (ii) and (iii)   C only (i) and (iii)
                D all of (i), (ii) and (iii)   E none of (i), (ii) and (iii)

22. A bag contains m blue and n yellow marbles. One marble is selected at random from the bag and its colour is noted. It is then returned to the bag along with k other marbles of the same colour. A second marble is now selected at random from the bag. What is the probability that the second marble is blue?

    A $\dfrac{m}{m+n}$ B $\dfrac{n}{m+n}$ C $\dfrac{m}{m+n+k}$ D $\dfrac{m+k}{m+n+k}$ E $\dfrac{m+n}{m+n+k}$

23. Which of the following have no real solutions?
    (i) $2x < 2^x < x^2$ (ii) $x^2 < 2x < 2^x$ (iii) $2^x < x^2 < 2x$
    (iv) $x^2 < 2^x < 2x$ (v) $2^x < 2x < x^2$ (vi) $2x < x^2 < 2^x$
    A (i) and (iii)   B (i) and (iv)   C (ii) and (iv)
                D (ii) and (v)   E (iii) and (v)

24. Which of the following is smallest?

    A $10 - 3\sqrt{11}$ B $8 - 3\sqrt{7}$ C $5 - 2\sqrt{6}$ D $9 - 4\sqrt{5}$ E $7 - 4\sqrt{3}$

25. Figure 1 shows a tile in the form of a trapezium, where $\alpha = 83\tfrac{1}{3}°$. Several copies of the tile are placed together to form a symmetrical pattern, part of which is shown in Figure 2. The outer border of the complete pattern is a regular 'star polygon'. Figure 3 shows an example of a regular 'star polygon'.

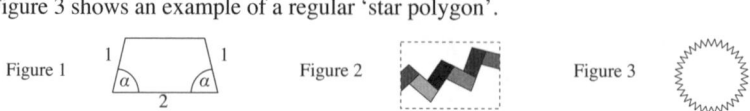

    Figure 1   Figure 2   Figure 3

    How many tiles are there in the complete pattern?
    A 48   B 54   C 60   D 66   E 72

Senior Challenge 2015 paper

1. What is $2015^2 - 2016 \times 2014$?

   A −2015   B −1   C 0   D 1   E 2015

2. What is the sum of all the solutions of the equation $6x = \dfrac{150}{x}$?

   A 0   B 5   C 6   D 25   E 156

3. When Louise had her first car, 50 litres of petrol cost £40. When she filled up the other day, she noticed that 40 litres of petrol cost £50.
   By approximately what percentage has the cost of petrol increased over this time?

   A 50%   B 56%   C 67%   D 75%   E 80%

4. In the diagram, the smaller circle touches the larger circle and also passes through its centre. What fraction of the area of the larger circle is outside the smaller circle?

   A $\dfrac{2}{3}$ B $\dfrac{3}{4}$ C $\dfrac{4}{5}$ D $\dfrac{5}{6}$ E $\dfrac{6}{7}$

5. The integer n is the mean of the three numbers 17, 23 and $2n$. What is the sum of the digits of n?

   A 4   B 5   C 6   D 7   E 8

6. The numbers 5, 6, 7, 8, 9, 10 are to be placed, one in each of the circles in the diagram, so that the sum of the numbers in each pair of touching circles is a prime number. The number 5 is placed in the top circle.
   Which number is placed in the shaded circle?

   A 6   B 7   C 8   D 9   E 10

7. Which of the following has the largest value?

   A $\dfrac{\left(\frac{1}{2}\right)}{\left(\frac{3}{4}\right)}$ B $\dfrac{1}{\left(\frac{\left(\frac{2}{3}\right)}{4}\right)}$ C $\dfrac{\left(\frac{\left(\frac{1}{2}\right)}{3}\right)}{4}$ D $\dfrac{1}{\left(\frac{2}{\left(\frac{3}{4}\right)}\right)}$ E $\dfrac{\left(\frac{1}{\left(\frac{2}{3}\right)}\right)}{4}$

8. The diagram shows eight small squares. Six of these squares are to be shaded so that the shaded squares form the net of a cube.
   In how many different ways can this be done?

   A 10   B 8   C 7   D 6   E 4

9. Four different straight lines are drawn on a flat piece of paper. The number of points where two or more lines intersect is counted.
   Which of the following could **not** be the number of such points?

   A 1   B 2   C 3   D 4   E 5

10. The positive integer n is between 1 and 20. Milly adds up all the integers from 1 to n inclusive. Billy adds up all the integers from $n + 1$ to 20 inclusive. Their totals are the same. What is the value of n?

    A 11   B 12   C 13   D 14   E 15

Senior Challenge 2015 paper 121

11. Rahid has a large number of cubic building blocks. Each block has sides of length 4 cm, 6 cm or 10 cm. Rahid makes little towers built from three blocks stacked on top of each other. How many different heights of tower can he make?

    A 6   B 8   C 9   D 12   E 27

12. A circle touches the sides of triangle *PQR* at the points *S*, *T* and *U* as shown. Also $\angle PQR = \alpha°$, $\angle PRQ = \beta°$ and $\angle TSU = \gamma°$. Which of the following gives γ in terms of α and β?

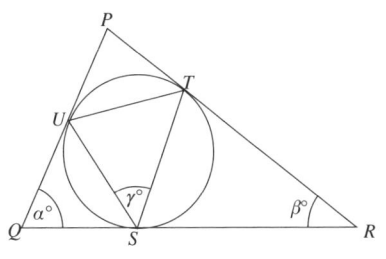

    A $\frac{1}{2}(\alpha + \beta)$ B $180 - \frac{1}{2}(\alpha + \beta)$
    C $180 - (\alpha + \beta)$ D $\alpha + \beta$
    E $\frac{1}{3}(\alpha + \beta)$

13. The Knave of Hearts tells only the truth on Mondays, Tuesdays, Wednesdays and Thursdays. He tells only lies on all the other days. The Knave of Diamonds tells only the truth on Fridays, Saturdays, Sundays and Mondays. He tells only lies on all the other days. On one day last week, they both said, "Yesterday I told lies." On which day of the week was that?

    A Sunday   B Monday   C Tuesday   D Thursday   E Friday

14. The triangle shown has an area of 88 square units. What is the value of *y*?

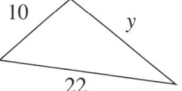

    A 17.6   B $2\sqrt{46}$ C $6\sqrt{10}$ D $13\sqrt{2}$ E $8\sqrt{5}$

15. Two vases are cylindrical in shape. The larger vase has diameter 20 cm. The smaller vase has diameter 10 cm and height 16 cm. The larger vase is partially filled with water. Then the empty smaller vase, with the open end at the top, is slowly pushed down into the water, which flows over its rim. When the smaller vase is pushed right down, it is half full of water.
    What was the original depth of the water in the larger vase?

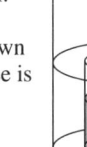

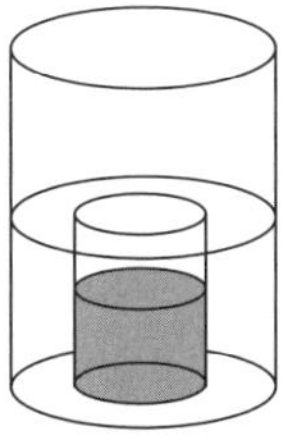

    A 10 cm   B 12 cm   C 14 cm   D 16 cm   E 18 cm

16. Fnargs are either red or blue and have 2, 3 or 4 heads. A group of six Fnargs consisting of one of each possible form is made to line up such that no immediate neighbours are the same colour nor have the same number of heads. How many ways are there of lining them up from left to right?

    A 12   B 24   C 60   D 120   E 720

17. The diagram shows eight circles of two different sizes. The circles are arranged in concentric pairs so that the centres form a square. Each larger circle touches one other larger circle and two smaller circles. The larger circles have radius 1. What is the radius of each smaller circle?

    A $\frac{1}{3}$ B $\frac{2}{5}$ C $\sqrt{2}-1$ D $\frac{1}{2}$ E $\frac{1}{2}\sqrt{2}$

18. What is the largest integer k whose square k^2 is a factor of $10!$?
    [$10! = 10 \times 9 \times 8 \times 7 \times 6 \times 5 \times 4 \times 3 \times 2 \times 1.$]

    A 6   B 256   C 360   D 720   E 5040

19. Three squares are arranged as shown so that their bases lie on a straight line. Also, the corners P, Q and R lie on a straight line. The middle square has sides that are 8 cm longer than the sides of the smallest square. The largest square has sides of length 50 cm.
    There are two possible values for the length (in cm) of the sides of the smallest square. Which of the following are they?

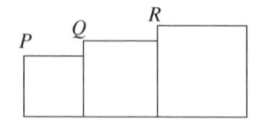

    A 2, 32   B 4, 42   C 4, 34   D 32, 40   E 34, 42

20. A square ink pad has sides of length 1 cm. It is covered in black ink and carefully placed in the middle of a piece of white paper. The square pad is then rotated 180° about one of its corners so that all of the pad remains in contact with the paper throughout the turn. The pad is then removed from the paper. What area of paper, in cm^2, is coloured black?

    A $\pi + 2$ B $2\pi - 1$ C 4   D $2\pi - 2$ E $\pi + 1$

21. The diagram shows a triangle XYZ. The sides XY, YZ and XZ have lengths 2, 3 and 4 respectively. The lines AMB, PMQ and SMT are drawn parallel to the sides of triangle XYZ so that AP, QS and BT are of equal length. What is the length of AP?

    A $\dfrac{10}{11}$ B $\dfrac{11}{12}$ C $\dfrac{12}{13}$ D $\dfrac{13}{14}$ E $\dfrac{14}{15}$

22. Let $f(x) = x + \sqrt{x^2 + 1} + \dfrac{1}{x - \sqrt{x^2 + 1}}$. What is the value of $f(2015)$?

    A -1 B 0   C 1   D $\sqrt{2016}$ E 2015

23. Given four different non-zero digits, it is possible to form 24 different four-digit numbers containing each of these four digits. What is the largest prime factor of the sum of the 24 numbers?

    A 23   B 93   C 97   D 101   E 113

24. Peter has 25 cards, each printed with a different integer from 1 to 25. He wishes to place N cards in a single row so that the numbers on every adjacent pair of cards have a prime factor in common.
    What is the largest value of N for which this is possible?

    A 16   B 18   C 20   D 22   E 24

25. A function, defined on the set of positive integers, is such that $f(xy) = f(x) + f(y)$ for all x and y. It is known that $f(10) = 14$ and $f(40) = 20$. What is the value of $f(500)$?

    A 29   B 30   C 39   D 48   E 50

Answers and solutions

Junior Challenge 2007
solutions

1. **C** $0.1 + 0.2 + 0.3 \times 0.4 = 0.3 + 0.12 = 0.42$.

2. **D** The train arrived $5 + 42 = 47$ minutes after 17:40, that is at 18:27.

3. **B** Note that 7 divides 35, 49 and 7, so it divides 354970. So the remainder is 2.

4. **E** Of the options given, only 27, which is three less than a multiple of 5, namely 30, and three more than a multiple of 6, namely 24, has both of the properties in the question.

5. **E** The area of the large square may be considered to consist of thirteen equal squares (nine of which are shaded) plus eight 'half squares' and four 'quarter squares' (all of which are unshaded).
So the total unshaded area is $\left(4 + 8 \times \frac{1}{2} + 4 \times \frac{1}{4}\right)$ squares = 9 squares. Hence half of the large square is shaded.

6. **A** When put in their correct places on the number line, the order of the fractions is: $-\frac{1}{3}, -\frac{1}{5}, -\frac{1}{7}, \frac{1}{6}, \frac{1}{4}$.

7. **D** If the top triangle is painted black, then any one of the three remaining triangles may also be painted black. Similarly, if the top triangle is painted white, then any one of the three remaining triangles may also be painted white. So there are six different ways.

8. **D** From the information, we see that Amy is to the left of both Ben and Chris. So the three are in the order Amy, Ben, Chris or the order Amy, Chris, Ben. So D is certainly true and the others are all false either in one case or in both.

9. **C** As ST is parallel to UV, $\angle PRT = 132°$ (corresponding angles).
So $\angle PRQ = 48°$ (angles on a straight line).
From the exterior angle of a triangle theorem, $\angle SQP = \angle QPR + \angle PRQ$, so $x = 134 - 48 = 86$.

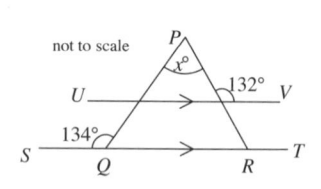

10. **D** The values of the five expressions are: A $\frac{3}{4}$; B $\frac{1}{4}$; C $\frac{1}{8}$; D 2; E $\frac{1}{2}$.

Junior Challenge 2007 solutions

11. A The number of times each bar is used is: A 4; B 6; C 8; D 7; E 7.

12. A The total number of spots which the six ladybirds have is $6 \times 12 = 72$. So the number of spots which the pine ladybird has is $72 - (2 + 10 + 14 + 18 + 24) = 4$.

13. D If R is $(-5, 4)$ then $PQ = PR = 6$. If R is $(7, 1)$ or if R is $(-6, 1)$ then R lies on the perpendicular bisector of PQ (the line $y = 1$), so in both cases $PR = QR$. If R is $(7, -2)$, then $QP = QR = 6$. However if R is $(-6, -2)$, then $PQ = 6, QR = 7$ and $PR > 7$, so triangle PQR is scalene.

14. E The thickness of the line is 0.2 mm, that is 0.0002 m. So, in order to cover an area of one square metre, the length of the line would need to be $\frac{1}{0.0002}$ m, that is 5000 m.

15. C We consider the different possible choices from the top row. If 1 is chosen, then the options are 1, 5, 9 and 1, 6, 8 giving products 45 and 48 respectively. If 2 is chosen, the options are 2, 4, 9 and 2, 6, 7 giving products 72 and 84 respectively. Finally, if 3 is chosen, the options are 3, 4, 8 and 3, 5, 7 giving products 96 and 105. So 105 is the maximum.

16. B The six marked angles, together with the six interior angles of the two triangles, comprise all of the angles around five separate points. So the required sum is $(5 \times 360 - 2 \times 180)° = 1440°$.

17. C The only possible cubes have edge size 1 or 2. It takes 8 of the former to replace one of the latter, so William needs to cut as many cubes of edge size 2 as possible, namely 3. The number of one inch cubes, therefore, is $2 \times 3 \times 6 - 3 \times 8$, that is 12. So the smallest number of cubes is $3 + 12 = 15$.

18. B The hundreds column shows us that $J = 1$ or 2. [We can't carry more than 2 from the units to the tens; and 2 plus the biggest feasible values 7, 8, 9 for the three letters is only 26.] The units column shows that $J + M$ is a multiple of 10 and it can't be 0 (or else $J + M = 0$); so $J + M = 10$ and $M = 9$ or 8 respectively. Also, the sum of the units column is $10 + C$, so there is exactly 1 to carry to the tens column. The tens column now tells us that $J + C + 1 = 10J$. So $J = 2$ is not possible and therefore $J = 1, C = 8$ and $M = 9$.

19. A If the semicircle with diameter PQ is rotated through 180° about Q, the new shape formed has the same area as the original shape. It consists of a semicircle of diameter 6 cm and a semicircle of diameter 2 cm. So its area is $\left(\frac{1}{2} \times \pi \times 3^2 + \frac{1}{2} \times \pi \times 1^2\right)$ cm², that is 5π cm².

20. **E** Range Hill scored only three points in the match and these were scored in the second half. They represent 10% of the total points scored. As Boarwarts Academy also scored three points in the second half, the proportion of points scored after halftime was 20%, that is $\frac{1}{5}$.

21. **B** Let the list be 3, 4, a, b, c, d, e, f, g, h. We can see that $c = 3$ and $e = 4$. So the list now reads 3, 4, $a, b, 3, d, 4, f, g, h$. Now, the only pairs of letters two apart from each other are a, d and d, g. Therefore $d = 2$ and the list is 3, 4, a, b, 3, 2, 4, f, g, h. The only pair now one apart are f, h. The list is 3, 4, a, b, 3, 2, 4, 1, g, 1. Now a, b are the only pair zero apart. So $a = b = 0$ and $g = 2$.

22. **D** Four of the given values for d may be rejected since $143 = 11 \times 13$; $153 = 3 \times 51$; $567 = 3 \times 189$; $183 = 3 \times 61$. However, 173 and 577 are both prime, so $d = 7$.

23. **E** Let the length of the longer side of each rectangle be l. Then the length of each shorter side is $l - x$. So $y = l + l - x$ and hence $l = \frac{1}{2}(y + x)$.

24. **C** Pages 1 to 9 inclusive require 9 digits; pages 10 to 99 inclusive require 180 digits. So, in total, 189 digits are required to number all of the pages before the three-digit page numbers commence with page number 100. This leaves 663 digits, so the last page in the book is the 221st page which has a three-digit number, namely page 320.

25. **B** Imagine unfolding the final triangle once. Then one edge of the final triangle is inside the new shape obtained; and the other two triangle edges have 'mirror image' copies. So the new shape has at most 4 edges. After unfolding once more, one of these edges is now on the inside; and the remaining edges get mirror images again. So the shape obtained (the original shape) has no more than 6 edges. The diagrams below show that 3, 4, 5 and 6 sides are all possible.

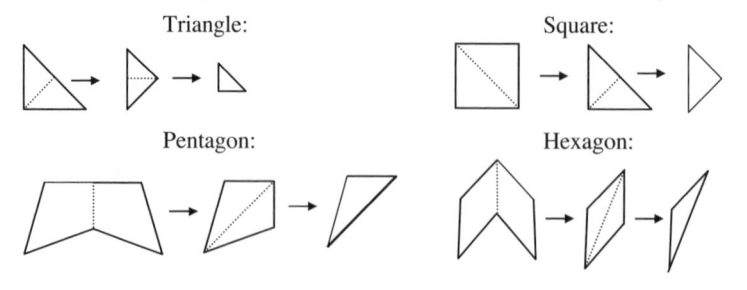

Junior Challenge 2008 solutions

1. **D** The results of the five calculations are 9, 11, 14, 25, 24 respectively.

2. **E** For it to be possible to draw a figure without taking the pen off the paper and without drawing along an existing line, there must be at most two points in the figure at which an odd number of lines meet. Only E satisfies this condition.

3. **B** $\frac{2}{40} = \frac{1}{20} = \frac{5}{100} = 5\%$.

4. **C** The unmarked interior angle on the right of the triangle $= (360 - 324)° = 36°$. So, by the exterior angle theorem, $x = 100 - 36 = 64$.

5. **E** The cost of 1 kg of potatoes is £1.25 ÷ 2.5 = 50 p. So the cost of 1 tonne, that is 1000 kg, is 1000 × 50 p = £500.

6. **D** Adam Ant walks 24 cm, whilst Annabel Ant walks 32 cm.

7. **C** In terms of length, 1 arm = 2 forearms = 4 hands = 8 middle fingers = 16 thumbs. So 4 arms have the same total length as 64 thumbs.

8. **A** From the diagram, in which all lengths are in cm, it can be seen that the perimeter
   $= [4 × 1 + 3 × 3 + x + (3 - x)]$ cm
   $= 16$ cm.

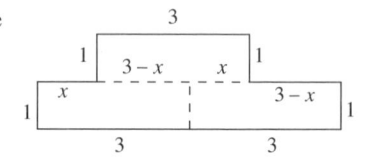

9. **E** The values of the five expressions are $\frac{1}{6}, \frac{1}{12}, \frac{1}{20}, \frac{1}{30}, \frac{1}{42}$ respectively.

10. **B** Consider one corner of the cube. There are three faces which meet there, and each pair of them has an edge in common. So three different colours are needed. No other colours will be needed provided that opposite faces are painted in the same colour since opposite faces have no edges in common.

11. **E** The 120 tons of ice which remain represent two-thirds of the original cargo. So one-third of the original cargo was 60 tons.

12. **C** Consider the sculpture to consist of three layers, each of height 1. Then the volumes of the bottom, middle and top layers are 5, 2, 5 respectively. So the volume of the sculpture is 12.
    (*Alternatively: the sculpture consists of a* 3 × 3 × 3 *cube from which two* 2 × 2 × 2 *cubes have been removed. The* 2 × 2 × 2 *cubes have exactly one* 1 × 1 × 1 *cube (the cube at the centre of the* 3 × 3 × 3 *cube) in common. So the volume of the sculpture* $= 27 - (2 × 8 - 1) = 12$.)

13. **C** New shapes may be formed by joining *PX* to *XR* (quadrilateral) or *SP* to *RQ* (parallelogram) or *XS* to *RQ* (trapezium). Triangle *SPX* shows that *PX* and *SX* have different lengths; and *PX* and *PQ* have different lengths because *XR* is shorter than *SR*. So there are no other places to position the triangle.

Junior Challenge 2008 solutions

14. D As the original cube was divided into eight cubes of equal size, these smaller cubes have side equal to half the side of the original cube. So each of the new cubes originally occupied one corner of the large cube and hence has three faces painted blue and three faces unpainted. So the fraction of the total surface area of the new cubes which is blue equals one half.

15. B A rate of 1 metre per 1000 years is equivalent to 1 mm per year, that is just under three thousandths of 1 mm per day.

16. A Of the five alternatives, only A and B have straight lines in the ratio 2:15:20. However, B would be formed by repeatedly moving forward 2 units, turning right, moving forward 20 units, turning right, moving forward 15 units, turning right.

17. B Consider the leading diagonal: $p \times 1 \times \frac{1}{8} = 1$ so $p = 8$.
Consider the bottom row: $u \times 4 \times \frac{1}{8} = 1$ so $u = 2$.
Consider the left-hand column: $p \times s \times u = 8 \times s \times 2 = 1$ so $s = \frac{1}{16}$.
Consider the non-leading diagonal: $r \times 1 \times u = r \times 1 \times 2 = 1$ so $r = \frac{1}{2}$.
Therefore $r + s = \frac{1}{2} + \frac{1}{16} = \frac{9}{16}$.

18. B Let my age now be x. So Granny's age is $4x$. Considering five years ago: $4x - 5 = 5(x - 5)$, giving $x = 20$. So Granny is 80 and I am 20.

19. D As $QS = SR$, $\angle SRQ = \angle SQR = x°$.
So $\angle QST = 2x°$ (exterior angle theorem). Also $\angle TQS = 2x°$ since $QT = TS$.
As $PT = QT$, $\angle TPQ = \angle TQP = 20°$.
Consider the interior angles of triangle PQR: $20 + (20 + 2x + x) + x = 180$. So $4x + 40 = 180$, hence $x = 35$.

20. A Consider the nine numbers from 1 to 9 inclusive: each digit appears once, with the exception of zero. Now consider the 90 two-digit numbers from 10 to 99 inclusive: each of the 10 digits makes the same number of appearances (9) as the second digit of a number and the digits from 1 to 9 make an equal number of appearances (10) as the first digit of a number, but zero never appears as a first digit. There is a similar pattern in the 900 three-digit numbers from 100 to 999 inclusive with zero never appearing as a first digit, but making the same number of appearances as second or third digit as the other nine digits. This leaves only the number 1000 in which there are more zeros than any other digit, but not enough to make up for the fact that zero appears far fewer times than the other nine digits in the numbers less than 1000. (*It is left to the reader to check that* 0 *appears* 192 *times,* 1 *appears* 301 *times and each of* 2 *to* 9 *appears* 300 *times.*)

21. **A** Consider the third column: $2♩ + ♥ = 13$ [1]
Consider the second row: $♩ + 2♥ = 11$ [2]
$2 \times [2] - [1]$ $3♥ = 9$, so $♥ = 3$.

(Although their values are not requested, it is now straightforward to show that $♩ = 5$, ☼ $= 4$.)

22. **D** The only such occasions occur when the clock changes from 09 59 59 to 10 00 00; from 19 59 59 to 20 00 00 and from 23 59 59 to 00 00 00.

23. **B** Let the 7-digit code be $abcdefg$. It may be deduced that $a = 3$ since $b + c + d + e = 16$ and $a + b + c + d + e = 19$. By using similar reasoning, it may be deduced that $b = c = e = f = g = 3$. As $a + b + c + d = 16$, $d = 7$; so the code is 3337333.

24. **E** Let the other such list of numbers be $a, 1; b, 2; c, 3; d, 4$ and note that $a + b + c + d = 8$ since there are 8 numbers in the list.
If $d = 4$, then exactly two of a, b, c equal 4, but this would make $a + b + c + d > 8$, so $d \neq 4$.
Similar reasoning shows that $d \neq 3$, so $d = 1$ or $d = 2$.
If $d = 2$, then exactly one of a, b, c equals 4 and the remaining two both equal 1 since $a + b + c + d = 8$. So we have $a, 1; b, 2; c, 3; 2, 4$ and it is b which must equal 4 since we already have more than one 2. However, as a and c are now both equal to 1, we have $1, 1; 4, 2; 1, 3; 2, 4$ and this is not correct.
So $d = 1$ and we have $a + b + c = 7$ and $a, b, c \neq 4$. Clearly $a \neq 1$, since that would give at least two 1s so $a = 2$ or $a = 3$.
If $a = 2$, then we have $2, 1; b, 2; c, 3; 1, 4$ with $b + c = 5$ and $b, c \neq 4$. So $b = 2, c = 3$ or vice versa. This gives either $2, 1; 2, 2; 3, 3; 1, 4$ (incorrect), or $2, 1; 3, 2; 2, 3; 1, 4$ (the example given in the question).
Finally, if $a = 3$, then we have $3, 1; b, 2; c, 3; 1, 4$ with $b + c = 4$. The possibilities are $3, 1; 1, 2; 3, 3; 1, 4$ or $3, 1; 2, 2; 2, 3; 1, 4$ or $3, 1; 3, 2; 1, 3; 1, 4$ but only the first of these describes itself correctly. So the total number of 1s and 3s is 6.

25. **D** Let the lengths of the sides of the squares, in increasing order, be $a, b, c, d, e, f, g, h, i$ respectively. So $h = 10$.
Note that $c = 2b - a$ and $d = 2c - 2a = 4b - 4a$. Also, $e = 2d - a = 8b - 9a$.
As $h = 2e - 2a - b = 15b - 20a$, we may deduce that $15b - 20a = 10$, that is $3b - 4a = 2$.
Since a and b are positive integers less than 10, the only possibilities are $a = 1$, $b = 2$ or $a = 4, b = 6$. However, $h = 10$ therefore b cannot be greater than 4. So $a = 1$ and $b = 2$. It may now be deduced that $c = 4 - 1 = 3$; $d = 8 - 4 = 4$; $e = 16 - 9 = 7$. Also $2g = 2e + d$, so $g = 9$.
Now the length of the side of the larger square is $2h + e + g = 20 + 7 + 9 = 36$, so its area is $36^2 = 1296$.

(Note that it was not necessary to find the values of f and i, but it is now quite simple to deduce that $f = 8$ and $i = 18$.)

Junior Challenge 2009
solutions

1. **B** $9002 - 2002 = 7000$ so $9002 - 2009 = 7000 - 7 = 6993$.

2. **B** Each of faces 1, 4 and 5 has four axes of symmetry, whilst each of faces 2, 3 and 6 has two axes of symmetry only.

3. **D** The values of the left-hand sides of the expressions are 0, 16, 28, 36 and 40 respectively.

4. **E** Each of points A, B, C and D is 1 unit from the origin, but the point $(1, 1)$ is at a distance $\sqrt{2}$ units from the origin.

5. **D** The problem may be solved by dividing each of the alternatives in turn by 7, but the prime factorisation of 1001, i.e. $1001 = 7 \times 11 \times 13$, leads to the conclusion that 111 111, which is 111×1001, is a multiple of 7.

6. **B** Triangle ABM has base 3 units and height 3 units, so its area is $\frac{1}{2} \times 3 \times 3$ units^2, that is $4\frac{1}{2}$ units^2.

7. **C** The time difference is 12 hours and 12 minutes, that is 732 minutes.

8. **E** Removing tile A or tile B or tile D has the effect of reducing the perimeter by a distance equal to twice the side of one tile, whilst removing tile C increases the perimeter by that same distance. Removing tile E, however, leaves the length of the perimeter unchanged.

9. **A** $\frac{20}{11} = 1\frac{9}{11} = 1.818181...$, so only two different digits appear.

10. **B** The triangle in the centre of the diagram is equilateral since each of its sides is equal in length to the side of one of the squares. The sum of the angles at a point is $360°$, so $x = 360 - (90 + 90 + 60) = 120$.

11. **C** The first thirteen terms of the sequence are $-3, 0, 2, -1, 1, 2, 2, 5, 9, 16, 30, 55, 101, ...$

12. **A** The increase in Gill's weight is 45 kg, which is 9 times her weight in 1988. So the percentage increase in weight is 900%.
    (The problem refers to Q14 in the very first Schools Mathematical Challenge – the forerunner of the current Junior and Intermediate Mathematical Challenges – in 1988. This was 'Weighing the baby at the clinic was a problem. The baby would not keep still and caused the scales to wobble. So I held the baby and stood on the scales while the nurse read off 78 kg. Then the nurse held the baby while I read off 69 kg. Finally I held the nurse while the baby read off 137 kg. What is the combined weight of all three (in kg)?
    A 142 B 147 C 206 D 215 E 284.')

13. **D** Let the ten consecutive integers be $x - 4, x - 3, x - 2, x - 1, x, x + 1, x + 2, x + 3, x + 4$ and $x + 5$ respectively. The sum of these is $10x + 5$ so $10x + 5 = 5$, that is $x = 0$. Hence the largest of the integers is 5.

Junior Challenge 2009 solutions

14. E The sum of Karen's two marks was 78×2, that is 156. So her mark for Mathemagics was $156 - 72$, that is 84.

15. E If Matt takes 12 jellybeans then he will have taken at least one of each flavour unless he takes all 8 watermelon jellybeans and either all 4 vanilla jellybeans or all 4 butter popcorn jellybeans. In this case the 4 remaining jellybeans will all be of the flavour he has yet to take, so taking one more jellybean ensures that he will have taken at least one of each flavour.

16. D 20% of the 80% is 16% of the kettle's capacity. Therefore the volume of water left in the kettle after Keith has poured out 20% of the original amount is 64% of the kettle's capacity. So when full, the kettle holds $\frac{1152}{64} \times 100$ ml, that is 1800 ml.

17. A The tiling pattern may be considered to be a tessellation by the shape shown, so the required ratio is 1:1.

18. B The lowest common multiple of 2, 3, 4, 5 and 6 is required. Of these numbers, 2, 3 and 5 are prime whilst $4 = 2^2$ and $6 = 2 \times 3$. So their lowest common multiple is $2^2 \times 3 \times 5$, that is 60.

19. A Adjacent angles on a straight line add up to 180°, so $\angle GJF = 180° - 111° = 69°$. In triangle FGJ, $GJ = GF$ so $\angle GFJ = \angle GJF$. Therefore $\angle FGJ = (180 - 2 \times 69)° = 42°$. As $FGHI$ is a rhombus, $FG = FI$ and therefore $\angle GIF = \angle FGI = 42°$. Finally, from triangle FJI, $\angle JFI = (180 - 111 - 42)° = 27°$.

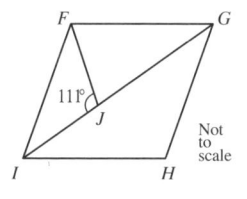

20. D Let the numbers in the boxes be as shown in the diagram. Then $b = 90 - a$; $c = 12 + a$; $d = b + 78 = 168 - a$. Also, $e = 90 + c = 102 + a$; $f = 90 + d = 258 - a$. So $x = e + f = 102 + a + 258 - a = 360$.

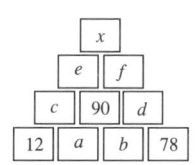

21. E The diagrams below show how the total number of edges of the resulting three pieces may be 9, 10, 11 or 12. However, 12 is the maximum value of the total number of edges since the original number of edges is four and any subsequent cut adds a maximum of four edges (by dividing two existing edges and adding the new 'cuts').

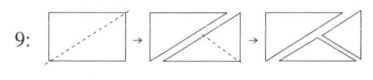

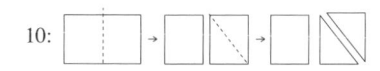

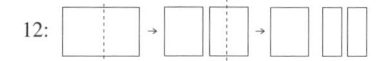

22. **D** In order to reach a 9 in three steps, the first zero must be one of the three adjacent to the 2 and the second zero must be one of the five adjacent to a 9. The table shows the number of such routes to that point.
So the total number of different routes is 25.

	1	2	4
1	1	2	5
2	2	1	3
4	5	3	1

23. **C** Let the value of a green note and the value of a blue note be g zogs and b zogs respectively. Then $3g + 8b = 46$ and $8g + 3b = 31$. Adding these two equations gives $11g + 11b = 77$, so $b + g = 7$.
Therefore $3g + 3b = 21$. Subtracting this equation from the original equations in turn gives $5b = 25$ and $5g = 10$ respectively. So $b = 5, g = 2$ and $2g + 3b = 19$.

24. **C** Let the lengths a, b, c, d, e, f be as shown in the diagram. Then the sum of the perimeters of the four labelled parallelograms is
$2(a + e) + 2(b + d) + 2(b + f) + 2(c + e)$
$= 2(a + b + c + d + e + f) + 2(b + e)$
$=$ perimeter of $WXYZ$ + perimeter of shaded parallelogram.
So the perimeter of the shaded parallelogram is $((11 + 8 + 4 + 5) - 21)$ cm = 7 cm.

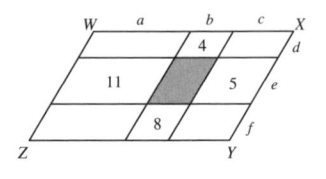

25. **B** Let the number of boys in Miss Quaffley's class be b and the number of girls be g. Then the number of teddy bears is $\frac{1}{3}(b + g)$. Also, in total, the boys took out $12b$ library books last term and the girls took out $17g$ books. The total number of books taken out by the bears was $9 \times \frac{1}{3}(b + g)$ that is $3(b + g)$.
So $12b + 17g + 3(b + g) = 305$, that is $15b + 20g = 305$, that is $3b + 4g = 61$.
Clearly, b and g are positive integers. The positive integer solutions of the equation $3b + 4g = 61$ are $b = 3, g = 13; b = 7, g = 10; b = 11, g = 7; b = 15, g = 4; b = 19, g = 1$.
However, there is one further condition: the number of teddy bears, that is $\frac{1}{3}(b + g)$, is also a positive integer and of the five pairs of solutions above, this condition is satisfied only by $b = 11, g = 7$.
Check: the 11 boys take out 132 books, the 7 girls take out 119 books and the 6 teddy bears take out 54 books, giving a total of 305 books.
(*The equation $3b + 4g = 61$ in which b and g both represent positive integers is an example of a Diophantine equation.*)

Junior Challenge 2010 solutions

1. **B** The expression = 2010 + 2010 − 2010 − 2010 + 2010
   = (2010 − 2010) + (2010 − 2010) + 2010 = 2010.

2. **E** In A, the letter T is incorrect; in B it is U which is incorrect; in C and D the incorrect letters are M and K respectively.

3. **A** 2010 mm = 2.01 m so, of the alternatives given, only a table could be expected to have a length of 2010 mm.

4. **D** Let X be on the top face of the cube. If the base is placed on a horizontal surface, then A, B, C, E will all be on vertical faces of the cube and D will be on the base, opposite X.

5. **D** Each of the five outer circles is divided into six regions, giving 30 regions in total. In addition, there is one region in the centre of the diagram and one region between the circles and the sides of the square. So, in all, there are 32 regions.

6. **C** The values of the expressions are A 12; B 15; C 16; D 15 and E 12.

7. **A** As 2, 5 and 10 are all factors of the correct product, this product is a multiple of 100. So the last digit and the last-but-one digit are both zero.

8. **D** If the mean of y and z is x, then $y + z = 2x$. So the sum of the interior angles of the triangle is $(x + y + z)° = 3x°$. So $3x = 180$, that is $x = 60$.

9. **A** One year is, at most, 366 days, so one-third of a year is less than 125 days. No month is longer than 31 days, so 4 months is also less than 125 days, as is 17.5 weeks which equals 122.5 days. However 3002 hours equals 125 days 2 hours, so this is the longest of the five periods of time.

10. **E** Third prize is worth one-sixth of the total prize money, so Mrs Keat received half of that amount, that is one-twelfth of the total.

11. **C** Divide the whole figure into horizontal strips of height 1 unit: its area is $(3 + 6 + 8 + 8 + 8 + 6 + 3)$ units^2 = 42 units^2. Similarly, the unshaded area is $(1 + 4 + 6 + 4 + 1)$ units^2 = 16 units^2. So the shaded area is 26 units^2.
    Alternative solution: notice that if the inner polygon is moved a little, the answer remains the same – because it is just the difference between the areas of the two polygons. So, although we are not told it, we may assume that the inner one is so positioned that the outer shaded area can be split neatly into 1 by 1 squares – and there are 26 of these.

Junior Challenge 2010 solutions 139

12. C There are 36 people to be seated so at least five tables will be required. The number of circular tables must be even. However, five rectangular tables will seat 40 people and three rectangular and two circular will seat 34. So at least six tables are needed. Two rectangular and four circular tables do seat 36 people: so six is the minimum number of tables.

13. B It is necessary to find a route for which the line is broken the first time it passes through any intersection and solid when it passes through that intersection for the second time. Only the route which starts at B and heads away from D satisfies this condition.

14. D The average number of vehicles per day $\approx \dfrac{300\,000\,000}{44 \times 365} \approx \dfrac{300\,000\,000}{40 \times 400}$
$= \dfrac{300\,000\,000}{16\,000} \approx \dfrac{300\,000\,000}{15\,000} = 20\,000$.

15. C The two shaded regions measure 3 by 7 and 1 by 6, so the total area outside the overlap is 27 units^2.

16. E As 108 marks represented 18% of the final total, 6 marks represented 1% of the final total. So this total was 600.

17. D As triangle *PQR* is equilateral, $x + 2y = 3x - y = 5y - x$. Equating any two of these expressions gives $2x = 3y$.
The only pair of given values which does not satisfy this equation is $x = 10, y = 6$.

18. D The other times that this has happened previously are when Sam's age in years went from 1 to 2; from 4 to 5; from 16 to 17 and from 36 to 37.
Note that since primes other than 2 are odd, the only squares which need to be checked, other than 1, are of even numbers.

19. C Villages which have more than two roads leading to them (or from them) must all be visited more than once as a single visit will involve at most two roads. So Bentonville, Pencaster and Wytham must all be visited more than once. The route Home, Bentonville, Greendale, Wytham, Bentonville, Pencaster, Home, Wytham, Horndale, Pencaster, Home starts and finishes at Home and visits both Greendale and Horndale exactly once so the minimum number of villages is three.

20. B The seven numbers must total 49 if their mean is to be 7. The largest possible number will occur when the other six numbers are as small as possible, that is 1, 2, 3, 4, 5, 6. So the required number is $49 - 21 = 28$.

21. C The first and last hexagons both contribute 5 cm to the perimeter of the pattern. Every other hexagon in the pattern contributes 4 cm to the perimeter. The first and last thus contribute 10 cm, so we need another $2000 \div 4 = 500$ hexagons. Therefore the total number of hexagons required is 502.

22. E The prime numbers less than 20 are 2, 3, 5, 7, 11, 13, 17, 19. It is not possible for 2 to be one of the six numbers Kiran wrote down, since that would give one of the pairs an odd sum, whereas both of the other pairs would add up to an even number. The sum of the remaining 7 primes is 75 which is a multiple of 3. The sum of the six primes making up the three pairs must also be a multiple of 3 since each pair has the same total. So the odd prime not used in the six pairs must be a multiple of 3 too. Therefore 3 is the odd prime not used. So each pair totals $72 \div 3$, that is 24, and the pairs are $5 + 19, 7 + 17, 11 + 13$.

23. E The number of sides of the polygon is equal to the number of corners it has. As no dot is at more than one corner, the maximum number of corners is 16. So the maximum possible number of sides is 16, provided that a 16-sided figure may be drawn. The figure on the right shows one of several ways in which this can be achieved.

24. B In the 21st Century, to obtain a sequence of two years or more then either a 2 or a 0 must be repeated in each year, or the sequence include years such as 2011, 2033, 2044 etc. So the only sequence after that mentioned in the question will be from 2020 to 2030, but this is too short.

In the 22nd Century, either a 2 or a 1 must be repeated. The first such sequence is 2110 to 2129 which does include 20 years, one of which is 2120.

25. A The three-digit number RRR is equal to 111 multiplied by the single digit R. So $PQPQ \times R = 639027 \div 111 = 5757$. Now $PQPQ$ equals the two-digit number PQ multiplied by 101. So $PQ \times R = 5757 \div 101 = 57$. The only ways in which 57 may be expressed as the product of a two-digit number and a single digit are 57×1 and 19×3. So $P = 5, Q = 7, R = 1$ or $P = 1, Q = 9, R = 3$. In both cases, $P + Q + R = 13$.

Junior Challenge 2011 solutions

1. **B** $2 \times 0 \times 1 + 1 = 0 \times 1 + 1 = 0 + 1 = 1$.

2. **E** If the sum of the digits is a multiple of 3 then the number is a multiple of 3. The sums of the digits of the given numbers are 6, 9, 12, 15, 18, so they are all multiples of 3.
    (*Can you prove that all numbers consisting of three consecutive digits are multiples of 3? Hint: let the second digit be n.*)

3. **B** In the diagram, the extra cells which need to be lit are shown in black.
    So, in total, 24 cells are lit in a bold 'o'.

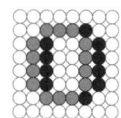

4. **C** 100 kg = 100 000 g. So the sum of money in £1 coins which would have the same mass as the world's largest coin is £(100 000 ÷ 10) = £10 000.
    (*The coin was sold for $4m (£2.6m) at an auction in Vienna in June 2010.*)

5. **B** One third is equal to four twelfths. Hence the children ate eight twelfths of the bar between them. Each child ate one twelfth of the bar, so old Mother Hubbard had eight children.

6. **E** The six marked angles are the interior angles of the two large triangles which make up the star shape in the diagram, so their sum is $2 \times 180° = 360°$.

7. **D** There are 9 bushels in a barrel. Each bushel is 4 pecks, so there are 36 pecks in a barrel. Therefore 35 more pecks are needed.

8. **A** Let the original square have side $3x$. Then its perimeter is $12x$.
   The perimeter of the octagon is $2 \times 4x + 3 \times 3x + 3 \times x = 8x + 9x + 3x = 20x$.
   So the required ratio is $12:20 = 3:5$.

9. **A** $1 + 2 + 3 + 4 + 5 + 6 + 7 + 8 + 9 = 45$ is the sum of the digits of each such number. As 45 is a multiple of 9, each such number is a multiple of 9 and so too is the difference between two of them. Thus the smallest feasible difference is 9. The two numbers 123 456 798 and 123 456 789 show that this can occur.

10. **C** The diagram shows the number of lines which meet at the vertices P, Q, R, S, T. When the path around the diagram passes through a vertex, it uses up two of the edges. So, apart from the first and last vertex used, each vertex must have an even number of edges meeting at it. So we are obliged to use R or S as the first vertex, and the other as the last. The path $RQPTSRPS$, together with its reverse, shows that either is a possible start. (It is a fact that such a path can be drawn through a connected graph precisely when either all, or all but 2, vertices have an even number of edges meeting there.)

11. **C** A line segment which is parallel to two sides of the rectangle has been added to the diagram, as shown. The angle marked $p°$ is equal to the angle marked $x°$ as these are alternate angles between parallel lines. So $x = p$. Similarly $y = q$. The angles marked $p°$ and $q°$ together form one interior angle of an equilateral triangle. Therefore $x + y = p + q = 60$.

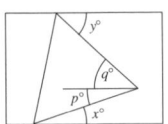

12. **E** ● = ■ + ▲ = ▲ + ▲ + ▲ = 3▲. Therefore ♦ = ● + ■ + ▲ = 3▲ + 2▲ + ▲ = 6▲.

13. **E** The mean of $\frac{2}{3}$ and $\frac{4}{9}$ is $\left(\frac{2}{3} + \frac{4}{9}\right) \div 2 = \left(\frac{6}{9} + \frac{4}{9}\right) \div 2 = \frac{10}{9} \div 2 = \frac{5}{9}$.
   (*Note that the mean of two numbers lies midway between those two numbers.*)

14. **A** Let the area of the shaded face be x cm^2. Then the cuboid has two faces of area x cm^2 and four faces of area $4x$ cm^2. So its total surface area is $18x$ cm^2. Therefore $18x = 72$, that is $x = 4$.
    So the area of one of the visible unshaded faces is 4×4 cm$^2 = 16$ cm^2.

15. **A** In order that the figure has rotational symmetry of order 2, the three squares which appear in black must be shaded. When this has been done, we note that the broken lines shown are both lines of symmetry. So the minimum number of squares which must be shaded is 3.

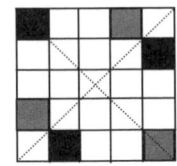

Junior Challenge 2011 solutions

16. **B** The smallest possible number of votes the winner could receive corresponds to the situation in which the numbers of votes received by each of the candidates are as close together as possible.
As $83 \div 4 = 20.75$, at least one of the candidates receives 21 votes or more. However, it is not possible for the winner to receive 21 votes, since there are still 62 votes to be allocated which makes it impossible for each of the other three candidates to receive fewer than 21 votes. So the winner must receive more than 21 votes. If the numbers of votes received by the candidates are 22, 21, 20, 20 then there is a winner and, therefore, 22 is the smallest number of votes the winner could receive.

17. **D** The lengths in minutes of the fifth set and the whole match are 491 and 665 respectively.
So the required fraction is $\dfrac{491}{665} = \dfrac{491 \times 3}{665 \times 3} \approx \dfrac{1500}{2000} = \dfrac{3}{4}$.

18. **C** Until Peri reaches Granny's, he travels 9m in every 10 days. So he takes 90 days to travel the first 81m of his journey. There remains a distance of 9m to be covered and so, after a further 9 days, Peri is at Granny's. Therefore the length of Peri's journey is 99 days, that is 14 weeks 1 day. So Peri arrives at Granny's on Tuesday.

19. **D** Of the given numbers, 2, 3 and 5 are all prime and therefore appear in the list. In addition, 1 appears in the list as it is the units digit of 11 and also of many other primes. However, all numbers with units digit 4 are even and therefore not prime, because the only even prime is 2. So only 1, 2, 3, 5 appear in the list.

20. **A** Let the length of the side of each cube be x cm. Then the volume of the solid is $7x^3$ cm^3. Therefore $7x^3 = 875$, that is $x^3 = 125$. So $x = 5$. The surface area of the solid comprises five of the faces of each of six cubes. Each face has area 25 cm^2 so the required area is $5 \times 6 \times 25$ cm$^2 = 750$ cm^2.

21. **B** In total the train travels 27 km + 29 km = 56 km.
So the combined time for these two parts of the journey is $\dfrac{56}{96}$ hours = $\dfrac{7}{12}$ hours = 35 minutes.
The total journey time, therefore, is 38 minutes. So Gill arrives at 09:38.

22. **D** Let the numbers of stamps bought by Evariste and Sophie be x and y respectively. Then $1.1x + 0.7y = 10$, that is $11x + 7y = 100$. As 100 has remainder 2 when divided by 7, we need a multiple of 11 which is two more than a multiple of 7. The multiples of 11 less than 100 are 11, 22, 33, 44, 55, 66, 77, 88, 99. Of these only 44 is two more than a multiple of 7. So the only positive integer solutions of the Diophantine equation $11x + 7y = 100$ are $x = 4, y = 8$. Therefore Evariste buys 4 stamps, costing £4.40, and Sophie buys 8 stamps, costing £5.60.

23. E Let $\angle RTS = x°$. Then $\angle RST = x°$ as $RS = RT$.
Let $\angle QUS = y°$. Then $\angle QSU = y°$ as $QS = QU$.
As RSQ is a straight line, $x + y + 40 = 180$; so $x + y = 140$.

Now $\angle TPU = 180° - \angle TRS - \angle SQU$
$= 180° - (180 - 2x)° - (180 - 2y)°$
$= 180° - 180° + 2x° - 180° + 2y°$
$= 2(x + y)° - 180°$
$= 2 \times 140° - 180°$
$= 100°$.

24. D (We may assume that the party is initially on the near bank and wishes to cross to the far bank.)
If an adult crosses to the far bank then there has to be a child waiting there to bring the raft back (unless an adult immediately brings the raft back – but this represents a wasted journey). This is possible only if the first two crossings involve both children crossing to the far bank and one of them staying there whilst the other brings the raft back. The third crossing involves the first adult crossing to the far bank and on the fourth crossing the child waiting on the far bank brings the raft back to the near bank. So after four crossings, one of the adults is on the far bank and the remainder of the party is on the near bank. This procedure is repeated so that after eight crossings, both adults are on the far bank and both children are on the near bank. A ninth and final crossing then takes both children to the far bank.

25. C The three trapezia have 12 edges in total. Whenever two trapezia are joined together the total number of edges is reduced by at least 2. Therefore the maximum possible value of N is $12 - 2 \times 2 = 8$. As the shapes form a polygon, N cannot be less than 3. The diagrams below show that all values of N from 3 to 8 are indeed possible, so there are 6 different values of N.

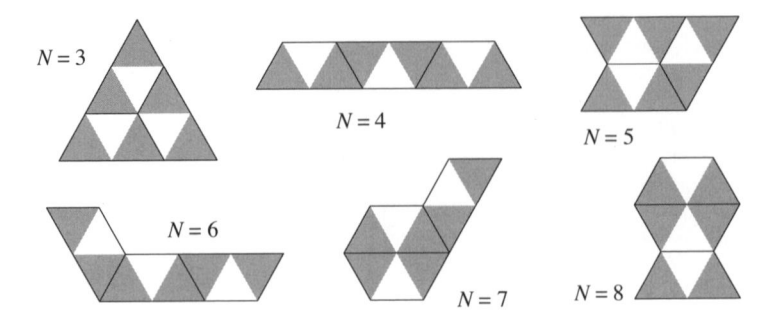

Junior Challenge 2012 solutions

1. **E** The smallest four-digit positive integer is 1000. Each of the subsequent integers up to and including 1022 has at least two digits the same. However, all digits of 1023 are different so this is the required integer.

2. **C** $1.01 \div 2 = 1 \div 2 + 0.01 \div 2 = 0.5 + 0.005 = 0.505$.

3. **E** An integer will have exactly one factor other than 1 and itself if, and only if, it is the square of a prime. Of the options given, the only such number is 25. Its factors are 1, 5, 25.

4. **C** None of the letters J, N, R has an axis of symmetry, so these letters cannot look the same when reflected in a mirror, no matter how the mirror is held. However, the letters U, I, O all have at least one axis of symmetry, so each may look the same when reflected in a mirror.

5. **D** $2012 - 1850 = 162$.

6. **D** The first two views of the cube show that I, M, U, O are not opposite K. So P is opposite K. Similarly, the second and third views show that I is opposite O. So the remaining two faces, M and U, must be opposite each other.

7. **B** Two medium cartridges can print as many pages as three small cartridges, i.e. 1800 pages. So three medium cartridges can print $1800 \times 3/2$ pages, i.e. 2700 pages. This is the same number of pages as two large cartridges can print, so one large cartridge can print $2700 \div 2$, i.e. 1350, pages.

8. **B** The 480 ml in Tommy's tankard represents three quarters of its capacity. So, one quarter of the capacity must be $480 \text{ ml} \div 3 = 160 \text{ ml}$.

9. **C** The person at position P can see exactly two of the other three people, so this person is Caz. The people he can see are at positions 1 and 2 and are Bea and Dan, each of whom can see exactly one person – Caz. This leaves Ali at position 3 – a position from which none of the three people can be seen, so all of the information given is consistent with Caz being at P.

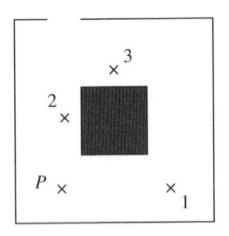

10. **E** The diagram shows the region of overlap, which has area 6 cm^2.

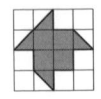

11. **B** We concentrate initially on the units digits of the numbers given, noting that the 3 comes first, so is positive. Now $3 + 7 = 10$ but there is no way to combine 5 and 9 to get a units digit 0. So we must use $3 - 7$. Hence, in the calculation, 67 must be preceded by a minus sign. Now $123 - 67 = 56$. So we need to get an extra 44 by combining 45 and 89. The only way to do this is $89 - 45$. So the correct calculation is $123 - 45 - 67 + 89$. It has two minus signs and one plus sign, so $p - m = 1 - 2 = -1$.

Junior Challenge 2012 solutions   147

12. **B** None of the pieces which Laura uses to make the 3 × 3 square can be more than 3 units long. Both the horizontal and vertical portions of the original shape are longer than 3 units, so at least two cuts will be required. Hence Laura will need at least three pieces and the diagrams on the right show that the task is possible using exactly three pieces.

13. **C** Note that p is a factor of both 15 and 18. So p is either 1 or 3. If $p = 1$ then $w = 15$. However, if $w = 15$ then r is not an integer.
So $p = 3, w = 5, x = 6$. The values of the other input factors may now be calculated: $r = 8, s = 10, v = 2, z = 7, q = 5, y = 4, t = 6$.
So $A + B + C + D + E = 6 + 25 + 48 + 40 + 42 = 161$.

×	p	q	r	s	t
v	A	10		20	
w	15	B	40		
x	18		C	60	
y		20		D	24
z			56		E

14. **A** Note that 96 is a multiple of 6, so the 97th symbol is the same as the first, the 98th symbol is the same as the second and the 100th and 101st symbols are the same as the fourth and fifth symbols respectively.

15. **E** In total, the fraction of tulips which are either yellow or red is $\frac{1}{2} + \frac{1}{3} \times \frac{1}{2} = \frac{2}{3}$. So one third of the tulips are pink or white. Of these, one quarter are pink, so the fraction of tulips which are white is $\frac{3}{4} \times \frac{1}{3} = \frac{1}{4}$.

16. **D** Normally, Beth reads pages 1, 4, 7, ... ; Carolyn reads pages 2, 5, 8, ... ; George reads pages 3, 6, 9, ... When Beth is away, Carolyn reads all the odd-numbered pages, whilst George reads all the even-numbered pages. So the pages which are read by the person who normally reads that page are numbered 5, 11, 17 (Carolyn) and 6, 12, 18 (George).

17. **A** The number of boys in the class is $(24 - 6) \div 2 = 9$. So there are 9 boys and 15 girls.
Hence the required ratio is 5 : 3.

18. **D** Note that the number which replaces x appears in both the row and the column. Adding the numbers in the row and the column gives $2 + 3 + 4 + 5 + 6 + 7 + 8 + x = 2 \times 21 = 42$. So $35 + x = 42$ and hence $x = 7$. The diagram shows one way in which the task may be accomplished.

19. **E** As $\angle QPS = 90°, \angle PSQ + \angle PQS = 90°$.
So, since the ratio of these angles is 1:5,
$\angle PSQ = 15°$ and $\angle PQS = 75°$.
Now $\angle QSR = \angle PQS$ (alternate angles).
So $\angle QSR = 75°$.

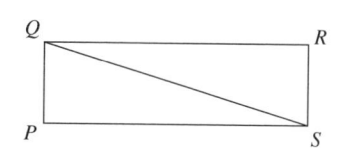

20. **A** 50 months = 4 years and 2 months; 50 weeks and 50 days = 57 weeks and 1 day, i.e. just over 1 year and 1 month. So Aroon is just over 55 years and 3 months old and will, therefore, be 56 on his next birthday.

21. **B** Exactly two dominoes have a '1' and exactly two dominoes have a '2' so the dominoes ▣ ▣ ▣ must be arranged as shown. So ▣ cannot be adjacent to ▣. Clearly, ▣ cannot be adjacent to ▣ either, but it is possible to form a ring with ▣ adjacent to ▣ or with ▣ adjacent to ▣. These are shown below. So only two of the dominoes cannot be placed adjacent to ▣.

22. **B** The original hexagon has been divided into seven regular hexagons and twelve equilateral triangles. Six equilateral triangles are equal in area to one smaller hexagon, so the large hexagon is equal in area to nine of the smaller hexagons. (This may also be deduced from the fact that their sides are in the ratio 3:1.) The shaded area consists of one smaller hexagon and six equilateral triangles, which is equivalent to the area of two of the smaller hexagons. So $\frac{2}{9}$ of the large hexagon is shaded.

23. **A** If either of the first two digits of the number is changed, the units digit will still be 0. Therefore the new number will be either 000 or a non-zero multiple of 10 and so will not be prime. If the units digit is changed then the possible outcomes are 201, 202, 203, 204, 205, 206, 207, 208, 209. The even numbers are not prime and neither are 201 (3 × 67), 203 (7 × 29), 205 (5 × 41), 207 (3 × 69), 209 (11 × 19).
So none of the numbers on Peter's list is prime.

24. **D** After 500 games, I have won $500 \times \frac{49}{100} = 245$ games. So I have lost 255 games. Therefore I need to win the next 10 games to have a 50% success rate.

25. **A** The sum of the interior angles of a triangle is 180°.
Therefore $5x + 3y + 3x + 20 + 10y + 30 = 180$, i.e. $8x + 13y = 130$.
As x and y are both positive integers, it may be deduced that x is a multiple of 13.
Also, since $y \geqslant 1, x \leqslant \frac{117}{8}$ so the only possible value of x is 13. If $x = 13$ then $y = 2$, so $x + y = 15$.

Junior Challenge 2013 solutions

1. **E** All of the alternatives involve subtracting a number from 1. The largest result, therefore, will correspond to the smallest number to be subtracted, i.e. 0.00001.

2. **E** Their average height is $\dfrac{2.1 + 1.4}{2}$ m = 1.75 m.

3. **C** Triangle *BCD* is isosceles, so $\angle BCD = \angle BDC = 65°$.
The sum of the interior angles of a triangle is 180° so
$\angle CBD = (180 - 2 \times 65)° = 50°$.
Therefore $\angle ABE = 50°$ (vertically opposite angles). So
$\angle AEB = (180 - 90 - 50)° = 40°$.

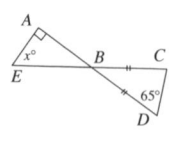

4. **C** Distance travelled = average speed × time of travel, so Gill travelled between 15 km and 20 km. Of the alternatives given, only 19 km lies in this interval.

5. **D** The diagram shows the four lines of symmetry.

6. **A** $((1 - 1) - 1) - (1 - (1 - 1)) = (0 - 1) - (1 - 0) = -1 - 1 = -2$.

7. **D** Let the number of balls collected by Roger be x. Then Andy collects $2x$ balls and Maria collects $(2x - 5)$ balls. So $x + 2x + 2x - 5 = 35$, i.e. $5x = 40$, i.e. $x = 8$. So Andy collected 16 balls.

8. **A** The number 3 on the top ruler (which is 7cm from the left-hand end) aligns with the 4 on the bottom one (which is 6cm from the right-hand end). Thus $L = 7 + 6 = 13$.

9. **B** Let there be b boys and g girls in the family. Then Peter has g sisters and $(b - 1)$ brothers. So $g = 3(b - 1)$. Louise has $(g - 1)$ sisters and b brothers. So $g - 1 = 2b$. Therefore $2b + 1 = 3b - 3$, i.e. $b = 4$. So $g = 9$. Therefore there are 4 boys and 9 girls in the family, i.e. 13 children in total.

10. **E** The top and bottom faces of the stack and the two touching faces form two pairs of opposite faces.
So the total number of pips on these four faces is $2 \times 7 = 14$. Therefore the total number of pips on the top and bottom faces of the stack is $14 - 5 = 9$.

11. **C** After Usain has run 100 m, his mum has run 50 m and Turbo has 'run' 10 m. So the distance between Usain's mum and Turbo is 40 m.

12. **E** Figure *ABEFGJ* itself is a hexagon. There are three hexagons congruent to *ABCLIJ*; two hexagons congruent to *ABDMHJ*; four hexagons congruent to *ABCKIJ*; two hexagons congruent to *ABDLHJ*. So in total there are twelve hexagons.

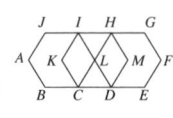

Junior Challenge 2013 solutions

13. **D** After the first coat, half of the paint is left. So after the second coat, the volume of paint remaining is one third of half of the capacity of the tin, i.e. one sixth of three litres = 500 ml.

14. **B** Let the two equal sides of the isosceles triangle have length a and the other side have length b. Then $2a + b = 20$. Since the sum of the lengths of any two sides of a triangle is greater than the length of the third, $2a > b$. Hence $4a > 2a + b$. So $4a > 20$, i.e. $a > 5$. Also $a < 10$ since $2a + b = 20$. So the possibilities are $a = 6, b = 8; a = 7, b = 6; a = 8, b = 4$; and $a = 9, b = 2$.

15. **A** When he starts to come down the hill, the Grand Old Duke of York has 90% of his men left. He loses 15% of these, so at the bottom of the hill he has 85% of 90% of the original number left. As $\frac{85}{100} \times 90 = 76\frac{1}{2}$, this means that $76\frac{1}{2}\%$ of his men were still there when they reached the bottom of the hill.

16. **B** The sum of the ages of the four children is $12 + 14 + 15 + 15 = 56$. Each year on their birthday, this sum increases by 4. So the number of years before the sum reaches 100 is $(100 - 56) \div 4 = 11$. Therefore their ages will first total 100 in 2024.

17. **E** Let x cm be the length of the ⌣ shape. Although x is not given, it is clear that $x > 1$. The lengths, in cm, of the perimeters of pieces A, B, C, D, E are $4 + 6x$, $2 + 10x, 7 + 5x, 6 + 6x, 1 + 11x$ respectively. As $4 + 6x < 6 + 6x$, the piece with the longest perimeter is B, C, D or E. As $x > 1$, it may be deduced that $7 + 5x < 6 + 6x < 2 + 10x < 1 + 11x$, so E has the longest perimeter.

18. **A** Let the weights, in kg, of baby, nurse and me be x, y, z respectively. Then $x + z = 78; x + y = 69; y + z = 137$. Adding all three equations gives $2x + 2y + 2z = 284$, so $x + y + z = 284 \div 2 = 142$.
(*To find the combined weight, it is not necessary to find the individual weights, but baby weighs 5kg, nurse weighs 64 kg and I weigh 73 kg.*)

19. **D** For every 2 senior members in the swimming club there are 3 junior members. For every 5 senior members there are 2 veteran members. The lowest common multiple of 2 and 5 is 10, so it may be deduced that the number of senior members is a multiple of 10. For every 10 senior members in the swimming club there are 15 junior members and 4 veteran members. So the total number of members is a multiple of 29. Of the alternatives given, the only multiple of 29 is 58.

20. **B** The 'long knight' needs to move exactly seven squares to the right and exactly seven squares upwards. Although it is possible to move seven squares to the right in three moves (1, 3 and 3), in doing so it could move upwards by a maximum of five squares (3, 1 and 1). Similarly, it could move seven squares upwards in three moves, but could then move a maximum of five squares to the right. In four moves, the number of squares moved to the right must be even, since it is the sum of four odd numbers. So at least five moves are required and the diagram shows one way in which the task may be achieved in five moves.

21. **C** As 5 is a prime number, it must lie in a 5 × 1 rectangle. So the only possibility is the rectangle which covers the top row of the grid. Now consider 6: there is insufficient room for a 6 × 1 rectangle so it must lie in a 3 × 2 rectangle. There are only two such rectangles which include 6 but do not include either 4 or 3. If 6 comes in the middle of the top row of a 2 × 3 rectangle then there is space for a 3 × 1 rectangle including 3. But then there is not enough space for a rectangle including 4. So 6 must be placed in the rectangle shown. There is now insufficient room to place 4 in a 4 × 1 rectangle so it must lie in the 2 × 2 square shown, which includes the shaded square. This leaves the grid to be completed as shown.

22. **E** The diagram shows the totals of the rows and columns. The circled numbers are the total of the numbers in the two main diagonals. Note, by considering the average values of the rows and columns, that each should total 34. Row 2 and column 2 are both 2 short. So their common entry, 13, needs to increase by 2. So 13 must be interchanged with 15. (This change also reduces row 4 and column 3 by 2 and increases the main diagonal by 2, thus making all the sums equal 34 as desired.) So the sum of the numbers to be swapped is 28.

23. **D** Let the points awarded for a win and a draw be w and d respectively. Then $7w + 3d = 44$. The only positive integer solutions of this equation are $w = 2$, $d = 10$ and $w = 5, d = 3$. However, more points are awarded for a win than for a draw so we deduce that 5 points are awarded for a win and 3 points for a draw. So the number of points gained by my sister's team is $5 \times 5 + 2 \times 3 = 31$.

24. **B** Each of the overlapping areas contributes to the area of exactly two squares. So the total area of the three squares is equal to the area of the non-overlapping parts of the squares plus twice the total of the three overlapping areas i.e. $(117 + 2(2 + 5 + 8))$ cm^2 = $(117 + 30)$ cm^2 = 147 cm^2. So the area of each square is $(147 \div 3)$ cm^2 = 49 cm^2. Therefore the length of the side of each square is 7 cm.

25. **C** By arranging the tiles in suitable positions it is possible to place the 1 × 1 spotted square in any one of four corners of the steel sheet and then to place the grey square in any one of the other three corners. The other two corners will then be occupied by black squares. So, in total, there are $4 \times 3 = 12$ different looking installations.)

Junior Challenge 2014 solutions

154   Ten Further Years of Mathematical Challenges

1. **D** $(999 - 99 + 9) \div 9 = (900 + 9) \div 9 = 909 \div 9 = 101$.

2. **B** There are 24 hours in one day, so $\frac{1}{12}$ of a day is 2 hours. Therefore the number of minutes in $\frac{1}{12}$ of a day is $2 \times 60 = 120$.

3. **C** The seats between us are T18 to T38 *inclusive*, that is, all the seats before seat 39 except for seats 1 to 17. So the number of seats is $38 - 17 = 21$.

4. **E** $987\,654\,321 \times 9 = 8\,888\,888\,889$.

5. **A** The smallest 4-digit number is 1000 and the largest 3-digit number is 999. They differ by 1.

6. **A** Let the width of each strip be 1. Then the square has side 5 and perimeter 20. The grey strips contribute 4 to the perimeter, so the fraction of the perimeter which is grey is $\frac{4}{20} = \frac{1}{5}$.

7. **B** $2002 - 4102 = -2100$. So $2014 - 4102 = -2100 + 12 = -2088$.

8. **A** Prime numbers have exactly two distinct factors, so 1 is not a prime number as it has exactly one factor. Of the others, 12, 1234 and 123 456 are all even numbers, so are not prime as the only even prime is 2. Also, $123 = 3 \times 41$ and 12 345 is clearly a multiple of 5, so neither of these is prime. Therefore none of the numbers in the list is prime.

9. **E** The area of a triangle $= \frac{1}{2} \times$ base $\times$ height. If we let the length of the sides of each square in the grid be 1, then the area of triangle PQR is $\frac{1}{2} \times 3 \times 2 = 3$. The area of triangle XYZ is $\frac{1}{2} \times 6 \times 3 = 9$. So the required fraction is $\frac{3}{9} = \frac{1}{3}$.

10. **D** The angles at a point sum to $360°$, so the largest angle in the triangle which includes the angle marked $x°$ is equal to $(360 - 90 - 90 - 60)° = 120°$. This triangle is isosceles as the sides of the three squares in the figure are equal to the sides of the equilateral triangle. So the triangle has angles $120°$, $x°$ and $x°$. Therefore $x = \frac{1}{2}(180 - 120) = 30$.

11. **D** The third term of the sequence equals $1 + 2 = 3$. Now consider the fourth term: it is the sum of the first three terms. However, as the first two terms sum to the third term, the sum of the first three terms is twice the third term, i.e. $2 \times 3 = 6$. So the fourth term is twice the third term. Similar reasoning applies to each subsequent term, i.e. each term after the third term is equal to twice the term which precedes it. Therefore the sequence is 1, 2, 3, 6, 12, 24, 48, 96, ...

12. **B** As $7Q2ST - P3R96 = 22222$, it follows that $7Q2ST = P3R96 + 22222$. Looking at the units column: $2 + 6 = T$, so $T = 8$. Looking at the tens column, as $2 + 9 = 11$, we deduce that $S = 1$ and that 1 is carried to the hundreds column. Looking at the hundreds column: the carry of $1 + 2 + R$ must equal 12 since the sum has 2 in the hundreds column. So $R = 9$ and there is a carry of 1 to the thousands column. Looking at this column: the carry of $1 + 2 + 3 = Q$, so $Q = 6$. Finally, since there is no carry to the next column, $2 + P = 7$, so $P = 5$. Therefore the calculation is $76218 - 53996 = 22222$ and $P + Q + R + S + T = 5 + 6 + 9 + 1 + 8 = 29$.

Junior Challenge 2014 solutions 155

13. **A** The diagram shows part of the given diagram after a rotation so that the diagonal shown is horizontal. The perpendicular height of triangle *P* is shown and it can be seen that this is also the perpendicular height of triangle *Q*. The diagonals of a rectangle bisect each other, so triangles *P* and *Q* have bases of equal length and the same perpendicular height. Therefore their areas are equal.

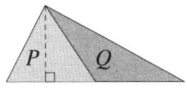

14. **D** One million millimetres is (1 000 000 ÷ 1000) m = 1000 m = 1 km.

15. **E** Consider, for example, the bottom left-hand corner of the envelope (see Figure 1). The two flaps overlap, so that the sum of the angles marked *x* and *y* is greater than 90°.
So when the flaps are unfolded, as in Figure 2, the angle marked *z* is less than 180°.
Therefore the correct answer is E.

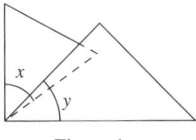

    Figure 1 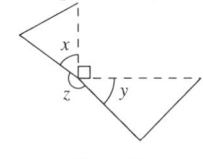   Figure 2

16. **E** If A is true then B is true which cannot be so since we are told only one statement is true. Hence A is false which is what E says. So E is the one true statement. [For completeness, we note that C and D must be false because we are told that exactly one statement is true; and B is false because A is false.]

17. **C** Whichever route is chosen, it must include section *BD*. We will divide the route into two sections. The first will include stations *A*, *B*, *C* and will finish at *D*. The second will start at *D* and include stations *E*, *F*, and *G*. 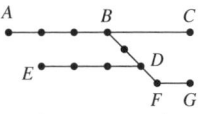
Clearly the first section cannot be traversed without visiting at least one station more than once and the route $A - B - C - B - D$ visits only B more than once so it is an optimal solution. Also, traversing the second section involves visiting D more than once as two branches lead from it. If $D - E - D$ is part of the route then two stations are visited more than once. However, if $D - G - D$ is part of the route then only *F* is visited more than once. So to traverse the second section, it is necessary to visit at least two stations (one of which is *D*) more than once. Therefore, the complete route must involve visiting at least 3 stations more than once. An example of an optimum route is $A - B - C - B - D - F - G - F - D - E$. The stations visited twice are *B, D,* and *F*.

18. **E** The units digit of any power of 5 is 5 so the units digit of $1 + 5^6$ is 6. Therefore the units digits of the calculations in the 5 options are 2, 1, 0, 9, 8 in that order. So the only calculation which could be correct is E. Checking this gives $1 + 5^6 - 8 = 1 + 15\,625 - 8 = 15\,626 - 8 = 15\,618$.

19. **C** Since Jack won 4 games, Jill lost 4 games for which she was awarded 4 points. So the number of games she won is $(10 - 4) \div 2 = 3$. Therefore, they played 7 games in total.

20. **B** Let the smallest number of chocolates required be n. Then $q + n > p - n$, that is $2n > p - q$. Therefore $n > \frac{1}{2}(p - q)$. Since $p > q$ and p and q are both odd, $\frac{1}{2}(p - q)$ is a positive integer. So the smallest possible value of n is $\frac{1}{2}(p - q) + 1 = \frac{1}{2}(p - q + 2)$.

21. **D** Both the top and bottom layers of 9 cubes can be seen to contain 5 cubes with at least one face printed grey. The bottom layer could contain more than 5. In the middle layer, two cubes with grey faces are visible and there could be more. Therefore at least 12 cubes must have at least one face painted grey, which means that the largest number of cubes which Pablo can leave with no faces painted grey is $27 - 12 = 15$.

22. **C** In order to increase the result of the calculation (the quotient) by 100, the number to be divided (the dividend) must be increased by 100×18, that is 1800. So the new dividend needs to be $952\,473 + 1800$, that is $954\,273$. So the two digits which need to be swapped are 2 and 4.

23. **D** Note first that the sum of the first 9 positive integers is 45. Therefore, when the four numbers in each of the three lines are added together the total is 45 plus the sum of the numbers in the three corner circles, each of which contributes to the sum of two lines of circles. So if the number in the top circle is x, the total of all 3 lines is $45 + 2 + 5 + x = 52 + x$. As all three lines of circles must have the same total, $52 + x$ must be a multiple of 3. The possible values of x are 2, 5 and 8 but 2 and 5 have already been assigned. So $x = 8$ and the sum of each line is $60 \div 3 = 20$. The diagram shows one way of completing the task.

24. **C** Note that rectangles B, C, E and G are all congruent. Two of these are shaded grey and two are hatched, so the difference between the area of the hatched region and the area shaded grey is the difference between the area of square D of side 1 and the sum of the areas of triangles A, F and H. These are all isosceles right-angled triangles with hypotenuse 1 and the lower diagram shows how a square of side 1 may be divided into 4 such triangles. So the required difference in area is $1 - \frac{3}{4} = \frac{1}{4}$.

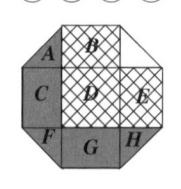

25. **A** If the die is rolled around a single vertex it covers, in turn, 6 small triangles making up a regular hexagon. It uses three different faces, repeated twice. An example is shown on the right. However, if it is rolled out from that hexagon in any direction, that will use the fourth face. The face that ends up covering each small triangle in the grid is always the same, regardless of the path taken to reach that triangle. Using these facts, it is easy to complete the diagram as shown. So, whichever route through the grid is taken, the '1' is face down when it reaches the shaded triangle.

Junior Challenge 2015 solutions

1. **A** The values of the expressions are: A 6, B 4, C 2, D −4, E 0.
    (*Alternative method: since every expression contains the integers 1, 2, 3 and 4, the expression which has the largest value is that in which the sum of the integers preceded by a minus sign is smallest. This is expression A.*)

2. **E** At 22:22, there are $60 - 22 = 38$ minutes to 23:00. There are then a further 60 minutes to midnight. So the number of minutes which remain until midnight is $38 + 60 = 98$.

3. **D** The value of $\dfrac{12\,345}{1 + 2 + 3 + 4 + 5} = \dfrac{12\,345}{15} = \dfrac{2469}{3} = 823$.

4. **A** The calculations required to find the value of x are:
$p = 105 - 47 = 58$; $q = p - 31 = 58 - 31 = 27$;
$r = 47 - q = 47 - 27 = 20$;
$s = r - 13 = 20 - 13 = 7$; $t = 13 - 9 = 4$;
$x = s - t = 7 - 4 = 3$.
(*Note that the problem may be solved without finding the values of four of the numbers in the pyramid. Finding these is left as an exercise for the reader.*)

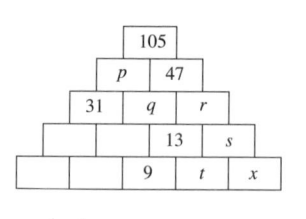

5. **B** Let the required number be x. Then $\frac{x}{3} - \frac{x}{4} = 3$. Multiplying both sides by 12 gives $4x - 3x = 36$. So $x = 36$.

6. **B** The sum of the exterior angles of any polygon is 360°. So $y = 360 - (110 + 120) = 360 - 230 = 130$. The sum of the angles on a straight line is 180°, so $x = 180 - y = 180 - 130 = 50$.

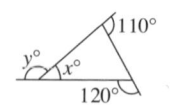

7. **A** The units digit of $123\,456\,789 \times 8$ is 2, since $9 \times 8 = 72$. So, if the statement in the question is correct then the two digits which are in a different order are 1 and 2, whose sum is 3. As a check, $123\,456\,789 \times 8$ is indeed $987\,654\,312$.

8. **C** All of the options are odd and therefore give a remainder of 1 when divided by 2. Two of the options, 3 and 9, give remainder 0 when divided by 3. Two other options, 5 and 11, give remainder 2 when divided by 3, and 7 is the only option which gives remainder 1 when divided by 3.

9. **D** The man has rowed the equivalent of just over 25 000 miles in approximately 13 years. So the mean number of 'miles' rowed per year is approximately $\frac{25\,000}{13} \approx \frac{26\,000}{13} = 2000$.

10. **E** If m and n are positive integers, then $mn > m + n$ unless at least one of m or n is equal to 1, or $m = n = 2$. So, to maximise the expression, we need to place multiplication signs between 2 and 3 and between 3 and 4. However, we need to place an addition sign between 1 and 2 because $1 + 2 \times 3 \times 4 = 25$, whereas $1 \times 2 \times 3 \times 4 = 24$.

11. **D** It can be established that 2 is not one of the three primes to be summed since the sum of 2 and two other primes is an even number greater than 2 and therefore not prime. The smallest three odd primes are 3, 5, 7 but these sum to 15 which is not prime. The next smallest sum of three odd primes is $3 + 5 + 11 = 19$, which is prime. So 19 is the smallest prime which is the sum of three different primes.

12. **B** The question tells us that 2 kg is two-thirds of the weight of the fish. So one-third of its weight is 1 kg and therefore its weight is 3 kg.

13. **A** We denote the label joining m and n as $(m + n)$. The labels which are multiples of 3 are $(1 + 2), (1 + 5), (1 + 8), (2 + 4), (2 + 7), (3 + 6), (4 + 5), (4 + 8), (5 + 7), (7 + 8)$. So 10 of the labels are multiples of 3.

14. **E** The primes and the number of illuminated bars which represent them are: $2 \to 5, 3 \to 5, 5 \to 5, 7 \to 3$. So all four prime digits are represented by a prime number of illuminated bars.

Junior Challenge 2015 solutions 159

15. C Of the options given, 23 × 34, 56 × 67 and 67 × 78 are all not divisible by 5, so may be discounted. Also 34 is not divisible by 4 and 45 is odd, so 34 × 45 may also be discounted as it is not divisible by 4. The only other option is 45 × 56. As a product of prime factors, $45 \times 56 = 2^3 \times 3^2 \times 5 \times 7$, so it is clear that it is divisible by all of the integers from 1 to 10 inclusive.

16. D The size of each interior angle of an equilateral triangle is 60°. As the sum of the interior angles of a triangle is 180°, $x + p + 60 = 180$, so $p = 120 - x$. Similarly, $q = 120 - y$. Each interior angle of a square is a right angle and the sum of the angles on a straight line is 180°, so $p + q + 90 = 180$. Therefore $120 - x + 120 - y + 90 = 180$, that is $330 - (x + y) = 180$. So $x + y = 330 - 180 = 150$.

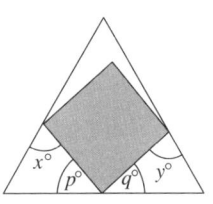

17. B If the Knave of Hearts is telling the truth then the Knave of Clubs is lying, which means that the Knave of Diamonds is telling the truth, but the Knave of Spades is lying. Alternatively, if the Knave of Hearts is lying then the Knave of Clubs is telling the truth, which means that the Knave of Diamonds is lying, but the Knave of Spades is telling the truth. In both cases, we can determine that two of the Knaves are lying, although it is not possible to determine which two they are.

18. B The fraction $\dfrac{5274}{36\,918} = \dfrac{2637}{18\,459} = \dfrac{1}{7}$, as given in the question.

19. D The first six positive cubes are 1, 8, 27, 64, 125, 216. Clearly, 64 cannot be the sum of three positive cubes as the sum of all the positive cubes smaller than 64 is $1 + 8 + 27 = 36$. Similarly, 125 cannot be the sum of three positive cubes as the largest sum of any three positive cubes smaller than 125 is $8 + 27 + 64 = 99$. However, we note that $27 + 64 + 125 = 216$, so 216 is the smallest cube which is the sum of three positive cubes.

20. C When the pyramid is viewed from above, it can be seen that the total area of the horizontal part of the surface of the pyramid (excluding its base) is the same as that of a square of side 4 metres, that is 16 m². The area of the base of the pyramid is also 16 m². Finally the total area of the vertical part of the pyramid is equal to $(4 \times 1 + 4 \times 2 + 4 \times 3 + 4 \times 4)$ m² = 40 m². So the total surface area of the pyramid is $(16 + 16 + 40)$ m² = 72 m².

21. C The diagram shows part of the wall of width 4800 mm and the four equally spaced pictures, each of width 420 mm. Let x be the required distance, that is the distance from the centre of each of the two pictures in the middle of the wall to a vertical line down the centre of the wall (marked by a broken line). Then the distance between the centres of any two adjacent pictures is $2x$. Note that the distance between the centres of the two pictures on the extremes of the wall is $(4800 - 2 \times 210)$ mm = 4380 mm. Therefore $2x + x + x + 2x = 4380$. So $x = 4380 \div 6 = 730$. Hence the required distance is 730 mm.

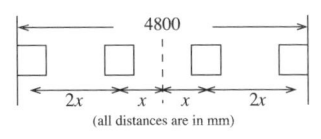

22. **E** In the diagram, the shaded small equilateral triangles have been divided into those which lie within the highlighted large equilateral triangle and the twelve small equilateral triangles which lie outside the large triangle.
Note that the unshaded star shape in the centre of the large triangle is made up of twelve small equilateral triangles, so the small triangles outside the large triangle could be moved into the large triangle so that the large triangle is shaded completely and the rest of the hexagon is unshaded as in the lower diagram.
The lower diagram shows that the hexagon may be divided into six congruent triangles, three of which are shaded and three of which are unshaded. So the required fraction is $\frac{1}{2}$.

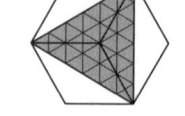

23. **D** The diagram shows some of the lengths of sides which may be deduced from the information given in the question. Note that the rectangle measures 5 cm by 5.5 cm. The sum of the areas of the four glass squares is $(1 + 4 + 9 + 16)$ cm^2 = 30 cm^2. However, the total region of the rectangle occupied by the four squares is equal to $(5 \times 5.5 - 1.5)$ cm^2 = 26 cm^2. So the area of the overlap is $(30 - 26)$ cm^2 = 4 cm^2.

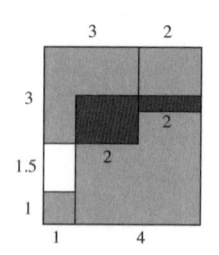

24. **B** For a number to be a multiple of 45 it must be a multiple of 5 and also of 9. In order to be a multiple of 5, a number's units digit must be 0 or 5. However, the units digit of a palindromic number cannot be 0, so it may be deduced that any palindromic number which is a multiple of 45 both starts and ends in the digit 5. In order to make the desired number as large as possible, its second digit should be 9 and for it to be as small as possible its second digit should be 0. So, if possible, the numbers required are of the form '59x95' and '50y05'. In addition, both numbers are to be multiples of 9 which means the sum of the digits of both must be a multiple of 9. For this to be the case, $x = 8$ and $y = 8$, giving digit sums of 36 and 18 respectively. So the two required palindromic numbers are 59895 and 50805. Their difference is 9090.

25. **E** The exterior angle of a triangle is equal to the sum of its two interior and opposite angles. Applying this theorem to triangle UZX:
$\angle VUW = z° + x°$.
Similarly, in triangle WYX: $y° = \angle XWY + x°$, so $\angle XWY = y° - x°$.
As $VU = VW$, $\angle VUW = \angle VWU$ and also $\angle VWU = \angle XWY$ because they are vertically opposite angles. Therefore $\angle VUW = \angle XWY$. So $z° + x° = y° - x°$ and hence $x = \frac{1}{2}(y - z)$.

Junior Challenge 2016 solutions

1. **B** The values of the expressions are: A 15, B 7, C 26, D −14, E $7\frac{1}{2}$. Of these, 7 is closest to 0.
2. **A** $60\,000 - 21 = 60\,000 - 20 - 1 = 59\,980 - 1 = 59\,979$.
3. **E** The number of laps is $5000 \div 400 = 50 \div 4 = 12\frac{1}{2}$.
4. **C** There are 41 years from January 1859 to January 1900 and a further 114 years to January 2014. So, since Åle died in August 2014, its age in years when it died was $41 + 114 = 155$.
5. **A** $\frac{1}{25} = \frac{4}{100} = 0.04$. So $\frac{1}{25} + 0.25 = 0.04 + 0.25 = 0.29$.

162   Ten Further Years of Mathematical Challenges

6. **C**   Let there be g girls in Gill's school. Then there are $(g - 30)$ boys at the school. So $g + g - 30 = 600$. Therefore $2g = 630$, that is $g = 315$.

7. **A**   As a distance of 8 km is roughly equal to 5 miles, $1.2 \text{ km} \approx \frac{1.2 \times 5}{8}$ miles $= \frac{6}{8}$ miles $= 0.75$ miles.

8. **A**   By factorising the numerator, it is seen that;
$$\frac{2+4+6+8+10+12+14+16+18+20}{1+2+3+4+5+6+7+8+9+10} = \frac{2(1+2+3+4+5+6+7+8+9+10)}{1+2+3+4+5+6+7+8+9+10} = 2.$$

9. **E**   All four numbers may be obtained: $36 = 20 + 16$; $195 = 201 - 6$; $207 = 201 + 6$; $320 = 20 \times 16$.

10. **D**   When a square is folded exactly in half, the shape obtained is a rectangle or a right-angled isosceles triangle. So to determine which of the given shapes can be obtained from a second fold we need to test which shapes form a rectangle or a right-angled isosceles triangle when joined with the image formed when the shape is reflected about an edge. Of the options given, only D does not do this. Of the others, shape A is formed by using fold line 1 first, followed by fold line 3. For shape B the fold lines are 3 followed by 4. For shapes C and E, which are similar, the fold lines are 2 followed by 5.

11. **C**   A number is divisible by 4 if and only if its last two digits are divisible by 4. Since 34 is not divisible by 4, we deduce that 1234 is not a multiple of 4. Of the other options, 12 is even and so is a multiple of 2; the sum of the digits of 123 is 6, which is a multiple of 3, so 123 is a multiple of 3; 12 345 has a units digit of 5 and so is a multiple of 5. Finally, 123 456 is even and has a digit sum of 21, a multiple of 3. So 123 456 is a multiple of 2 and of 3 and is therefore a multiple of 6.

12. **B**   Five hundred and twenty five thousand six hundred minutes is equal to
$$\frac{525\,600}{60} \text{ hours } = 8760 \text{ hours } = \frac{8760}{24} \text{ days } = 365 \text{ days}.$$
So the length of time in the song is the number of minutes in a year, unless it is a leap year.

13. **C**   The position of the 5 is immaterial to the question asked, so let it be placed in the top circle. Now 4 differs by 1 from 5 so neither a nor d equals 4. Therefore either $b = 4$ or $c = 4$. It doesn't matter which it is, because the answer will be symmetric. So let $b = 4$. Since 3 differs by 1 from 4, neither a nor c can be 3, so $d = 3$. This leaves us with 1 and 2 to place. As 2 cannot be next to 3, $c \neq 2$ so $c = 1$ and $a = 2$. Therefore the sum of the numbers in the two circles adjacent to the circle containing 5 is $3 + 2 = 5$.

14. **D**   As $AB = AC$, triangle ABC is isosceles. So $\angle ABC = \angle ACB = \frac{1}{2}(180° - 40°) = 70°$ as $\angle BAC = 40°$ and the angle sum of a triangle is 180°. Triangle BCD is also isosceles as $BD = BC$, so $\angle BDC = \angle BCD = 70°$. Considering triangle ABD: $\angle BDC = \angle DAB + \angle ABD$ as an exterior angle of a triangle is equal to the sum of the two interior opposite angles. So $\angle ABD = \angle BDC - \angle DAB = 70° - 40° = 30°$.

Junior Challenge 2016 solutions 163

15. **E** All four expressions are perfect squares: $1^3 + 2^3 = 1 + 8 = 9 = 3^2$;
    $1^3 + 2^3 + 3^3 = 1 + 8 + 27 = 36 = 6^2$; $1^3 + 2^3 + 3^3 + 4^3 = 1 + 8 + 27 + 64 = 100 = 10^2$; $1^3 + 2^3 + 3^3 + 4^3 + 5^3 = 1 + 8 + 27 + 64 + 125 = 225 = 15^2$.
    (*It is not a coincidence that all four expressions are squares: the sum of the cubes of the first n integers is equal to the square of the sum of the first n integers for all positive integers n. For example*: $1^3 = 1^2$; $1^3 + 2^3 = (1 + 2)^2$; $1^3 + 2^3 + 3^3 = (1 + 2 + 3)^2$; $1^3 + 2^3 + 3^3 + 4^3 = (1 + 2 + 3 + 4)^2$ *etc.*)

16. **B** We imagine all the squares being black and consider changing as few as possible to white in order to satisfy the conditions required. First note that the colour of the centre square has no effect on the symmetries involved. So we will leave that black. If we change one corner to white, the opposite corner must also be changed to white to give the rotational symmetry. The diagram still has reflective symmetry. If you instead try changing a non-corner square to white, the opposite one must be. And you again have reflective symmetry. That shows we need to change more than two squares. The rotational symmetry means that the next possiblity is to change 4 squares to white. And the diagram shown shows that it is possible, with four white squares, to have rotational but not reflective symmetry. That means that, in the problem as stated, the maximum number of black squares is 5.

17. **C** Initially there are 48 children of whom $\frac{3}{8}$ are boys and $\frac{5}{8}$ are girls, so there are 18 boys and 30 girls. When more boys join, there are still 30 girls but now they form $\frac{3}{8}$ of the total. So the total number of pupils is now $\frac{8}{3} \times 30 = 80$, of whom $80 - 30 = 50$ are boys. Hence the number of boys joining is $50 - 18 = 32$.

18. **D** First note that when two numbers are added together the only possible carry from any column is 1. Now, looking at the tens column of the sum, we see that $E + E$ leaves a total of E in the column. Since E is non-zero, the only way that this can happen is that there is a carry of 1 from the units column. So we have $1 + E + E = 10 + E$, so $1 + E = 10$, that is $E = 9$. Looking at the units column we see that $E + E = 18$, so $S = 8$ and there is a carry of 1 to the tens column. The addition sum may now be solved: $899 + 899 = 1798$. So $X = 7$.

19. **B** Let p be the total number of pears. Then $12 + \frac{p}{9} = \frac{1}{2}\left(p - \frac{p}{9}\right) = \frac{4p}{9}$. So $12 = \frac{3p}{9} = \frac{p}{3}$. Therefore $p = 3 \times 12 = 36$. So the number of pieces of fruit in each box is $\frac{12 + 36}{3} = 16$.

20. **E** The length of s, half the perimeter of the cyclic quadrilateral, is $\frac{1}{2}(4 + 5 + 7 + 10)$ cm $= 13$ cm. So the required area, in cm^2, is $\sqrt{(13-4)(13-5)(13-7)(13-10)} = \sqrt{9 \times 8 \times 6 \times 3} = \sqrt{9 \times 144} = 3 \times 12 = 36$.

21. **A** The area of the shaded triangle is $\frac{1}{2} \times 3 \times 6 = 9$. The area of the square grid is $6 \times 6 = 36$, and the area of the triangle which is not part of the area of the pentagon is $\frac{1}{2} \times 3 \times 3 = \frac{9}{2}$. So the area of the pentagon is $36 - \frac{9}{2} = \frac{63}{2}$. Hence the required fraction is $9 \div \frac{63}{2} = 9 \times \frac{2}{63} = \frac{2}{7}$.

22. **E** In order to join the four triangles together it is required to join together at least three pairs of edges, which consequently are not part of the perimeter of the resulting parallelogram. The four triangles have a total of 12 edges, so the maximum number of edges which can be part of the perimeter of the parallelogram is 12 − 3 × 2 = 6. For the perimeter to be as large as possible, all four 13 cm edges should be included together with two of the 12 cm edges, if this is possible. The diagram shows how it may be accomplished. So the largest possible perimeter is (4 × 13 + 2 × 12) cm = 76 cm.

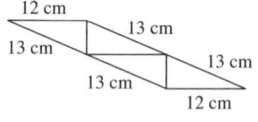

23. **B** Note first that the fourth square has side length 3, the fifth square has side length 4 and the sixth square has side length 7. As described in the question, the seventh square is placed alongside the sixth square, the fourth square and one of the first three unit squares. However, it may be seen that the side length of the seventh square is equal to the sum of the side lengths of the fifth and sixth squares, which is 4 + 7 = 11. Similarly, the eighth square is placed along the fourth, fifth and seventh squares, but its side length is the sum of the side lengths of the sixth and seventh squares, which is 7 + 11 = 18. The spiral sequence continues in the same way and therefore the side length of any subsequent square may be calculated by adding together the side lengths of the two previous squares in the sequence. So from the fourth square onwards the side lengths of the squares are 3, 4, 7, 11, 18, 29, 47, 76, 123, ... Hence the side length of the twelfth square is 123.
(*All of the positive integers in the sequence from the side length of the fourth square onwards are members of the sequence of Lucas numbers − a Fibonacci sequence with first term 2 and second term 1.*)

24. **D** First note that as there are four tiles to be placed and all three colours must be used, every arrangement of tiles consists of two of one colour and one each of the other two colours. Let the colours be R, G and B and consider the arrangements in which there are two tiles of colour R. These two tiles may be placed in six different ways: RR**, R*R*, R**R, *RR*, *R*R and **RR. For each of these arrangements of R tiles, there are two possible ways of placing the remaining G tile and B tile − the G tile may go in the first remaining space or the second remaining space and then there remains only one space for the B tile. So the number of arrangements in which there are two R tiles is 2 × 6 = 12. By the same reasoning, we see that there are 12 different arrangements in which there are two G tiles and 12 different arrangements in which there are two B tiles. So the total number of different arrangements is 3 × 12 = 36.

25. **D** First note that there are 25 squares on the board. As each domino occupies two squares, the number of squares left uncovered must be odd. The diagram on the right shows that it is possible for Beatrix to place the dominoes so that there are seven uncovered spaces when it is not possible for her to place any more dominoes. 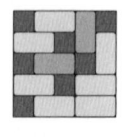
Of the options given, it is not possible to obtain eight uncovered spaces as the number of them must be odd and it has been shown that seven uncovered spaces is possible so the correct answer is seven.
(*For a proof that it is not possible to obtain more than seven uncovered spaces, please see the extended solutions on the UKMT website.*)

Intermediate Challenge
2007 solutions

1. **D** The date 18 years after 15 December 2005 will be 15 December 2023. Since a further 0.6 years, i.e. just over 7 months, will then elapse, the moon will next reach its highest point in the sky in 2024.

2. **C** There are forty dots in the 5 × 8 array and twenty of these are illuminated to form the letter 't'.

3. **E** Any line which passes though the centre of the square divides the square into two congruent shapes. An example is shown on the right.

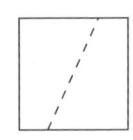

4. **E** The fraction of the cake which Victoria eats is $\frac{2}{3} - \frac{1}{4}$, that is $\frac{5}{12}$.

5. **D** (12340 + 12.34) ÷ 1234 = 12340 ÷ 1234 + 12.34 ÷ 1234 = 10 + 0.01 = 10.01.

6. **A** The average of the 9 numbers is 223, so they are 219, 220, ..., 226, 227. (*Note that the difference between the largest and smallest of 9 consecutive whole numbers is 8, irrespective of the sum of the numbers.*)

7. **B** The product = 1 × 3 × 4 × 6 × 7 × 8 × 9 × (2 × 5) × 10. The product of the first seven of these numbers is not a multiple of 10, so the original product is a multiple of 100, but not a multiple of 1000.

8. **B** The sum of the three numbers is $3x$, so $y + z = 2x$. Hence the mean of y and z is x.

9. **B** If there are f females and m males then $86 = 8f + 9m = 8(f + m) + m$. Now $86 = 8 \times 10 + 6 = 8 \times 9 + 14 = 8 \times 8 + 22...$. Only the first of these is feasible (because $f + m \geq m$). So $m = 6$ and $f = 4$.

10. **C** At each vertex of the triangle, four angles meet. In all, these twelve angles comprise six right angles, the three interior angles of the triangle and the three marked angles. So the sum of the marked angles = 3 × 360° − 6 × 90° − 180° = 360°.

11. **A** As the product of each pair has the same value, this value must be product of the smallest and largest numbers, that is 5 × 72. So the number which is paired with 10 is (5 × 72) ÷ 10, that is 36.

12. **A** The formula which gives C in terms of d is $C = \pi d$, so the graph of C versus d is a straight line which passes through the origin.

Intermediate Challenge 2007 solutions 167

13. E The area of the page inside the margins is 26 cm × 36 cm, that is 936 cm^2. So the percentage of the page occupied by the margins is $\frac{264}{1200} \times 100\%$, that is 22%.

14. A Both p and $-q$ are positive numbers. Hence $p + (-q)$ is the largest of the alternatives.

15. D Each interior angle of a regular pentagon is 108°, so $\angle SRQ = 108°$. As $SR = QR$, triangle SRQ is isosceles with $\angle RQS = \angle RSQ = \angle 36°$. Similarly, $\angle SRT = \angle STR = 36°$. So $\angle SUR = (180 - 2 \times 36)° = 108°$. From the symmetry of the figure, $\angle PUR = \angle PUS = (360° - 108°) \div 2 = 126°$.

16. D In total, there are 12^3 cubes with edge length 1 cm. Each of these centimetre cubes has 12 edges, so the sum of the lengths of these edges is 12 cm. Therefore the total length of the edges of all the centimetre cubes is 12^3 × 12 cm, that is 12^4 cm.

17. C The two watches will next agree when Grannie's watch has gained twelve hours relative to Grandpa's watch. Each hour, Grannie's watch gains one hour relative to Grandpa's watch, so it will take 12 hours for this to happen. At this time, both watches will show a time of 6 o'clock.

18. C From the second row we see that c, d, e are 1, 2, 4 in some order; and from the third column we see that $e > 2$. Hence $e = 4$ and we may now deduce that $g = 8$ and so $f = 5$. (*Although their values are not required, it is now also possible to deduce that* $c = 1$, $a = 3, b = 9, d = 2$.)

			Total
a	b		12
c	d	e	7
	f	g	13
Total 4	16	12	

19. E As each of the five given options is a member of the sequence, each is a multiple of 9. So we require the third factor of the number, that is the factor consisting of several 2s followed by a single 3, to be a multiple of 9 also. This is true if and only if the sum of its digits is a multiple of 9. For each number in the sequence, the number of 2s in its third factor equals the number of 0s in that number. The options given have 4, 6, 8, 10, 12 zeros, corresponding to their third factors having digital sums of 11, 15, 19, 23, 27 respectively. Of these, only 27 is a multiple of 9 so the correct answer is 20 000 000 000 007.

20. C Let O be the centre of the circle. Then $\angle POR = 90°$ as the angle subtended by an arc at the centre of a circle is twice the angle subtended by that arc at a point on the circumference of the circle. So triangle POR is an isosceles right-angled triangle with $PO = RO = 4$ cm. Let the length of PR be x cm. Then, by Pythagoras' Theorem, $x^2 = 4^2 + 4^2 = 2 \times 4^2$ and so $x = 4\sqrt{2}$.

21. B From the symmetry of the figure, the two circles must be concentric. Let their centre be O. Let the radius of the semicircles be r. Then the radius of the outer circle is $2r$ and, by Pythagoras' Theorem, the radius of the inner shaded circle is $\sqrt{r^2 + r^2}$, that is $\sqrt{2}r$.
So the radii of the two circles are in the ratio $\sqrt{2} : 2$, that is $1 : \sqrt{2}$, and hence the ratio of their areas is $1 : 2$.

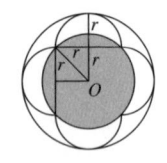

22. A The table shows the number on the face in contact with the table at the various stages described and also the numbers on the three faces of the die visible from the viewpoint in the question.

In contact with the table	5	1	2	3	5
Facing South	3	3	3	5	4
Facing East	1	2	6	6	6
Facing Up	2	6	5	4	2

As the '6' face is now facing East, the '1' face will be facing West.

23. C Note that
$$\frac{n^2}{n+4} = \frac{n^2 - 16}{n+4} + \frac{16}{n+4} = \frac{(n+4)(n-4)}{n+4} + \frac{16}{n+4} = n - 4 + \frac{16}{n+4}, (n \neq -4).$$
So when $n > 12$, the remainder when n^2 is divided by $n + 4$ is always 16. For $1 \leqslant n \leqslant 12$, the remainder when n^2 is divided by $n + 4$ is shown in the table below.

n	1	2	3	4	5	6	7	8	9	10	11	12
$n+4$	5	6	7	8	9	10	11	12	13	14	15	16
remainder	1	4	2	0	7	6	5	4	3	2	1	0

So there are 9 different remainders, namely 0, 1, 2, 3, 4, 5, 6, 7, 16.

24. D Firstly, there are 12 unit squares which contain an even number. Every 2×2 square in the diagram has entries which consist of two odd numbers and two even numbers and hence have an even total. There are 16 of these. Each 3×3 square in the diagram, however, has entries which consist of five odd numbers and four even numbers (giving an odd total), or four odd numbers and five even numbers (giving an even total). There are 4 of the latter: those with 8, 12, 14 or 18 in the centre. Every 4×4 square in the diagram has entries which consist of eight odd numbers and eight even numbers and hence have an even total. There are 4 of these. Finally, the full 5×5 square contains 13 odd numbers and 12 even numbers, giving an odd total. So the required number is $12 + 16 + 4 + 4$, that is 36.

25. E Let the radius of the semicircle be r and let the perpendicular height of the isosceles triangle be h. Then $\tan x° = \frac{h}{r}$.
Now the area of the semicircle $= \frac{1}{2}\pi r^2$, whilst the area of the triangle $= \frac{1}{2} \times 2r \times h = rh$. So $rh = \frac{1}{2}\pi r^2$, giving $\frac{h}{r} = \frac{\pi}{2}$.

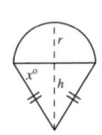

Intermediate Challenge
2008 solutions

1. **E** The clocks do not go forward or back this week, so there are seven 24-hour days, that is 168 hours.

2. **C** $2 + 3 + 5 \times 7 = 5 + 35 = 40$. As $40 = 2^3 \times 5$, the largest prime number which divides exactly into it is 5.

3. **B** $0.75 \div \frac{3}{4} = \frac{3}{4} \div \frac{3}{4} = 1$.

4. **B** The large square is made up of 25 small squares, 15 of which are shaded. So $\frac{15}{25}$ of the large square is shaded, corresponding to $\frac{15}{25} \times 100\% = 60\%$.

5. **D** In each of the fractions, the denominator is 18 and the sum of the digits of the numerator is also 18. So every numerator is a multiple of 9 and the even numerators are also multiples of 18. However, 873 is not a multiple of 18, so $\frac{873}{8 + 7 + 3}$ is the only expression not equal to a whole number.

6. **B** Let shape C have width 1 unit, height 1 unit and depth 1 unit. Then the volumes, in units³, of the five shapes are: A 2, B $2\frac{1}{2}$, C $\frac{1}{2}$, D $1\frac{1}{2}$, E 4. These total $10\frac{1}{2}$ units³, so we may deduce that the cube formed by the four shapes will have side 2 units and volume 8 units³. Hence B is the shape which is not required. The cube may be formed by placing C next to D to form a shape identical to A. This combination is then placed alongside A to form a shape identical to E. If shape E is now rotated through 180° about a suitable axis, it may be placed with the combination of shapes A, C and D to form a cube.

7. **D** Let the original number be x. Then $x^2 = 0.7x$, that is $x(x - 0.7) = 0$. So $x = 0$ or $x = 0.7$, but as x is non-zero it is 0.7.

8. **A** October has 31 days so, in any year, in October there are three days of the week which occur five times and four days which occur four times. As there were four Tuesdays and four Fridays, there could not have been five Wednesdays or five Thursdays, so the days which occurred five times were Saturday, Sunday and Monday. Hence October 1st fell on a Saturday, which means that October 31st was a Monday.

9. **D** Let the smaller cubes have side of length 1 unit. So the original cube had side of length 3 units and hence a surface area of 54 units², all of which was painted blue. The total surface area of the 27 small cubes is 27×6 units², that is 162 units². So the required fraction is $\frac{54}{162} = \frac{1}{3}$.

10. **C** In every triangle the length of the longest side is less than the sum of the lengths of the two other sides. So if the triangle has sides of length 5 cm and 6 cm, then the length of the third side is greater than 1 cm, but less than 11 cm. Hence the perimeter, p cm, of the triangle satisfies $12 < p < 22$. So 15 cm is the only one of Perry's suggested values which could be correct.

Intermediate Challenge 2008 solutions

11. E $S = 25\%$ of $60 = 15$. $U = \dfrac{60}{0 \cdot 8} = 75$. $M = \dfrac{80}{0 \cdot 25} = 320$. So $S + U + M = 410$.

12. C   In each of 6 possible directions, the view of the sculpture is as shown, with the outer square having side 3 units and the inner square having side 1 unit.
So the surface area of the sculpture is 6×8 units^2 = 48 units^2.

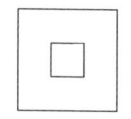

13. D   The sum of all 64 numbers is $64 \times 64 = 64^2$. The sum of the first 36 numbers is $36 \times 36 = 36^2$. So the sum of the remaining 28 numbers is $64^2 - 36^2 = (64 + 36)(64 - 36) = 2800$. Therefore the mean of these 28 numbers is 100.

14. B   Let A and B denote the ends of the first length of rope and C and D denote the ends of the second length of rope. Then Pat chooses one of 6 different possible combinations: $(A, B), (A, C), (A, D), (B, C), (B, D), (C, D)$. Sam now holds one untied length of rope and one tied loop of rope if, and only if, Pat has chosen (A, B) or (C, D) so the required probability is $\dfrac{2}{6} = \dfrac{1}{3}$.
(*Alternatively: Irrespective of whichever end Pat chooses first, Sam will hold one untied length of rope and one tied loop of rope if, and only if, Pat now chooses a particular one of the three remaining ends, namely the other end of the same rope. As each of the three ends is equally likely to be chosen, the required probability is $\tfrac{1}{3}$.*)

15. A   Notice that a single copy of the logo consists of four dots which lie in a straight line plus two other dots which lie on the perpendicular bisector of this line. These two dots are not evenly spaced above and below the line of four dots. Of the options given, only A has two lines of four dots with two more dots in the correct positions relative to each line.

16. D   The problem may be solved by firstly calculating the third and fourth terms of the sequence, but an algebraic method does reduce the amount of calculation involved. Let the first two terms be x and y respectively. Then the third term is $\tfrac{1}{2}(x + y)$, whilst the fourth term is $\tfrac{1}{4}(x + 3y)$. So the fifth term is $\tfrac{1}{8}(3x + 5y)$. Putting $x = \dfrac{2}{3}$ and $y = \dfrac{4}{5}$, we obtain $\dfrac{2 + 4}{8} = \dfrac{3}{4}$.

17. D   As the perimeter of the square has length 8, the square has side length 2. So the diameter of each of the circles is 1. The perimeter of the shaded region consists of four semi-circular arcs and four quarter-circle arcs, so it has length equal to three times the circumference of one circle, that is 3π.

18. C   The five options are: A 0.20088888...   B 0.20080000...   C 0.20080808...
D 0.20080080...   E 0.20082008....
So in ascending order they are B D C E A.

19. E Using 'the difference of two squares':

$(1+x+y)^2 - (1-x-y)^2 = (1+x+y+1-x-y)(1+x+y-1+x+y) = 2(2x+2y) = 4(x+y)$.

20. A Let the vertices of the quadrilateral be A, B, C, D as shown. Then, by Pythagoras' Theorem: $AC^2 = AD^2 + DC^2 = (7^2 + 9^2)\,\text{cm}^2 = 130\,\text{cm}^2$. Similarly, $AB^2 + BC^2 = AC^2$, so $AB^2 = (130 - 9)\,\text{cm}^2 = 121\,\text{cm}^2$. Therefore AB has length 11 cm and the area, in cm², of quadrilateral $ABCD$ is $\frac{1}{2} \times 9 \times 7 + \frac{1}{2} \times 3 \times 11 = 48$.

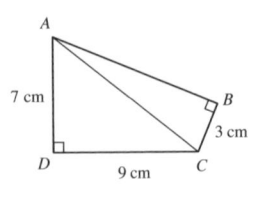

21. B The sum of the interior angles of a triangle is $180°$, so $\angle PRQ = (180 - \alpha - \beta)°$; hence $\angle QRM = \left(90 - \frac{\alpha}{2} - \frac{\beta}{2}\right)°$. As RN is perpendicular to PQ, $\angle NRQ = (90 - \beta)°$. So $\angle MRN = \left(90 - \frac{\alpha}{2} - \frac{\beta}{2}\right)° - (90 - \beta)° = \left(\frac{\beta}{2} - \frac{\alpha}{2}\right)°$.

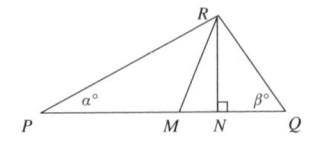

22. A Both £4.20 and £7.70 are multiples of 70p, so £C must also be a multiple of 70p. Of the options given, only £91 is a multiple of 70p, but it remains to check that a total cost of £91 is possible. If there are 7 children and 8 adults, then the total cost is $7 \times £4.20 + 8 \times £7.70 = £29.40 + £61.60 = £91$.

23. E The only digits which will appear the same when reflected in the glass table-top are 0, 1, 3 and 8. So it is necessary to find the number of times in a 24-hour period that the display on the clock is made up only of some or all of these four digits. The first of the digits, therefore, may be 0 or 1; the second digit may be 0, 1, 3 or 8; the third digit may be 0, 1 or 3; the fourth digit may be 0, 1, 3 or 8. So the required number is $2 \times 4 \times 3 \times 4 = 96$.

24. C As the figure has rotational symmetry of order 4, $ABEF$ is a square. Area $ABEF = 4 \times$ area $\triangle BDA = 4 \times \frac{1}{2}BD \times DA = 2BD^2 = 24\,\text{cm}^2$ so $BD = \sqrt{12}\,\text{cm} = 2\sqrt{3}\,\text{cm}$. As $ABEF$ is a square, $\angle ABD = 45°$ so $\angle CBD = 45° - 15° = 30°$. Therefore $\tan 30° = \frac{1}{\sqrt{3}} = \frac{CD}{BD} = \frac{CD}{2\sqrt{3}}$, so $CD = 2\,\text{cm}$.

25. E In the diagram on the right, triangle ABC represents the garden, CD represents the fence and E is the foot of the perpendicular from D to AC.
The two sections of the garden have the same perimeter so AD is 10 m longer than DB. Hence $AD = 30$ m and $DB = 20$ m. As $\angle AED$ and $\angle ACB$ are both right angles, triangles AED and ACB are similar. 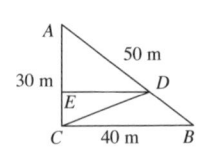
So $\frac{AE}{AC} = \frac{AD}{AB} = \frac{30}{50}$. Hence $AE = \frac{3}{5} \times 30\,\text{m} = 18\,\text{m}$. So $EC = (30 - 18)\,\text{m} = 12\,\text{m}$.
Also, $\frac{ED}{CB} = \frac{AD}{AB} = \frac{30}{50}$. Hence $ED = \frac{3}{5} \times 40\,\text{m} = 24\,\text{m}$.
Finally, by Pythagoras' Theorem: $CD^2 = EC^2 + ED^2 = (12^2 + 24^2)\,\text{m}^2 = 5 \times 12^2\,\text{m}^2$.
So the length of the fence is $12\sqrt{5}$ m.

Intermediate Challenge
2009 solutions

1. **B** $1 + 2^3 + 4 \times 5 = 1 + 8 + 20 = 29$.

2. **D** The first five non-prime positive integers are $1, 4, 6, 8, 9$.

3. **C** The values of these expressions are $5, 8, 9, 8, 5$ respectively.

4. **A** The two acute angles in the quadrilateral in the centre of the diagram are both $(180 - 2x)°$ and the two obtuse angles are both $y°$, so $360 - 4x + 2y = 360$. So $y = 2x$.

5. **D** Let the number be x. Then $x^2 = 2x^3$, that is $x^2(1 - 2x) = 0$. So $x = 0$ or $x = \frac{1}{2}$. However, x is positive, so the only solution is $x = \frac{1}{2}$.

6. **A** $\frac{4}{5} = \frac{12}{15}$ and $-\frac{2}{3} = -\frac{10}{15}$, so the number half way between these is $\frac{1}{2}\left(\frac{-10}{15} + \frac{12}{15}\right)$, that is $\frac{1}{15}$.

7. **C** As can be seen from the diagram, the square whose vertices are the centres of the original four circles has side of length 2 units and this distance is equal to the diameter of the circle through X, Y, Z and T.

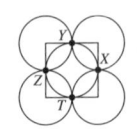

8. **A** The small square on top will be in the upper half of the divided figure. Now consider the figure formed by moving this square to become an extra square on the left of the second row, as shown. It may now be seen from the symmetry of the figure that the line PX splits the new figure in half – with that small square in the upper half. So the line PX does the same for the original figure.

9. **B** The ratio of goats to sheep is $100:155 = 20:31$.

10. **D** There are 51 houses numbered from 100 to 150 inclusive. Of these, 17 are multiples of 3, 11 are multiples of 5 and 4 are multiples of both 3 and 5. So the number of houses Fiona can choose from is $51 - (17 + 11 - 4) = 27$.

11. **E** Note that 2004 is a multiple of 3 (since its digit sum is a multiple of 3) and also a multiple of 4 (since its last two digits form a multiple of 4). So 2004 is a multiple of 12 and hence the part of the pattern between 2007 and 2011 is the same as the part of the pattern between 3 and 7.

12. **D** Let Y and Z be the points shown. The interior angle of a regular hexagon is $120°$, so $\angle XZY = 120° - 90° = 30°$. The side of the square has the same length as the side of the regular hexagon, so $YZ = XZ$. Hence triangle XYZ is isosceles and $\angle ZXY = \angle ZYX = \frac{1}{2}(180° - 30°) = 75°$.

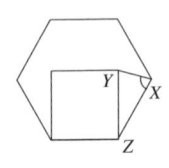

Intermediate Challenge 2009 solutions

13. **A** If the shaded regions in the top-right and bottom-left corners of the diagram are moved as shown, the area of the shaded region in both the top half and bottom half of the diagram is now that of a 3 × 2 rectangle which has a quarter of a circle of radius 2 removed from it. So the total shaded area is
$2(3 \times 2 - \frac{1}{4} \times \pi \times 2^2)$ cm² = $(12 - 2\pi)$ cm².

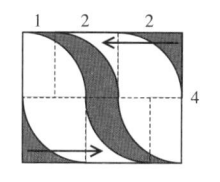

14. **E** If n is a positive integer then the units digit of 66^n is 6. So when a power of 66 is divided by 2, the units digit of the quotient is either 3 or 8. Now 66^{66} is clearly a multiple of 4, so $\frac{1}{2}(66^{66})$ is even and therefore has units digit 8 rather than 3.

15. **B** As $\frac{1}{x} = 3.5 = \frac{7}{2}, x = \frac{2}{7}$. So $x + 2 = \frac{16}{7}$. Hence $\frac{1}{x+2} = \frac{7}{16}$.

16. **B** If n is an odd prime, then $n^3 + 3$ is an even number greater than 3 and therefore not prime. The only even prime is 2 (which some would say makes it very odd!) and when $n = 2, n^3 + 3 = 11$ which is also prime. So there is exactly one value of n for which n and $n^3 + 3$ are both prime.

17. **D** Triangles *PRS* and *QPR* are similar because: $\angle PSR = \angle QRP$ (since $PR = PS$) and $\angle PRS = \angle QPR$ (since $QP = QR$). Hence $\frac{SR}{RP} = \frac{RP}{PQ}$, that is $\frac{SR}{6} = \frac{6}{9}$, that is $SR = 4$.

18. **B** For all positive integer values of p and q, $2p^2q$ and $3pq^2$ have a common factor of pq. They will also have an additional common factor of 2 if $q = 2$ and an additional common factor of 3 if $p = 3$. As the values of p and q are to be chosen from 2, 3 and 5, the largest possible value of the highest common factor will occur when $p = 3$ and $q = 5$. For these values of p and q, $2p^2q$ and $3pq^2$ have values 90 and 225 respectively, giving a highest common factor of 45.

19. **E** Let the time for which Mary drove at 70 mph be t hours. Then the total distance covered was $(55 \times 2 + 70 \times t)$ miles. Also, as her average speed over $(2 + t)$ hours was 60 mph, the total distance travelled was $60(2 + t)$ miles. Therefore $110 + 70t = 120 + 60t$, that is $10t = 10$, that is $t = 1$.
So, in total, Mary's journey took 3 hours.

20. **D** As can be seen from the figures below, the perimeter of the trapezium is $2 + 3\sqrt{2}$.

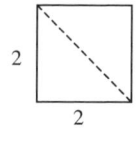

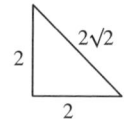

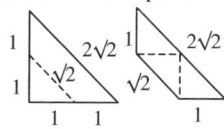

21. **E** Consider the top row of four dots. One can obtain a triple of dots by eliminating any one of the four – so there are four such triples. The same is true for each of the four rows, each of the four columns and the two main diagonals, giving 40 triples. In addition there are four diagonal lines consisting of exactly three dots, so there are 44 triples in total.

22. D If the first triangle selected to be shaded is a corner triangle, then the final figure will have at least one axis of symmetry provided that the second triangle selected is one of five triangles. For example, if A is chosen first then there will be at least one axis of symmetry in the final figure if the second triangle selected is B, D, E, G or H. The same applies if an inner triangle is selected first: for example, if B is chosen first then there will be at least one axis of symmetry in the final figure if the second triangle selected is A, C, F, G or H.

So, irrespective of which triangle is selected first, the probability that the final figure has at least one axis of symmetry is $\frac{5}{7}$.

23. C Firstly, note that the black squares have side 2 units. The pattern may be considered to be a tessellation of the shape shown on the right. So the ratio of squares to rectangles is 1:2 and hence the fraction coloured black is $\frac{4}{4 + 2 \times 48} = \frac{4}{100} = \frac{1}{25}$.

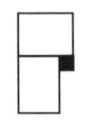

24. C Reading from the left, we number the statements I, II, III, IV and V.

Statement I is true if and only if $-1 < x < 1$; statement II is true if $x > 1$ or if $x < -1$. By considering the graph of $y = x - x^2$, which intersects the x-axis at $(0, 0)$ and $(1, 0)$ and has a maximum at $\left(\frac{1}{2}, \frac{1}{4}\right)$, it may be seen that statement V is true if and only if $0 < x < 1$.

We see from the table below that a maximum of three statements may be true at any one time.

	$x < -1$	$x = -1$	$-1 < x < 0$	$x = 0$	$0 < x < 1$	$x = 1$	$x > 1$
True statement(s)	II	none	I, III	none	I, IV, V	none	II

25. E As it is known that the fake coin is heavier than all of the others, it is possible in one comparison to identify which, if any, is the fake in a group of three coins: simply compare any two of the three coins – if they do not balance then the heavier coin is the fake, whereas if they do balance then the third coin is the fake. This means that it is possible to find the fake coin when $N = 9$ using two comparisons: the coins are divided into three groups of three and, using the same reasoning as for three individual coins, the first comparison identifies which group of three coins contains the fake. The second comparison then identifies which of these three coins is the fake. However, it is not possible to identify the fake coin in a group of four coins in one comparison only, so it is not always possible to identify the fake coin using two comparisons when $N = 10$. If less than four are put on each side for the first comparison and they balance, then there are more than three left and the fake coin amongst these cannot be identified in one further comparison. Alternatively, if more than three are put on each side for the first comparison and they do not balance, then the fake coin in the heavier group cannot be identified in one further comparison.

Intermediate Challenge
2010 solutions

1. **D** $10 + 10 \times 10 \times (10 + 10) = 10 + 10 \times 10 \times 20 = 10 + 2000 = 2010$.

2. **A** The sum of the interior angles of a quadrilateral is 360°, so the fourth angle is $(360 - 3 \times 80)° = 120°$.

3. **E** 2345 has units digit 5 and so is a multiple of 5; 23 456 is even; the digit sum of 234 567 is 27 so it is a multiple of 9; 2 345 678 is even. So if exactly one of the numbers is prime then it must be 23 456 789.

4. **A** The number of calories saved per day is $\frac{7000}{365} \approx \frac{7000}{350} = 20$.

5. **E** The values are A $\frac{1}{50}$, B $\frac{1}{60}$, C $\frac{1}{60}$, D $\frac{1}{50}$, E $\frac{1}{30}$.

6. **C** Triangle PQS is isosceles with $PS = QS$ so $\angle PQS = \angle SPQ = 20°$. Therefore $\angle PSR = 20° + 20° = 40°$ (exterior angle theorem). Triangle PSR is also isosceles, with $PS = PR$, so $\angle PRS = \angle PSR = 40°$.

7. **D** The Festival will next be held in Worcester in 2011. As it follows a three-year cycle, the Festival is held in Worcester when the number of the year leaves a remainder of 1 when divided by 3. So it will be held in Worcester in 2020, 2032, 2047 and 2077, but not in 2054.

8. **B** The next such display will be 03:12, that is in 41 minutes' time.

9. **C** The difference in perimeters is the total length of the edges which are hidden when the pieces are fitted together. These are eight straight edges of length 1 and four semicircular arcs of radius 1.
So the required difference is $8 \times 1 + 4(\frac{1}{2} \times 2 \times \pi \times 1) = 8 + 4\pi$.

10. **C** Every year, the day of the week on which a particular date falls is one day later than it fell the previous year unless February 29th has occurred in the meantime, in which case it falls two days later. As January 1st returned to a Monday after 11 years, it must have 'moved on' 14 days during that time, so February 29th occurred three times in those 11 years.

11. **B** If the first statement is true, then the three other statements are all false. If the first statement is false, however, then the second statement is the only true statement. Either way, exactly one of the four statements is true.

12. **D** When the cuboid is cut away, the surface area of the solid 'loses' two rectangles measuring 10 cm × 5 cm and two squares of side 5 cm. However, it also 'gains' two rectangles measuring 10 cm × 5 cm. So the surface area decreases by an area equal to one half of the area of one of the faces of the original cube, that is one twelfth of its original surface area.

13. **B** Let the prices of a fork handle and a candle be £x and £y respectively.
Then $x + y = 6.1$ and $x - y = 4.6$. Adding these two equations gives $2x = 10.7$.
So a fork handle costs £5.35 and a candle costs £0.75.
Therefore the required total is £10.70 + £3.00 = £13.70.

Intermediate Challenge 2010 solutions 179

14. C Adding the three equations gives $3x + 3y + 3z = 30$, so $x + y + z = 10$.
(*The equations may be solved to obtain* $x = 2, y = 3, z = 5$. *However, as the above method shows, this is not necessary in order to find the value of* $x + y + z$.)

15. E The line $y = 2x + 6$ intersects the y-axis when $x = 0$ and $y = 6$. It intersects the x-axis when $x = -3$ and $y = 0$. So E is the correct line.
(*Alternatively*: $y = 2x + 6$ may be rearranged to give $x = \tfrac{1}{2}y - 3$. So the required line looks the same as the line $y = \tfrac{1}{2}x - 3$ when the axes are drawn in the traditional way.)

16. E After x hours, the first clock will have gone forward $2x$ hours and the second clock will have gone back x hours. So the next time they agree is when $2x + x = 24$, that is when $x = 8$. The correct time then is 21:00.

17. A The volume of a cylinder of radius r and height h is $\pi r^2 h$. Replacing r by $2r$ and h by $3h$ multiplies this volume by 12.

18. A Let the distance from the chalet to the top of the mountain be x miles. Then, at 6 mph Supergran would take $\dfrac{x}{6}$ hours, whereas at 10 mph she would take $\dfrac{x}{10}$ hours.
So $\dfrac{x}{6} - \dfrac{x}{10} = 2$, that is $5x - 3x = 60$, so $x = 30$. Hence Supergran's departure time is 8 am and to arrive at 12 noon she should walk at $\dfrac{30}{4}$ mph, that is $7\tfrac{1}{2}$ mph.

19. B In one hour, the snail can reach points within 1 m of the corner at which it starts. So it can reach some of the points on the three faces which meet at that corner, but none of the points on the other three faces. On each of the three reachable faces, the points which the snail can reach form a quarter of a circle of radius 1 m. 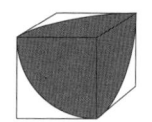
So the required fraction is $\dfrac{3 \times \tfrac{1}{4}\pi \times 1 \times 1}{6 \times 1 \times 1} = \dfrac{\pi}{8}$.

20. D If the difference between $\sqrt{n}$ and 7 is less than 1, then $6 < \sqrt{n} < 8$. Therefore $36 < n < 64$, so there are 27 possible values of n.

21. E The rooms are labelled A, B, C, D, E, F, G, X, Y as shown.
We look first at routes which visit no room more than once.
We need consider only routes which go from X to A, since each of these routes has a corresponding route which goes from X to C. For example, the route X A D E Y corresponds to the route X C D G Y. 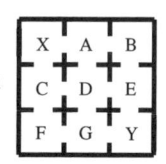
Routes which start X A then go to B or to D. There are three routes which start X A B, namely X A B E Y, X A B E D G Y and X A B E D C F G Y. There are also three routes which start X A D, namely X A D E Y, X A D G Y and X A D C F G Y.
The condition that a gap in a wall closes once a person has travelled through it means that it is not possible to visit a room more than once unless that room has at least four gaps leading into and out of it and the only such room is D. There

are two routes which start X A and visit D twice. These are X A D G F C D E Y and X A D C F G D E Y. So there are 8 routes which start X A and there are 8 corresponding routes which start X C so there are 16 routes in all.

22. E Curly's drink has squash and water in the ratio 1: 7, whilst the corresponding ratio for Larry's drink is 3 : 37. This ratio is less than 1 : 7. When some of Curly's mixture is poured into Larry's, the strength will be between 1 : 7 and 3 : 37, but not equal to either.

23. B Let the centre of the circle be O and let A and B be corners of one of the shaded squares, as shown. As the circle has area π units^2, its radius is 1 unit. So OB is 1 unit long. Let the length of the side of each of the shaded squares be x units. 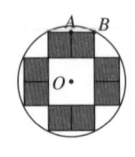
By Pythagoras' Theorem: $OB^2 = OA^2 + AB^2$, that is $1^2 = (2x)^2 + x^2$.
So $5x^2 = 1$. Now the total shaded area is $8x^2 = 8 \times \frac{1}{5} = 1\frac{3}{5}$ units^2.

24. B There is the possibility of using only 3s giving one possible number 333333. Let's suppose a second digit is used, say x. After the initial digit 3, there are 5 positions into which we can put either 3 or x. So there are 2 choices in each of these 5 positions and so $2^5 = 32$ possible choices – except that one such choice would be five 3s. So we get 31 choices. There are 9 possible values for x, namely 0, 1, 2, 4, 5, 6, 7, 8, 9. So this gives $9 \times 31 = 279$ numbers. Together with 333333, this gives 280 numbers.

25. D Let the length of the side of regular octagon be x units and let A, B, C, D, E, F be the points shown. So $AC = CE = x$. Now $\angle ACE = 135°$ (interior angle of regular octagon), so $\angle ACB = 45°$ and hence triangle ABC is an isosceles right-angled triangle with $AB = BC$. 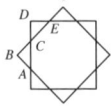
Also, by Pythagoras' Theorem: $AB^2 + BC^2 = AC^2 = x^2$ so $AB = BC = \frac{\sqrt{2}}{2}x$.
Similarly, $EF = \frac{\sqrt{2}}{2}x$.
Therefore $BF = \left(\frac{\sqrt{2}}{2}x + x + \frac{\sqrt{2}}{2}x\right)$ units $= x\left(1 + \sqrt{2}\right)$ units.
But we are given that $BF = \left(1 + \sqrt{2}\right)$ units so $x = 1$.
Now the area of the octagon formed by the overlap of the squares is equal to the area of one of these squares minus the sum of the area of four triangles, each of which is congruent to triangle CDE.
Thus, in square units, the required area is

$$\left(1 + \sqrt{2}\right)^2 - 4 \times \frac{1}{2} \times \frac{\sqrt{2}}{2} \times \frac{\sqrt{2}}{2} = 3 + 2\sqrt{2} - 1 = 2 + 2\sqrt{2}.$$

Intermediate Challenge
2011 solutions

182   Ten Further Years of Mathematical Challenges

1. **B** $4.5 \times 5.5 + 4.5 \times 4.5 = 4.5(5.5 + 4.5) = 4.5 \times 10 = 45$.
2. **A** The diameter is $(5 \times 0.3 + 2.1)$ mm $= (1.5 + 2.1)$ mm $= 3.6$ mm.
3. **E** $12 \div 3 = 4$, but this is the example given in the question. $23 \div 4 \neq 5$; $34 \div 5 \neq 6; 45 \div 6 \neq 7$. However, $56 \div 7 = 8$, so $s = 8$. {Note also that $67 \div 8 \neq 9$.}
4. **E** The difference between the angles is $\left(\dfrac{5}{10} - \dfrac{2}{10}\right) \times 180°$.
5. **C** Triangles A and C are each of area $\frac{1}{2} \times 5 \times 5$ cm^2. Triangles B and D are each of area $\frac{1}{2} \times 3 \times 3$ cm^2. So the shaded area is $[64 - (25 + 9)]$ cm$^2 = 30$ cm^2. 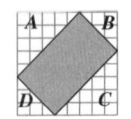
6. **B** The next palindromic number after 24942 is 25052, so the car travelled 110 miles in the two days.
7. **A** Alternate angles BDF and DFG are equal, so lines BD and FG are parallel. Therefore $\angle BCA = \angle FGC = 80°$ (corresponding angles). Consider triangle ABC: $x + 70 + 80 = 180$, so $x = 30$. 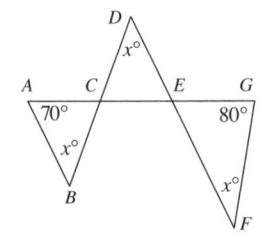
8. **E** The base of the open box is a square. Let its side be of length x cm. Then the total surface area of the box in cm^2 is $x^2 + 4 \times 2x = x^2 + 8x$. Hence $x^2 + 8x = 180$, that is $x^2 + 8x - 180 = 0$. Therefore $(x + 18)(x - 10) = 0$, which gives $x = -18$ or $x = 10$. As x is positive, it may be deduced that the open box has dimensions 10 cm × 10 cm × 2 cm. So its volume is 200 cm^3.
9. **A** In a triangle, an exterior angle is equal to the sum of the two interior, opposite angles. Repeatedly applying this theorem:
$p = 150 - 80 = 70$;
$q = p - 40 = 30; r = q - 20 = 10$.
Therefore $x = 180 - r = 170$. 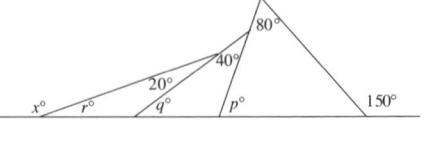
10. **E** One tonne = 1000kg = 1 000 000g. So the number of mice is $6\,000\,000 \div 20 = 300\,000$.
11. **E** $19\frac{1}{2} \times 20\frac{1}{2} = \left(20 - \frac{1}{2}\right) \times \left(20 + \frac{1}{2}\right) = 20^2 - \left(\frac{1}{2}\right)^2 = 400 - \frac{1}{4} = 399\frac{3}{4}$.
12. **D** $20 \div 11 = 1\frac{9}{11} = 1.818181\ldots$. So the first 2011 digits are 1006 '1's and 1005 '8's. Therefore the required total is $1006 \times 1 + 1005 \times 8 = 1006 + 8040 = 9046$.
13. **D** After the first mouse has eaten, $\frac{2}{3}$ of the cheese remains. After the second mouse has eaten, $\frac{2}{3}$ of $\frac{2}{3}$, that is $\frac{4}{9}$, of the cheese remains. Finally, after the third mouse has eaten, $\frac{2}{3}$ of $\frac{4}{9}$, that is $\frac{8}{27}$, of the cheese remains. So the mice ate $\frac{19}{27}$ of the cheese.

Intermediate Challenge 2011 solutions 183

14. **E** $3 = \frac{2+2^2}{2}$; $10 = \frac{4+4^2}{2}$; $15 = \frac{5+5^2}{2}$; $21 = \frac{6+6^2}{2}$. However $\frac{7+7^2}{2} = 28$ and $\frac{8+8^2}{2} = 36$, so 30 is not exactly halfway between a positive integer and its square.
(*Note that every number which is exactly halfway between a positive integer and its square is a triangle number. Can you explain why this is so?*)

15. **A** In each rotation which C makes, the radius of the arc it describes is 1 unit. In the first rotation, C turns through an angle of 120°, so it moves a distance $\frac{1}{3} \times 2 \times \pi \times 1$, that is $\frac{2\pi}{3}$. As it is the centre of the second rotation, C does not move during it. In the third rotation, C again turns through an angle of 120°, so the total distance travelled is $2 \times \frac{2\pi}{3} = \frac{4\pi}{3}$.

16. **C** The L-shape needs to be divided as shown since neither of the pieces is to be a square. Notice that one of the pieces must be turned over. The difference between the areas of the two pieces is 7 − 5 = 2.

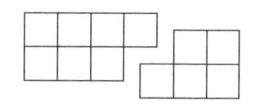

17. **C** The reduction of 15% off sale prices is equal to a reduction of 7.5% off the original prices. Therefore the total reduction on the original prices is (50 + 7.5)% = 57.5%.

18. **D** As the diagram shows, each equilateral triangle may be divided into four equilateral triangles of side 1, whilst the hexagon may be divided into six equilateral triangles of side 1.
Therefore the fraction of the whole shape which is shaded is
$\frac{6}{6 \times 4 + 6} = \frac{6}{30} = \frac{1}{5}$.

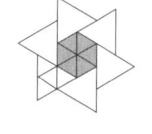

19. **B** As can be seen from the diagram, Manchester is 40km west of Leeds and 25 km south of it. Therefore, by Pythagoras' Theorem, the distance in km from Leeds to Manchester as the crow flies is $\sqrt{25^2 + 40^2} = 5\sqrt{5^2 + 8^2} = 5\sqrt{89}$.
Now $\sqrt{81} = 9$ and $\sqrt{100} = 10$, so $9 < \sqrt{89} < 10$.
This means that the required distance is between 45km and 50km and, of the options given, only 47km (corresponding to the approximation $\sqrt{89} \approx 9.4$) lies in this interval.
(*Please note that the distances given in this problem are all approximate.*)

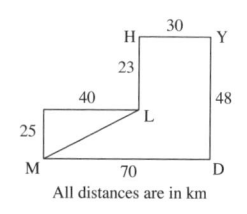

All distances are in km

20. **D** Let Max and Molly meet after the latter has travelled x miles. Then Max has travelled $(6 - x)$ miles. So $6 - x = 2x$, thus $x = 2$. Therefore Molly walks a total of 4 miles.

21. **B** Let $4x$ be the length of each side of the regular octagon. The diagram shows part of the figure. The four triangles shown in the diagram are all isosceles right-angled triangles. In such triangles the ratio of the length of the hypotenuse to the length of the shorter sides is $\sqrt{2} : 1$.

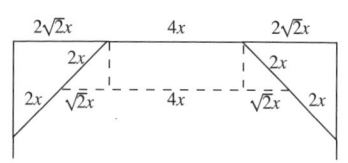

So in the larger triangles which have hypotenuse of length $4x$, the length of the shorter sides is $2\sqrt{2}x$, whilst the smaller triangles with hypotenuse $2x$ have shorter sides of length $\sqrt{2}x$.
Therefore the shaded square in the question has side of length $(4 + 2\sqrt{2})x$.
The length of the side of the outer square is $(4\sqrt{2} + 4)x = \sqrt{2}(4 + 2\sqrt{2})x$.
Therefore the two squares have sides in the ratio $1 : \sqrt{2}$, which means that their areas have ratio $1 : 2$.

22. **B** $5^p = 9$ and $9^q = 12$. Therefore $(5^p)^q = 12$, that is $5^{pq} = 12$. Similarly, as $12^r = 16$ then $5^{pqr} = 16$, as $16^s = 20$ then $5^{pqrs} = 20$ and, finally, as $20^t = 25$ then $5^{pqrst} = 25$. Therefore $pqrst = 2$.

23. **A** Points A, B, C, D and E are, respectively: the point where the large semicircle and the circle touch, the centre of the circle, the centre of the left-hand semicircle, the centre of the large semicircle and the centre of the right-hand semicircle. The radius of the circle is r m. In triangle BCD, CD has length 1m, BD has length $(2 - r)$ m, since AD is a radius of the semicircle of diameter 4m, and BC has length $(1 + r)$ m, since it is the sum of the radii of the left-hand semicircle and the circle. Therefore, by Pythagoras' Theorem:
$(1 + r)^2 = 1^2 + (2 - r)^2$, that is $1 + 2r + r^2 = 1 + 4 - 4r + r^2$. So $6r = 4$ and the radius of the circle is $\tfrac{2}{3}$m.
(*Note that triangle BCD is a 3,4,5 triangle with sides $\tfrac{3}{3}$m, $\tfrac{4}{3}$m and $\tfrac{5}{3}$m.*)

24. **C** Firstly we give examples to show that Paul's answer could have been any of A, B, D or E.
    A: If n is prime then the only factor of n other than itself is 1.
    B: Take $n = 4$. Its factors are 1, 2 and 4, and $1 + 2 = 3$.
    D: Take $n = 8$. Its factors are 1, 2, 4 and 8, and $1 + 2 + 4 = 7$.
    E : Take $n = 15$. Its factors are 1, 3, 5 and 15, and $1 + 3 + 5 = 9$.
We now show that Paul's answer cannot be C. If the sum were 5, then the factors of n other than itself would have to be 1 and 4, as we are not allowed to repeat any number in the sum. However, if 4 is a factor of n, then 2 is also a factor, which produces a contradiction.

25. **D** Let triangle CEF have area a. Note that $\angle AFD = \angle CFE$ (vertically opposite angles) and $\angle DAF = \angle ECF$ (alternate angles), so triangles ADF and CEF are similar.
Note also that the side AD is twice the length of the corresponding side CE.
Hence:
(i) triangle ADF has area $4a$ and;
(ii) AF has twice the length of the corresponding side CF.
View AF and CF as bases of the triangles ADF and CDF (which then share the same height). Therefore, by (ii), triangle ADF has twice the area of triangle CDF (area P), which thus is $2a$.
The area of triangle ACD is $6a$; so that of triangle ABC is also $6a$ and that of area Q is $5a$. So the required ratio is $2 : 5$.

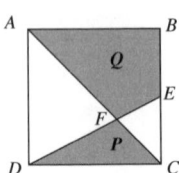

Intermediate Challenge
2012 solutions

1. **B** 3 is the only one of the four numbers which is prime. The sums of the digits of the other three numbers are 6, 9, 12 respectively. These are all multiples of 3, so 33, 333, 3333 are all multiples of 3.

2. **D** The following triples of positive integers all sum to 7:
$$(1, 1, 5), \ (1, 2, 4), \ (1, 3, 3); \ (2, 2, 3).$$
In only one of these are the three integers all different, so the required integers are 1, 2, 4 and their product is 8.

3. **E** The diagram shows that the interior angles of the polygon may be divided up to form the interior angles of six triangles. So their sum is $6 \times 180°$.

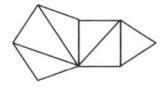

4. C The digits to be used must be 9, 8, 7, 6. If any of these were to be replaced by a smaller digit, then the sum of the two two-digit numbers would be reduced. For this sum to be as large as possible, 9 and 8 must appear in the 'tens' column rather than the 'units' column. So the largest possible sum is 97 + 86 or 96 + 87. In both cases the sum is 183.

5. D The difference between the two given times is 24 hours 50 minutes
= (24 × 60 + 50) minutes = (1440 + 50) minutes = 1490 minutes.

6. A The diagram shows the result of the successive reflections.

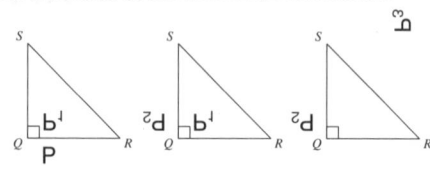

7. C The primes in question are 5 and 11. The only primes smaller than 5 are 2 and 3. However neither 8 nor 9 is prime so p and q cannot be 2 and 8, nor 3 and 9.

8. A Referring to the diagram, $a = 11 - 9 = 2$; $b = 11 - 5 - a = 4$; $f = 11 - 8 = 3$. So the values of c, d and e are 1, 6, 7 in some order. If $c = 1$ then $d = 6$, but then e would need to be 2, not 7. 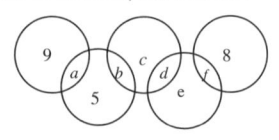
If $c = 6$, then $d = 1$ and $e = 7$ and this is a valid solution. Finally, if $c = 7$ then d would need to equal 0, which is not possible. So in the only possible solution, * is replaced by 6.

9. B 1% of 1 000 000 = 1 000 000 ÷ 100 = 10 000. So the least number of fleas which will be eradicated is 1 000 000 − 10 000 = 990 000.

10. D The table shows the first 12 positive integers, N, and the sum, S, of the factors of N excluding N itself. As can be seen, 12 is the first value of N for which this sum exceeds N, so 12 is the smallest abundant number.

N	1	2	3	4	5	6	7	8	9	10	11	12
S	0	1	1	3	1	6	1	7	4	8	1	16

(Note that for $N = 6$ the sum also equals 6. For this reason, 6 is known as a 'perfect number'. After 6, the next two perfect numbers are 28 and 496.)

11. C Opposite angles of a parallelogram are equal so $\angle QPS = 50°$.
Therefore $\angle QPT = 112°$ and, as triangle QPT is isosceles,
$\angle PQT = (180° - 112°) ÷ 2 = 34°$.
As $PQRS$ is a parallelogram, $\angle PQR = 180° - 50° = 130°$.
So $\angle TQR = 130° - 34° = 96°$.

12. B The values of the expressions are £5.40, £6.00, £5.40, £5.40, £5.40 respectively.

13. D In the rally, approximately 90 shots were hit per minute for a total of 132 minutes. As 90 × 130 = 11 700, D is the best alternative.

14. A The mean of the first three numbers is $\frac{1}{3}(20 + x)$; the mean of the last four numbers is $\frac{1}{4}(33 + x)$. Therefore $4(20 + x) = 3(33 + x)$, that is $80 + 4x = 99 + 3x$, so $x = 99 - 80 = 19$.

15. E $\frac{1}{2} + \frac{1}{3} \times \frac{1}{4} = \frac{1}{2} + \frac{1}{12} = \frac{7}{12}; \frac{1}{2} \div \frac{1}{3} = \frac{1}{2} + \frac{1}{3} \times \frac{4}{1} = \frac{1}{2} + \frac{4}{3} = \frac{11}{6}; \frac{1}{2} \times \frac{1}{3} \div \frac{1}{4} =$
$\frac{1}{2} \times \frac{1}{3} \times \frac{4}{1} = \frac{2}{3}; \frac{1}{2} - \frac{1}{3} \div \frac{1}{4} = \frac{1}{2} - \frac{1}{3} \times \frac{4}{1} = \frac{1}{2} - \frac{4}{3} = -\frac{5}{6}; \frac{1}{2} - \frac{1}{3} \times \frac{1}{4} = \frac{1}{2} - \frac{1}{12} = \frac{5}{12}$.

Of the fractions $\frac{7}{12}, \frac{11}{6}, \frac{2}{3}, -\frac{5}{6}, \frac{5}{12}$, the closest to 0 is $\frac{5}{12}$.

16. B As triangle ABC is equilateral, $\angle BAC = 60°$. From the symmetry of the figure, we may deduce that $AD = DE$ so triangle ADE is equilateral. The length of the side of this equilateral triangle = length of $DE = (5 + 2 + 5)$ cm = 12 cm. So $AF = AD - AF = (12 - 5)$ cm = 7 cm. By a similar argument, we deduce that $BD = 7$ cm, so the length of the side of triangle $ABC = (7 + 5 + 7)$ cm = 19 cm.

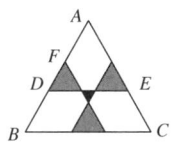

17. E The terms of the sequence are 6, 3, 14, 7, 34, 17, 84, 42, 21, 104, 52, 26, 13, 64, 32, 16, 8, 4, 2, 1, 4, 2, 1, ... As can be seen, there will now be no other terms in the sequence other than 4, 2 and 1. It can also be seen that the only values of n for which the n th term = n are 13 and 16.

18. C After traversing the first semicircle, Peri will be at the point $(8, 0)$; after the second semicircle Peri will be at $(4, 0)$ and after the third semicircle, Peri will be at the point $(2, 0)$.

19. A The diagram shows the original diagram enclosed within a square of side $2r$, where r is the radius of the original circle. The unshaded area of the square consists of four quadrants (quarter circles) of radius r. So the shaded area is $4r^2 - \pi r^2 = r^2(4 - \pi)$. Therefore the required fraction is

$$\frac{r^2(4 - \pi)}{\pi r^2} = \frac{4 - \pi}{\pi} = \frac{4}{\pi} - 1.$$

20. D Let the sides of the rectangle, in cm, be $4x$ and $5x$ respectively. Then the area of the square is $4x \times 5x$ cm$^2 = 20x^2$ cm^2. So $20x^2 = 125$, that is $x^2 = \frac{25}{4}$. Therefore $x = \pm\frac{5}{2}$, but x cannot be negative so the sides of the rectangle are 10 cm and 12.5 cm. Hence the rectangle has perimeter 45 cm.

21. A In the diagram, T is the foot of the perpendicular from Q to SR produced. Angles PQR and QRT are alternate angles between parallel lines so $\angle QRT = 60°$. Triangle QRT has interior angles of $90°$, $60°$, $30°$ so it may be thought of as being half of an equilateral triangle of side 1 unit, since the length of QR is 1 unit. So the lengths of RT and QT are $\frac{1}{2}$ and $\frac{\sqrt{3}}{2}$ units respectively.

Applying Pythagoras' Theorem to $\triangle QST$, $SQ^2 = ST^2 + QT^2 = \left(\frac{5}{2}\right)^2 + \left(\frac{\sqrt{3}}{2}\right)^2 = \frac{25}{4} + \frac{3}{4} = 7$. So the length of SQ is $\sqrt{7}$ units.

22. **E**   The median number of cups of coffee is the median of a sequence of 190 positive integers $(t_1, t_2, \ldots, t_{190})$. Let the sum of these terms be S.
The median of the 190 numbers is $\frac{1}{2}(t_{95} + t_{96})$. The alternatives imply that the median cannot be greater than 3.5. The next lowest possible value for the median would be 4. For this to be possible, $t_{95} + t_{96} = 8$.
If $t_{95} = t_{96} = 4$ then the minimum value for S would occur if all other values of t were as small as possible, that is the first 94 values would all equal 1 and the last 94 values would all equal 4. In this case, $S = 94 \times 1 + 2 \times 4 + 94 \times 4 = 478$, whereas we are told that 477 cups of coffee were sold. Any other values of t_{95} and t_{96} such that $t_{95} + t_{96} = 8$ would produce a larger minimum value of S. For example, if $t_{95} = 3$ and $t_{96} = 5$ then the minimum value of S would be $94 \times 1 + 3 + 5 + 94 \times 5$, that is 572. So the median of the 190 terms cannot be 4, but it is possible for it to be 3.5. If the first 94 terms all equal 1, $t_{95} = 3$ and $t_{96} = 4$ and the last 94 terms all equal 4 then $S = 477$ as required and the median is $\frac{1}{2}(3 + 4) = 3.5$.
So the maximum possible value of the median number of cups of coffee bought per customer is 3.5.

23. **C**   As in the solution for Q21, $\triangle PTS$ may be thought of as half an equilateral triangle, so TS has length 1 unit. Therefore $\triangle SRT$ is isosceles and, as $\angle TSR = 120°$, $\angle SRT = \angle STR = 30°$. So $\angle TRQ = 45° - 30° = 15°$. Using the exterior angle theorem in $\triangle TQR$, $\angle TQR = \angle STR - \angle TRQ = 30° - 15° = 15°$. So $\triangle TQR$ is isosceles with $TQ = TR$. However, $\triangle PRT$ is also isosceles with $PT = TR$ since $\angle PRT = \angle TPR = 30°$. Therefore $TQ = TP$, from which we deduce that PQT is an isosceles right-angled triangle in which $\angle PQT = \angle QPT = 45°$. So $\angle QPR = \angle QPT + \angle TPS = 45° + 30° = 75°$.

24. **D**   The nature of the spiral means that 4 is in the top left-hand corner of a 2×2 square of cells, 9 is in the bottom right-hand corner of a 3×3 square of cells, 16 is in the top left-hand corner of a 4×4 square of cells and so on. To find the position of 2012 in the grid, we note that $45^2 = 2025$ so 2025 is in the bottom right-hand corner of a 45×45 square of cells and note also that $47^2 = 2209$. The table below shows the part of the grid in which 2012 lies. The top row shows the last 15 cells in the bottom row of a 45×45 square of cells, whilst below it are the last 16 cells in the bottom row of a 47×47 square of cells.

2011 2012 2013 2014 2015 2016 2017 2018 2019 2020 2021 2022 2023 2024 2025
2194 2195 2196 2197 2198 2199 2200 2201 2202 2203 2204 2205 2206 2207 2208 2209

So 2195 lies below 2012.

25. **B**   The diagram shows part of the ceramic.
A and B are vertices of the outer octagon, which has O at its centre. The solid lines are part of the original figure, whilst the broken lines OA, OB, two broken lines which are parallel to AB and broken lines parallel to OA and OB respectively have been added. As can be seen, these lines divide $\triangle OAB$ into nine congruent triangles. The shaded portion of triangle has area equal to that of two of the triangles. So $\frac{2}{9}$ of the area of $\triangle OAB$ has been shaded. Now the area of the outer octagon is eight times the area of $\triangle OAB$ and the area of shaded portion of the design is eight times the area of the shaded portion of $\triangle OAB$ so the fraction of the octagon which is shaded is also $\frac{2}{9}$.

Intermediate Challenge 2013 solutions

1. **D** In order to be a multiple of 6, a number must be both even and a multiple of 3. Of the numbers given, only B 999 998 and D 999 996 are even. Using the rule for division by 3, we see that, of these two, only 999 996 is a multiple of 3.

2. **B** 180 000 eggs per hour is equivalent to 3000 eggs per minute, i.e. to 50 eggs per second.

3. **E** The figure is itself a quadrilateral. It can be divided into four small quadrilaterals labelled A, B, C, D. There are also four quadrilaterals formed in each case by joining together two of the smaller quadrilaterals: A and B; B and C; C and D; D and A.

4. **D** The number of seeds in a special packet is $1.25 \times 40 = 50$. So the number of seeds which germinate is $0.7 \times 50 = 35$.

5. **E** A wheatear travels the distance of almost 15 000 km in approximately 50 days. This is on average roughly 300 km per day.

6. **E** In order, the values of the expressions given are: $1 - 0 = 1$; $2 - 1 = 1$; $9 - 8 = 1$; $64 - 81 = -17$; $625 - 1024 = -399$.

7. **A** Only two colours are needed for the upper four faces of the octahedron. If, for example, blue and red are used then these four faces may be painted alternately red and blue. Consider now the lower four faces: every face adjacent to an upper blue face may be painted red and every face adjacent to an upper red face may be painted blue. So only two colours are required for the whole octahedron.

8. **D** Let the number of scores of 1 be n. Then the product of the scores is $1^n \times 2 \times 3 \times 5 = 30$. Therefore $1 \times n + 2 + 3 + 5 = 30$, i.e. $n = 20$. So Jim threw 23 dice.

9. **A** Let the length of the shorter sides of the cards be 1 unit. Then, by Pythagoras' Theorem, the length of the hypotenuse of each card is $\sqrt{1^2 + 1^2} = \sqrt{2}$. 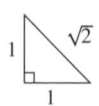
So the lengths of the perimeters of the five figures in order are: $4\sqrt{2}$; $4 + 2\sqrt{2}$; $4 + 2\sqrt{2}$; 6; $4 + 2\sqrt{2}$. Also, as $\left(\frac{3}{2}\right)^2 = \frac{9}{4} = 2\frac{1}{4} > 2$ we see that $\frac{3}{2} > \sqrt{2}$. Therefore, $4\sqrt{2} < 6 < 4 + 2\sqrt{2}$. So figure A has the shortest perimeter.

10. **C** The sum of the interior angles of a pentagon is 540° so $\angle ABC = 540° \div 5 = 108°$. Each interior angle of an equilateral triangle is 60°, so $\angle FBC = 60°$. Therefore $\angle ABF = 108° - 60° = 48°$. As $ABCDE$ is a regular pentagon, $BC = AB$. However, $BC = FB$ since triangle BFC is equilateral.
So triangle ABF is isosceles with $FB = AB$.
Therefore $\angle FAB = \angle AFB = (180° - 48°) \div 2 = 66°$.

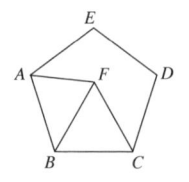

11. **C** We first look at $66 = 2 \times 3 \times 11$. Its factors involve none, one, two or all three of these primes. So the factors are 1, 2, 3, 11, 6, 22, 33, 66; and their sum is $144 = 12^2$. Similarly, we can check that the sum of the factors of 3, 22, 40 and 70 is, respectively, $4 = 2^2$, $36 = 6^2$, 90 and $144 = 12^2$. So 40 is the only alternative for which the sum of the factors is not a square number.

12. **D** As the words 'three' and 'five' contain 5 and 4 letters respectively, their 'sum' will be a 9-letter word. Of the alternatives given, only 'seventeen' contains 9 letters.

13. **B** The diagram shows the top-right-hand portion of the square. The shaded trapezium is labelled $QXYZ$ and W is the point at which ZY produced meets PQ. 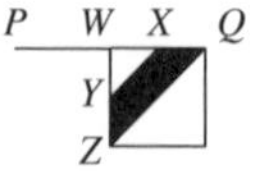
As $QXYZ$ is an isosceles trapezium, $\angle QZY = \angle ZQX = 45°$.
Also, as YX is parallel to ZQ, $\angle XYW = \angle WXY = 45°$. So WYX and WZQ are both isosceles right-angled triangles. As $\angle ZWQ = 90°$ and Z is at the centre of square $PQRS$, we deduce that W is the midpoint of PQ. Hence $WX = XQ = \frac{1}{4}PQ$.
So the ratio of the side-lengths of similar triangles WYX and WZQ is $1 : 2$ and hence the ratio of their areas is $1 : 4$.
Therefore the area of trapezium $QXYZ = \frac{3}{4} \times$ area of triangle $ZWQ = \frac{3}{32} \times$ area $PQRS$ since triangle ZWQ is one-eighth of $PQRS$. So the fraction of the square which is shaded is $4 \times \frac{3}{32} = \frac{3}{8}$.

Intermediate Challenge 2013 solutions

14. D As all the fractions are raised to the power 3, the expression which has the largest value is that with the largest fraction in the brackets. Each of these fractions is a little larger than $1\frac{1}{2}$. Subtracting $1\frac{1}{2}$ from each in turn, we get the fractions $\frac{1}{14}, \frac{1}{6}, \frac{1}{4}, \frac{3}{10}, 0$, the largest of which is $\frac{3}{10}$ (because $0 < \frac{1}{14} < \frac{1}{6} < \frac{1}{4} = \frac{2\frac{1}{2}}{10} < \frac{3}{10}$). Hence $\left(\frac{9}{5}\right)^3$ is the largest.

15. B From the information given, we may deduce that the number of coins is a multiple of each of 3, 5, 7. Since these are distinct primes, their lowest common multiple is $3 \times 5 \times 7 = 105$. So the number of coins in the bag is a multiple of 105. So there are 105 coins in the bag since 105 is the only positive multiple of 105 less than or equal to 200.

16. A The image of a straight line under a rotation is also a straight line. The centre of rotation, the point $(1, 1)$, lies on the given line and so also lies on the image. The given line has slope 1 and so its image will have slope -1. Hence graph A shows the image.

17. D The radius of each disc in the figure is equal to half the side-length of the square, i.e. $\frac{1}{\pi}$. Because the corners of a square are right-angled, the square hides exactly one quarter of each disc. So three-quarters of the perimeter of each disc lies on the perimeter of the figure. Therefore the length of the perimeter is $4 \times \frac{3}{4} \times 2\pi \times \frac{1}{\pi} = 6$.

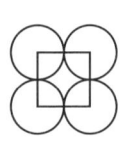

18. C The diagrams show isosceles triangles T and U. The perpendicular from the top vertex to the base divides an isosceles triangle into two congruent right-angled triangles as shown in both T and U. Evidently, by Pythagoras' Theorem, $h_1 = 4$ and $h_2 = 3$. So both triangles T and U consist of two '3, 4, 5' triangles and therefore have equal areas.

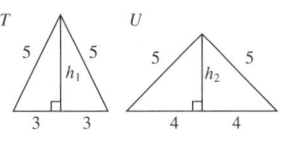

19. E $(x \div (y \div z)) \div ((x \div y) \div z) = \left(x \div \frac{y}{z}\right) \div \left(\left(\frac{x}{y}\right) \div z\right) = \left(x \times \frac{z}{y}\right) \div \left(\frac{x}{y} \times \frac{1}{z}\right)$
$= \frac{xz}{y} \div \frac{x}{yz} = \frac{xz}{y} \times \frac{yz}{x} = z^2$.

20. B Let the base AB of the triangle be the side of length 8 cm and let AC be the side of length 6 cm. So C must lie on the circle with centre A and radius 6 cm as shown. The area of the triangle is to be 7 cm^2, so the perpendicular from C to AB (or to BA produced) must be of length $\frac{7}{4}$ cm.
The diagram shows the four possible positions of C. However, since $\angle BAC_1 = \angle BAC_3$ and $\angle BAC_2 = \angle BAC_4$, these correspond to exactly two possibilities for the length of the third side AC. The diagrams below show the two possibilities.

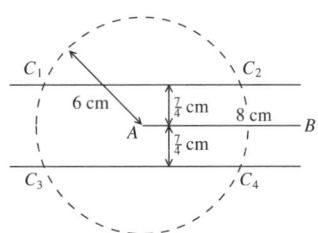

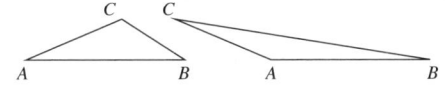

21. **B** The large square has area $196 = 14^2$. So it has side-length 14. The ratio of the areas of the inner squares is $4 : 1$, so the ratio of their side-lengths is $2 : 1$. Let the side-length of the larger inner square be $2x$, so that of the smaller is x. The figure is symmetric about the diagonal AC and so the overlap of the two inner squares is also a square which therefore has side-length 1. Thus the vertical height can be written as $x + 2x - 1$. Hence $3x - 1 = 14$ and so $x = 5$. Also, the two shaded rectangles both have side-lengths $2x - 1$ and $x - 1$; that is 9 and 4. So the total shaded area is 72.

22. **D** Let the radius of each semicircle be r. In the left-hand diagram, let the side-length of the square be $2x$. By Pythagoras' Theorem, $x^2 + (2x)^2 = r^2$ and so $5x^2 = r^2$. So this shaded area is $4x^2 = \frac{4r^2}{5}$. In the right-hand diagram, let the side-length of each square be y. Then by Pythagoras' Theorem, $y^2 + y^2 = r^2$ and so this shaded area is r^2. Therefore the ratio of the two shaded areas is $\frac{4}{5} : 1 = 4 : 5$.

23. **A** If Alfred is telling the truth, the other three are lying (as their statements would then be false) and we know this is not the case. Hence Alfred is lying. Similarly, if Horatio is telling the truth, the other three are lying which again cannot be the case. So Horatio is lying. Hence the two who are telling the truth are Bernard and Inigo. (A case where this situation would be realised would be if the brothers in descending order of age were Alfred, Bernard, Horatio and Inigo.)

24. **B** The length of the side of the triangle is equal to four times the radius of the arcs. So the arcs have radius $2 \div 4 = \frac{1}{2}$. In the first diagram, three semicircles have been shaded dark grey. The second diagram shows how these semicircles may be placed inside the triangle so that the whole triangle is shaded. Therefore the difference between the area of the shaded shape and the area of the triangle is the sum of the areas of three sectors of a circle. The interior angle of an equilateral triangle is $60°$, so the angle at the centre of each sector is $180° - 60° = 120°$. Therefore each sector is equal in area to one-third of the area of a circle. Their combined area is equal to the area of a circle of radius $\frac{1}{2}$. So the required area is $\pi \times \left(\frac{1}{2}\right)^2 = \frac{\pi}{4}$.

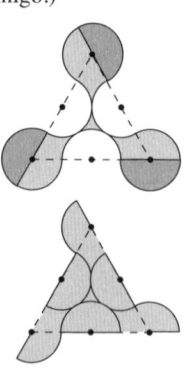

25. **D** $\left(10^{640} - 1\right)$ is a 640-digit number consisting entirely of nines. So $\dfrac{\left(10^{640} - 1\right)}{9}$ is a 640-digit number consisting entirely of ones. Therefore $\dfrac{10^{641} \times \left(10^{640} - 1\right)}{9}$ consists of 640 ones followed by 641 zeros. So $\dfrac{10^{641} \times \left(10^{640} - 1\right)}{9} + 1$ consists of 640 ones followed by 640 zeros followed by a single one. Therefore it has 1281 digits.

Intermediate Challenge
2014 solutions

1. **A**   25% of $\frac{3}{4}$ = $\frac{1}{4} \times \frac{3}{4}$ = $\frac{3}{16}$.

2. **D**   The first four options are the smallest positive integers which are both odd and not prime. However, the next largest odd numbers after 9, 15, 21 are 11, 17, 23 respectively and these are all prime. The next largest odd number after 25 is 27, which is not prime. So 25 is the smallest positive integer which satisfies all three conditions.

3. **E**   Clearly AD lies along one of the lines of symmetry of the figure. So $\angle FDA = \angle EDA = x°$. Triangle DEF is equilateral so $\angle EDF = 60°$.
The angles which meet at a point sum to $360°$, so
$x + x + 60 = 360$.
Therefore $x = 150$.

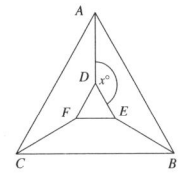

4. **C**   Since m is even, $m = 2k$ for some integer k. So $3m + 4n = 2(3k + 2n)$; $5mn = 2(5kn)$; $m^3n^3 = 8k^3n^3$ and $5m + 6n = 2(5k + 3n)$, which are all even. As n is odd, $3n$ is also odd. So $m + 3n$ is an even integer plus an odd integer and is therefore odd. The square of an odd integer is odd so $(m + 3n)^2$ is odd.

5. **E** In one complete cycle of 4 hours, the clock is struck $1 + 2 + 3 + 4 + 5 + 6 + 7 + 8 = 36$ times. So in 24 hours the clock is struck $6 \times 36 = 216$ times.

6. **E** The large shape consists of 21 small squares, so the required shape is made up of 7 small squares. So A and C may be eliminated. The diagram on the right shows that shape E is as required. It is left to the reader to check that neither B nor D was the shape used.

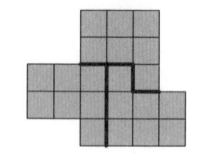

7. **B** Since 6 and 15 are factors of the integer, its prime factors will include 2, 3 and 5. So 10 and 30 will also be factors of the required integer. Seven of its factors are now known and as 1 must also be a factor, the required integer is 30, the factors of which are 1, 2, 3, 5, 6, 10, 15, 30.
(*Positive integers with exactly 8 factors are of the form pqr or pq^3 or p^7 where p, q, r are distinct primes.*)

8. **C** The missing die, if correctly placed in the figure, would show faces 1, 3, 5 placed in a clockwise direction around the nearest corner. An examination of each of the five proposed dice shows that only C has this property.

9. **A** Gill's car uses $p/100$ litres of petrol for every one kilometre travelled. So for a journey of length d km, $pd/100$ litres of petrol are required.

10. **B** A, B, C, D, E are the centres of the five semicircles. Note that AC joins the centres of two touching semicircles and therefore passes through the point of contact of the semicircles. So AC has length $2 + 2 = 4$. This also applies to all of the other sides of triangles ACD and BED. Hence both triangles are equilateral. So each of the nine arcs which make up the perimeter of the shaded shape subtends an angle of $60°$ at the centre of a semicircle. 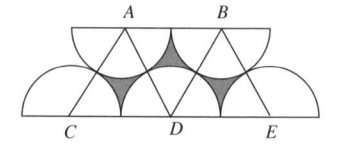
So the length of the perimeter of the shaded figure is $9 \times \frac{1}{6} \times 2 \times \pi \times 2 = 6\pi$.

11. **C** Precisely one of Jenny and Willie is telling the truth since the number of people is either even or odd. Similarly, precisely one of Sam and Mrs Scrubitt is telling the truth since the number of people is either a prime number or a number which is the product of two integers greater than one. So although it is not possible to deduce who is telling the truth, it is possible to deduce that exactly two of them are doing so.

12. **D** Let the width of each strip be 1 unit. Then the triangle has base 8 and perpendicular height 8. So its area is equal to $\frac{1}{2} \times 8 \times 8 = 32$. Looking from the right, the area of the first shaded strip is 1 unit of area less than the first unshaded strip. This difference of 1 unit also applies to the other three pairs of strips in the triangle, which means that the shaded area is 4 less than the unshaded area. So the total shaded area is $\frac{1}{2}(32 - 4) = 14$. Therefore the required fraction is $\frac{14}{32} = \frac{7}{16}$.

Intermediate Challenge 2014 solutions

13. **B** The smallest such number is $1 + 2 = 3$, whilst the largest is $99 + 100 = 199$. Every number between 3 and 199 may be written as $1 + n$ with $n = 2, 3, \ldots, 99$ or as $100 + n$ with $n = 1, \ldots, 99$. So in total there are $(199 - 3) + 1 = 197$ such numbers.

14. **B** Chris Froome's average speed $\approx \frac{3400}{84}$ km/h $\approx \frac{3400}{85}$ km/h $= \frac{200}{5}$ km/h $= 40$ km/h.

15. **E** Let Zac's number be x. Then $\frac{1}{2}x + 8 = 2x - 8$. So $x + 16 = 4x - 16$. Therefore $32 = 3x$, that is $x = 10\frac{2}{3}$.

16. **C** If the areas of the original and new triangles are the same then the product of the base and the perpendicular height must be the same for the two triangles. When the base of the original triangle is increased by 25%, its value is multiplied by $\frac{5}{4}$. So if the area is to remain unchanged then the perpendicular height must be multiplied by $\frac{4}{5}$, which means that its new value is 80% of its previous value. So it is decreased by 20%.

17. **D** The number of minutes in one week is $7 \times 24 \times 60$, which may be written as $7 \times (6 \times 4) \times (5 \times 3 \times 2 \times 2) = (7 \times 6 \times 5 \times 4 \times 3 \times 2) \times 2$. So the number of weeks in $8 \times 7 \times 6 \times 5 \times 4 \times 3 \times 2 \times 1$ minutes is $8 \div 2 = 4$.

18. **B** The point (m, n) is hidden if and only if m and n share a common factor greater than 1. So (6, 2) is hidden by (3, 1) since 6 and 2 have common factor 2. Also (6, 3) is hidden by (2, 1) whilst (6, 4) is hidden by (3, 2). However, 6 and 5 have no common factor other than 1 and therefore (6, 5) is not a hidden point.

19. **C** Note that $8^m = (2^3)^m = 2^{3m} = (2^m)^3$ and $27 = 3^3$; so $2^m = 3$. Therefore $4^m = 2^m \times 2^m = 9$.

20. **D** Each exterior angle of a regular pentagon is $\frac{1}{5} \times 360° = 72°$. So each of the five circular arcs has radius 2 and so subtends an angle of $(180 + 72)°$ at a vertex of the pentagon. Therefore the area of each of the five shaded major sectors is $\frac{252}{360} \times \pi \times 2^2 = \frac{7}{10} \times \pi \times 4 = \frac{14\pi}{5}$. So the total shaded area is 14π.

21. **D** Firstly suppose that any two knights X and Y win x and y bouts respectively and that x is at least as large as y. The difference between their total scores would be the same as if X had won $x - y$ bouts and Y had won none, since each of the separate totals would have been reduced by the same amount, namely $20y$. A similar procedure applies to losses. For example, if X won 3 and lost 6, while Y won 8 and lost 2, the difference between their total scores is the same as if X won 0 and lost 4, while Y won 5 and lost 0. In each case the difference is 32.
This argument shows that, in the case of the Black Knight, B, and the Red Knight, R, the smallest number of bouts will be achieved when one of B, R wins all his bouts and the other loses all his bouts. Also B has to score one more point than R. The possible scores for the knight who wins all his bouts are 20, 40, 60, 80, 100, 120, ... while the possible scores for the knight who loses all his bouts are 17, 34, 51, 68, 85, 102, 119, 136, ...
The first two numbers to differ by 1 are 119 and 120. Thus the Black Knight has a total of 120 corresponding to winning all of his 6 bouts and the Red Knight has a total of 119 corresponding to losing all of his 7 bouts.

22. B Let $a = a_1 a_2$ where a_2 is the largest square dividing a. Note that a_1 is then a product of distinct primes. Similarly write $b = b_1 b_2$ and $c = c_1 c_2$. Since ab is a square, $a_1 b_1$ must be a square; so $a_1 = b_1 = k$ say. Similarly $c_1 = k$. The smallest possible value of k is 2 (since a is not a square); and the smallest possible values for a_2, b_2, c_2 are 1, 4 and 9 in some order. This makes $a + b + c = 2 + 8 + 18 = 28$.

23. A Let the radius of the circle be r and let the angle of the sector be $a°$.
Then the perimeter of the sector is $2r + \frac{a}{360} \times 2\pi r$.
This equals $2\pi r$, the circumference of the original circle.
So $2r + \frac{a}{360} \times 2\pi r = 2\pi r$.
Therefore the fraction of the area of the disc removed is
$\frac{a}{360} = \frac{2\pi r - 2r}{2\pi r} = \frac{\pi - 1}{\pi}$.

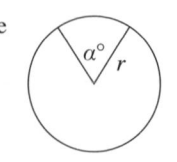

24. A There are 9000 four-digit integers. To calculate the number of these which have four different digits, we note that we have a choice of 9 for the thousands digit. We now have a choice of 9 for the hundreds digit (since we can choose 0 as a possible digit). After these two digits have been chosen, we have a choice of 8 for the tens digit and then 7 for the units digit. So the number of four-digit numbers in which all digits are different is $9 \times 9 \times 8 \times 7$.
Therefore the number of four-digit numbers which have at least one digit repeated is $9000 - 9 \times 9 \times 8 \times 7 = 9(1000 - 9 \times 8 \times 7) = 9 \times 8 \times (125 - 9 \times 7) = 72 \times (125 - 63) = 72 \times 62$.

25. E Let each side of the octagon have length x. The octagon may be divided into eight triangles by joining the centre of the circle to the vertices of the octagon. One such triangle is shown. Each of these triangles has one side of length 1 (the radius of the smaller circle), one side of length 2 (the radius of the larger circle) and one side of length x. So all eight triangles are congruent. Therefore $\angle AOB = 360° \div 8 = 45°$. 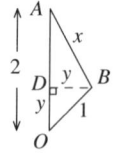
Let D be the foot of the perpendicular from B to AO. Then triangle BDO is an isosceles right-angled triangle.
Let $OD = DB = y$. Applying Pythagoras' Theorem to triangle BDO:
$y^2 + y^2 = 1$. So $y = \frac{1}{\sqrt{2}}$.
Applying Pythagoras' Theorem to triangle ADB:
$x^2 = (2-y)^2 + y^2 = \left(2 - \frac{1}{\sqrt{2}}\right)^2 + \left(\frac{1}{\sqrt{2}}\right)^2 = 4 - 2 \times 2 \times \frac{1}{\sqrt{2}} + \frac{1}{2} + \frac{1}{2} = 5 - \frac{4}{\sqrt{2}} = 5 - 2\sqrt{2}$.
So the length of the perimeter is $8x = 8\sqrt{5 - 2\sqrt{2}}$.
(Note that the length of AB may also be found by applying the Cosine Rule to triangle OAB.)

Intermediate Challenge 2015 solutions

1. **A** $1 - 0.2 + 0.03 - 0.004 = 0.8 + 0.026 = 0.826$.

2. **E** The number of steps climbed per minute $\sim \dfrac{1600}{12} = \dfrac{400}{3} \sim 130$.

3. **E** Half of a third, plus a third of a quarter, plus a quarter of a fifth equals
$\dfrac{1}{6} + \dfrac{1}{12} + \dfrac{1}{20} = \dfrac{10 + 5 + 3}{60} = \dfrac{18}{60} = \dfrac{3}{10}$.

4. **C** The sum of the exterior angles of a convex polygon equals 360°. The angle marked $p°$ is the exterior angle of a regular pentagon. So $p = 360 \div 5 = 72$. The angle sum of a triangle equals 180°, so $q = 180 - 90 - 72 = 18$. The angle marked $r°$ is the interior angle of a regular pentagon, so $r = 180 - 72 = 108$. The angles marked $q°, r°$ and $x°$ lie along a straight line, so $x = 180 - (q + r) = 180 - (18 + 108) = 54$.

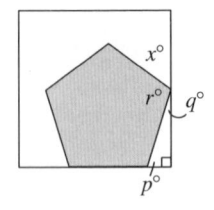

5. **B** $1^6 = (1^3)^2, 3^4 = (3^2)^2, 4^3 = 64 = 8^2$ and 5^2 are all squares. However, $2^5 = 32$ and is not a square.

6. **D** Let the length of the side of the regular hexagon be a. Then its perimeter is $6a$. Therefore the perimeter of the equilateral triangle is also $6a$, so the length of each of its sides is $2a$. The diagrams show that the equilateral triangle may be divided up into 4 equilateral triangles of side a, whereas the regular hexagon may be divided into 6 such triangles. So the required ratio is $4 : 6 = 2 : 3$.

7. **E** The tetrahedron has 6 edges and 4 vertices, so the required product is $6 \times 4 = 24$.

8. **B** The two-digit squares are 16, 25, 36, 49, 64 and 81. Of these, only 49 and 81 differ by 1 from a multiple of 10.

9. **B** The sum of the exterior angles of a convex polygon equals 360°. Therefore $p + r + t + v + x = 360°$. Similarly, $q + s + u + w + y = 360°$. Therefore $p + q + r + s + t + u + v + w + x + y = 720°$.

10. **C** $2^2 \times 3^3 \times 5^5 \times 7^7$ is of the form $2^2 \times$ an odd number. It therefore has the form $4(2n + 1) = 8n + 4$ where n is a positive integer and so leaves a remainder of 4 when divided by 8.

11. **D** As the 3 numbers have mean 7, their sum equals $3 \times 7 = 21$. For one of the numbers to be as large as possible the other two numbers must be as small as possible. They must also be different and so must be 1 and 2. Hence the largest possible of the three numbers equals $21 - (1 + 2) = 18$.

12. **D** If the ant moves alternately from white square to black square and from black to white, then it will end on a white square after 4 moves. So it must find a way to move from white to white or from black to black. However, there is only one pair of adjacent black squares and only one of white. To reach that pair of black squares, the ant must move to one side then climb up to one of the pair. That uses up 3 moves, and the fourth must take it to the other black square of that pair. Thus the two black squares in that pair are possible end points.

If, instead, the ant uses the white pair, it must first move to one side, then climb up to one of the white pair then across to the other square of that pair. That uses 3 moves. The fourth move can then take it to any of the three adjoining black squares. This gives 6 end squares, but these include the two already identified. So there are just 6 possible end squares which are black.

Intermediate Challenge 2015 solutions 199

13. A Three vertical lines have been added to the diagram. These divide the original diagram into 4 rectangles. In each of these, a diagonal divides the rectangle into two triangles of equal area, one shaded and one unshaded. So the total shaded area in the original rectangle is equal to the total unshaded area and is therefore equal to half the area of the original rectangle. So the total shaded area is $\frac{1}{2} \times 3 \times 14\,\text{cm}^2 = 21\,\text{cm}^2$.

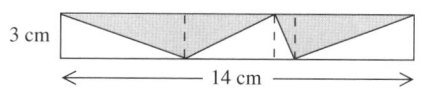

14. C Suppose the first three terms of the sequence are a, b, c. Then $c = \frac{1}{2}(a + b)$ and so $a + b = 2c$. The mean of the first three terms is then $\frac{1}{3}(a + b + c) = \frac{1}{3}(2c + c) = c$, so the fourth term is c. Similarly, the following terms are all equal to c. Since one of these terms is 26 and $a = 8$ then $b = 2c - a = 52 - 8 = 44$.

15. C The stripes are of equal width, so the width of each stripe is $(72 \div 6)\,\text{cm} = 12\,\text{cm}$. The diagram shows that the difference between the areas of any two adjacent stripes is equal to the area of a rectangle of width 12 cm and height h cm. By similar triangles, $\frac{h}{12} = \frac{24}{72}$. So $h = \frac{12 \times 24}{72} = 4$. So the required area is $12 \times 4\,\text{cm}^2 = 48\,\text{cm}^2$.

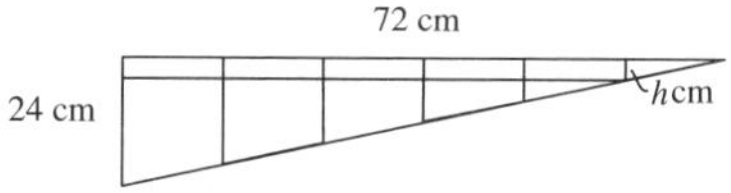

16. D All four values cannot be prime. If this were so, both $m \times n$ and $m \div n$ would be prime which can happen only if m is prime and $n = 1$. If m is an odd prime then $m + 1$ is even and at least 4, hence not prime, while if $m = 2$ then $m - 1$ is not prime but $m + 1 = 3$ is. Thus three prime values are the most we can have.

17. D The 12 pentagonal panels have a total of $12 \times 5 = 60$ edges. The 20 hexagonal panels have a total of $20 \times 6 = 120$ edges. So in total the panels have 180 edges. When the panels are sewn together, two edges form each join. So the number of joins is $180 \div 2 = 90$.

18. A Let the weights in kg of the box, 1 plate and 1 cup be b, p and c respectively. Then: $b + 20p + 30c = 4.8$ (i); $b + 40p + 50c = 8.4$ (ii). Subtracting (i) from (ii): $20p + 20c = 3.6$ (iii). So $10p + 10c = 1.8$ (iv). Subtracting (iv) from (i): $b + 10p + 20c = 3$. So the required weight is 3 kg.

19. A The small numbers in the figure show the lengths in cm of each line segment. The larger numbers inside the figure show the areas in cm² of each square or trapezium. (The area of a trapezium is $\frac{1}{2}(a + b)h$ where a and b are the lengths of the parallel sides and h is the perpendicular distance between them.) So the area of the shaded portion in cm² is $11 \times 11 - (1 + 12 + 4 + 15 + 9 + 14 + 16 + 15) = 35$. (See the extended solutions for a beautifully elegant solution of this problem.)

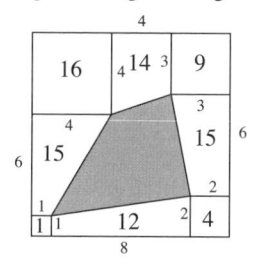

20. C There are 3 different possibilities for the first character. The second character may be any digit from 0 to 9 inclusive, so it has 10 different possibilities. The third character differs from the second digit, so has 9 different possibilities. Once the second and third characters are determined, the fourth character is also determined since it is the units digit of the sum of the second and third characters.
So, the number of different codes is $3 \times 10 \times 9 = 270$.

21. D Let the area of each rectangle be Y. Then the total shaded area is $2(Y - X) + X = 2Y - X$. Therefore $X = \frac{1}{8}(2Y - X)$. So $8X = 2Y - X$, that is $9X = 2Y$. Therefore $\frac{X}{Y} = \frac{2}{9}$.

22. B Let the length of the sides of each small square be x. Then the shaded area is $24x^2$. Let the perimeter of the square be divided into eight line segments, each of length y, and four line segments of length z. Some of these are labelled in the diagram. By Pythagoras' Theorem in triangle ABC:
$y^2 + y^2 = (5x)^2$, that is $2y^2 = 25x^2$. 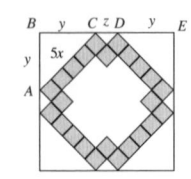
So $y = \frac{5}{\sqrt{2}}x = \frac{5\sqrt{2}}{2}x$. Similarly, in the triangle with hypotenuse CD:
$x^2 + x^2 = z^2$, that is $2x^2 = z^2$. So $z = \sqrt{2}x$. Therefore the length of the side of the large square is $2y + z = 5\sqrt{2}x + \sqrt{2}x = 6\sqrt{2}x$. So the area of the large square is $(6\sqrt{2}x)^2 = 72x^2$. Hence the required fraction is $\frac{24x^2}{72x^2} = \frac{1}{3}$.

23. B The permutations which follow UKIMC in dictionary order are UKMCI, UKMIC, UMCIK, UMCKI, UMICK, UMIKC, UMKCI, UMKIC. There are eight of these, so UKIMC is 112th in the list.

24. E In the diagram V is the point where the perpendicular from P meets TS. Let the side of the square $RSTU$ be x. So the radius of the arc from R to T is x. Therefore SP has length x, PV has length $x - 8$ and VS has length $x - 1$. Applying Pythagoras' Theorem to triangle PVS:
$(x - 8)^2 + (x - 1)^2 = x^2$. So $x^2 - 16x + 64 + x^2 - 2x + 1 = x^2$.
Therefore $x^2 - 18x + 65 = 0$, so $(x - 5)(x - 13) = 0$. 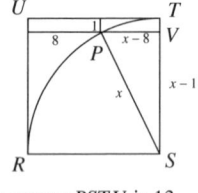
Hence $x = 5$ or $x = 13$, but $x > 8$ so the length of the side of the square $RSTU$ is 13.

25. D Points A, B, C, D, E, F on the perimeter of the triangle are as shown. Let AD have length x so that DB has length $3x$. Let the perpendicular from C to AB have length $4h$. So, by similar triangles, the perpendicular from E to DB has length h. The area of triangle ABC is $\frac{1}{2} \times 4x \times 4h = 8xh$. The area of triangle DBE is $\frac{1}{2} \times 3x \times h = \frac{3}{2}xh$.
So the area of triangle DBE is $\frac{3}{16}$ of the area of triangle ABC. 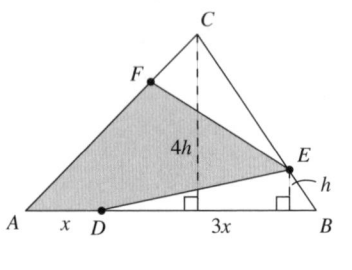
Similarly, by drawing perpendiculars to CB from A and from F, it may be shown that the area of triangle FEC is $\frac{3}{16}$ of the area of triangle ABC.
So the fraction of the area of the triangle that is shaded is $1 - \frac{3}{16} - \frac{3}{16} = \frac{5}{8}$.

Intermediate Challenge
2016 solutions

1. **B** $6116 - 2016 = 4100$, so $6102 - 2016 = 4100 - 14 = 4086$.
2. **D** The difference between the given options and 1 is $\frac{1}{8}, \frac{1}{7}, \frac{1}{10}, \frac{1}{11}$ and $\frac{1}{10}$ respectively. As $\frac{1}{11}$ is the smallest of these fractions, $\frac{10}{11}$ is closest to 1.
3. **B** The values of the five expressions are 5, 13, 25, 41 and 61 respectively. Of these, only 25 is non-prime.

4. **E** Amrita bakes every 5 days and Thursdays come every 7 days. So the next time Amrita bakes on a Thursday will be in 35 days time since 35 is the lowest common multiple of 5 and 7.

5. **A** By train, the distance in miles of the second sign from Edinburgh is $200 - 3\frac{1}{2}$. This sign is halfway between London and Edinburgh, so the distance in miles between the two cities is $2(200 - 3\frac{1}{2}) = 400 - 7 = 393$.

6. **C** Let g and s be the number of goats and sheep respectively. Then $s = 2g$ and $12 = s - g = 2g - g = g$. Hence the number of animals is $s + g = 3g = 36$.

7. **C** The angles at a point sum to $360°$ so $75 + z = 360$ and $y + x = 360$. Therefore $75 + z + y + x = 720$. The sum of the interior angles of a hexagon is $4 \times 180° = 720°$. Therefore $27 + 24 + y + 23 + 26 + z = 720$, so $75 + z + y + x = 27 + 24 + y + 23 + 26 + z$. Hence $75 + x = 27 + 24 + 23 + 26 = 100$. So $x = 100 - 75 = 25$.

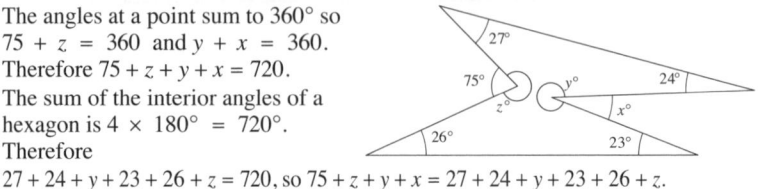

8. **E** $2.017 \times 2016 - 10.16 \times 201.7 = 201.7 \times 20.16 - 10.16 \times 201.7$
   $= 201.7(20.16 - 10.16) = 201.7 \times 10 = 2017$.

9. **C** Bertie travelled 5.5 m in 19.6 s, which is just less than one-third of a minute. So his average speed was approximately 16.5 m per minute, which is equal to 990 m in one hour, as $16.5 \times 60 = 990$. Now 990 m = 0.99 km, so Bertie's approximate average speed was 1 km per hour.

10. **E** The sum of the interior angles of a quadrilateral is $360°$, so $x + 5x + 2x + 4x = 360$, that is $12x = 360$. Therefore $x = 30$ and the angles of the quadrilateral, taken in order, are $30°$, $150°$, $60°$ and $120°$. The diagram shows the shape of the quadrilateral. Since $30 + 150 = 180$, we see that AB and DC are parallel. Since it has no equal angles, it is not a rhombus or a parallelogram so it is a trapezium.

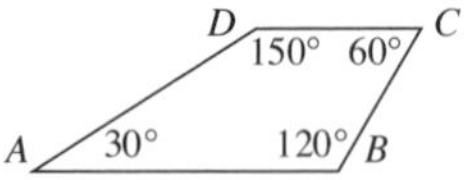

11. **D** When the net is folded up to form the rhombicuboctahedron, the left-hand edge of the square marked X is joined to the right-hand edge of the square marked E so that the eight squares at the centre of the net form a band around the solid. In this band, the square opposite square P is the square which is four squares away from P, that is square D. So if the square marked P is placed face down on a table, then the square marked D will be facing up.

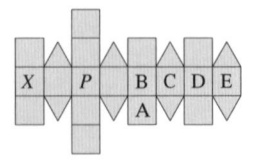

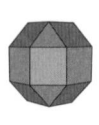

12. **D** Assume that $a > b$. Then $a + b = 7$ and $a - b = 2$. Adding these two equations together gives $2a = 9$. So $a = \frac{9}{2}$ and hence $b = 7 - \frac{9}{2} = \frac{14-9}{2} = \frac{5}{2}$. Therefore $a \times b = \frac{9}{2} \times \frac{5}{2} = \frac{45}{4} = 11\frac{1}{4}$.

Intermediate Challenge 2016 solutions   203

13. **B** In the seven lines each of the integers from 1 to 7 is used twice and each of the integers from 8 to 14 is used once. So the sum of the numbers in the seven lines is $(1 + 2 + \ldots +14) + (1 + 2 + \ldots +7) = 105 + 28 = 133$. Therefore the total of the numbers in each line is $133 \div 7 = 19$.
It is left as an exercise for the reader to show that it is possible to complete the diagram so that the total of the three numbers in each line is indeed 19.

14. **D** Let there be g girls and b boys in Tegwen's family. Then, as she has the same number of brothers as she does sisters, $b = g - 1$. Also, each of her brothers has 50% more sisters than brothers. Therefore $g = \frac{3}{2}(b - 1)$. So $b + 1 = \frac{3}{2}(b - 1)$ and hence $2b + 2 = 3b - 3$. Rearranging this equation gives $b = 5$. So $g = 5 + 1 = 6$. Therefore there are $5 + 6 = 11$ children in Tegwen's family.

15. **A** Let the length of the side of the square be $2x$ cm. Then, using Pythagoras' Theorem in the triangle shown, $(2x)^2 + x^2 = 1^2$. So $4x^2 + x^2 = 1$. Therefore $x^2 = \frac{1}{5}$ and the area of the square is $4x^2$ cm$^2 = \frac{4}{5}$ cm^2.

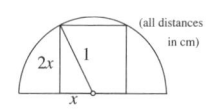

16. **B** The prime factorisation of $24 = 2^3 \times 3$. Therefore all multiples of 24 must include both 2^3 and 3 in their prime factorisation. Of the options given, only the last includes 2^3. As it is also a multiple of 3, it is a multiple of 24.

17. **B** Let the radius of the dashed circle be r cm. Then one of the equal areas is bounded by circles of radii of 14 cm and r cm, whilst the other is bounded by circles of radii of r cm and 2 cm. So $\pi \times 14^2 - \pi r^2 = \pi r^2 - \pi \times 2^2$. Dividing throughout by π gives $196 - r^2 = r^2 - 4$. So $2r^2 = 200$, that is $r^2 = 100$. Therefore $r = 10$ (since $r > 0$).

18. **C** Let the length of each of the shorter sides of the triangle be x cm and the length of its hypotenuse be y cm. Then, by Pythagoras' Theorem: $x^2 + x^2 = y^2$. So $y^2 = 2x^2$. Also, $x^2 + x^2 + y^2 = 72$, so $4x^2 = 72$, that is $x^2 = 18$. Now the area of the triangle, in cm^2, is $\frac{1}{2} \times x \times x = \frac{1}{2}x^2 = 9$.

19. **B** From the information given, there are at least two 9s in the list, since 9 is the mode, and at least one number greater than 10, since 10 is the mean. So there are at least three numbers greater than 8 in the list. Therefore the list must contain at least six numbers, as the median of the numbers is 8. Moreover, it is possible to find suitable lists of six numbers with sum 60 (as the mean is 10), for example 1, 2, 7, 9, 9, 32.

20. **D** In the diagram, O is the centre of the lower semicircle, A and C are the points of intersection of the two semicircles and B is the point at the centre of the rectangle and also of the overlap. Now OA is a radius of the semicircle so OA has length 5 cm. Also OB is half the height of the rectangle so has length 4 cm. Angle ABO is a right angle. So triangle ABO is a (3, 4, 5) triangle and hence $AC = 2 \times 3 \text{ cm} = 6 \text{ cm}$.

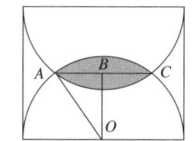

21. **A** Let a be the side length of the octagon and b be as shown on the diagram. The square in the centre is a by a, each rectangle is a by b and the triangles are each half of a b by b square. Applying Pythagoras' Theorem to a triangle shows that $a^2 = 2b^2$. So the shaded area is $b^2 + ab = b^2 + \sqrt{2}b^2 = b^2(1 + \sqrt{2})$. Similarly the total area of the figure is $a^2 + 4ab + 2b^2 = 4b^2 + 4\sqrt{2}b^2 = b^2(4 + 4\sqrt{2})$. Therefore the ratio required is $(1 + \sqrt{2}) : (4 + 4\sqrt{2}) = 1 : 4$.

22. **E** For brevity, let T denote a truth teller and L a liar. Clearly each T has to have an L on each side. Each L either (i) has a T on each side or (ii) has an L on one side and a T on the other side. The largest number of Ts will occur if (i) is always the case. This gives the arrangement TLTLTL… which, since 2 divides 2016, joins up correctly after going round the table. In this case the number of Ts is $\frac{1}{2} \times 2016$. The smallest will occur if case (ii) always is the case. This gives the arrangement LLTLLTLLT… which, since 3 divides 2016, also joins up correctly. In this case the number of Ts is $\frac{1}{3} \times 2016$. The difference is $\frac{1}{6} \times 2016 = 336$.

23. **B** The diagram shows part of the figure, to which have been added A and C, centres of two of the quarter-circle arcs, B and D, points of intersection of two arcs, and E, the centre of the small circle. In cm, the radii of each arc and the small circle are R and r respectively. Firstly, note that $\angle BCD$ is a right angle as arc BD is a quarter of a circle. Therefore, by Pythagoras' Theorem $R^2 + R^2 = 2^2$ so $R = \sqrt{2}$. Consider triangle ACE: from the symmetry of the figure we deduce that $\angle AEC = \frac{1}{4} \times 360° = 90°$. So, by Pythagoras' Theorem $(R + r)^2 + (R + r)^2 = (2R)^2 = 4R^2$. Therefore $(R + r)^2 = 2R^2 = 2 \times 2 = 4$. Hence $R + r = 2$, so $r = 2 - R = 2 - \sqrt{2}$.

(all distances in cm)

24. **C** Let the distance from the bottom of the escalator to the top be d. Then, when she stands still, Aimee travels $d/60$ every second. When she is walking, Aimee travels $d/90$ every second. So when Aimee walks up the working escalator, the distance which she travels every second is $\dfrac{d}{60} + \dfrac{d}{90} = \dfrac{3d + 2d}{180} = \dfrac{5d}{180} = \dfrac{d}{36}$. So the required number of seconds is 36.

25. **D** The tiled area may be considered to be a tessellation of the figure shown, except for the dotted lines. For every hexagonal tile, there are two triangular tiles. The diagram shows that the area of each hexagonal tile is 24 times the area of each triangular tile. As there are two triangular tiles to each hexagonal tile, the ratio of the fraction of the floor shaded black to that which is shaded grey is $2 : 24 = 1 : 12$. Therefore, in the repeating pattern of tiles, the fraction which is shaded black is 1/13.

The exact ratios given are for the infinite plane. Since we are dealing with a finite floor, this is approximate since the edges are unpredictable, but close to correct since the numbers involved are large.

Senior Challenge 2006 solutions

1. **E** The resulting length of the bedframe would be 80% of 2.10 m, that is 1.68 m.

2. **A** Subtracting the second equation from the first: $6x - y - (6y - x) = 21 - 14$. So $7x - 7y = 7$, that is $x - y = 1$.
(*The equations may be solved to give $x = 4, y = 3$, but it is not necessary to do this in order to find the value of $x - y$.*)

3. **A** The overlapping region of the two squares is bounded by a pentagon. Two of the interior angles of this pentagon are vertically opposite the given angles of size $x°$ and $y°$, whilst the other three interior angles are all right angles. So $x + y + 3 \times 90 = 540$, that is $x + y = 270$.
(*The diagram on the right also demonstrates that $x + y = 270$.*)

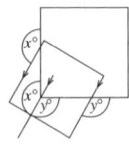

4. **C** $\sqrt{2^4 + \sqrt{3^4}} = \sqrt{16 + \sqrt{81}} = \sqrt{16 + 9} = \sqrt{25} = 5$.

5. **A** As 2006 is not a leap year, January 1st, 2007 will fall one day later in the week than January 1st, 2006, that is on a Monday. So there will be 53 Mondays in 2007 and 52 of each of the other days of the week.

6. **D** $1 \times 2 \times (3 \oplus 4 + 5) \times (6 \times 7 + 8 + 9) = 2006$, that is $2 \times (3 \oplus 4 + 5) \times (42 + 8 + 9) = 2006$, that is $(3 \oplus 4 + 5) \times 59 = 1003$, that is $3 \oplus 4 + 5 = 17$, that is $3 \oplus 4 = 12$. So $\oplus$ should be replaced by $\times$.

7. **B** The pyramid has $2n$ edges and $n + 1$ faces, so the required difference is $2n - (n + 1)$, that is $n - 1$.

8. **C** Matt black paint reflects 3% of light, so the superblack paint reflects only 0.3% of light. Hence it absorbs 99.7% of light.

9. **C** Each spoke of the London Eye is about $\frac{1}{20}$ mile long. As 1 mile is approximately 1600 m, this means that the radius of the giant wheel is roughly 80 m. So the circumference is approximately 500 m.

10. **B** Let a, b, c, d, e, f be the numbers in the squares shown. Then the sum of the numbers in the four lines is $1 + 2 + 3 + \ldots + 9 + b + n + e$ since each of the numbers in the corner squares appears in exactly one row and one column. So $45 + b + n + e = 4 \times 13 = 52$, that is $b + n + e = 7$. Hence b, n, e are 1, 2, 4 in some order.
If $b = 2$ then $a = 2$; if $b = 4$ then $a = 0$. Both cases are impossible, so $b = 1$ and $a = 3$.
This means that $n = 2$ or $n = 4$. However, if $n = 2$ then $c = 10$, so $n = 4$ and $c = 8$.
(*The values of the other letters are $e = 2, d = 7, f = 6$.*)

11. **E** Let the smallest of the three even numbers be n. Then the other two numbers are $n + 2$ and $n + 4$. So $4n + 2(n + 4) = 3(n + 2) + 2006$, that is $6n + 8 = 3n + 2012$, that is $n = 668$.

12. **E** It is necessary to test only $n = 2, n = 3, n = 5$ since the other two possible values are not prime. $2! + 1 = 3$, which is prime; $3! + 1 = 7$, which is prime; but $5! + 1 = 121$, which is not prime. So $n = 5$ provides the counterexample.

13. **D** Disc A may have any one of three colours and, for each of these, disc B may have two colours. So these two discs may be coloured in six different ways.
If discs C and D have the same colour, then they may be coloured in two different ways and, for each of these, disc E may have two colours. So the discs may be coloured in 24 different ways if C and D are the same colour. However, if discs C and D are different

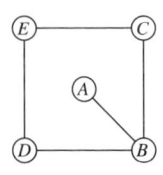

Senior Challenge 2006 solutions

colours, then C may have one of two colours, but the colours of discs D and E are then determined. So the discs may be coloured in 12 different ways if C and D are different colours. In total, therefore, the discs may be coloured in 36 different ways.

14. B Let Rachel and Heather have x and x^2 pennies respectively. So $x + x^2 = 100n$, where x and n are positive integers. We require, therefore, that $x(x + 1) = 100n = 2^2 \times 5^2 \times n$. Now x and $x + 1$ cannot both be multiples of 5, so their product will be a multiple of 25 if and only if x or $x + 1$ is a multiple of 25. The smallest value of x which satisfies this condition is 24 which is a multiple of 4 so 24×25 is a multiple of 100. Therefore Rachel has 24 pennies, Heather has 576 pennies and, in total, they have £6.

15. C Let O be the centre of square $PQRS$. The medians of triangle PSR intersect at T so $OT = \frac{1}{3}OS$.
Hence the area of triangle PTR is one third of the area of triangle PSR, that is one sixth of the area of square $PQRS$. So the required fraction = $\frac{1}{6} + \frac{1}{2} = \frac{2}{3}$.

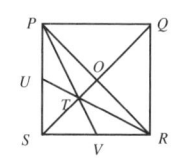

16. C As $\alpha + \beta = 90°$, $\sin \alpha = \cos \beta$; $\cos \alpha = \sin \beta$. So $\sin \alpha \sin \beta = \sin \alpha \cos \alpha$; $\sin \alpha \cos \beta = \sin^2 \alpha$; $\cos \alpha \sin \beta = \cos^2 \alpha$; $\cos \alpha \cos \beta = \cos \alpha \sin \alpha$. As $\alpha < \beta$, $\alpha \neq 45°$. So $\sin \alpha \neq \cos \alpha$. Thus three of the four expressions have different values.

17. E The trapezium in question is shown as $ABCD$ in the diagram. The coordinates of its vertices are $A(0, k), B(0, 2), C(4, 5), D(4, k)$. Using Pythagoras' Theorem: $BC = \sqrt{4^2 + 3^2} = 5$.
The perimeter of $ABCD = (2 - k) + 5 + (5 - k) + 4 = 16 - 2k$.
The area of $ABCD = 4(2 - k) + \frac{1}{2} \times 4 \times 3 = 14 - 4k$. So $16 - 2k = 14 - 4k$, that is $k = -1$.
(*In the diagram it was assumed that $k > 0$, although it transpires that $k < 0$. However, this does not affect the validity of the solution.*)

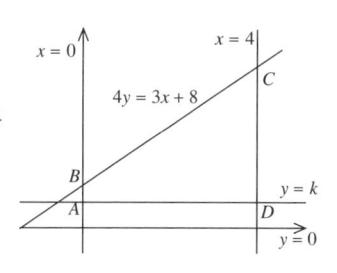

18. D It is not possible for all five statements to be true at the same time since if $a < b, a < 0$, $b < 0$ are all true then $\frac{1}{a} < \frac{1}{b}$ is not true since $\frac{1}{b} - \frac{1}{a} = \frac{a-b}{ab}$ which is negative. However, when these three statements are true, $a^2 > b^2$ is also true, so it is possible for four of the statements to be true at the same time.

19. C Let the length of the tunnel and the distance from the front of the train to the entrance of the tunnel when the engineer receives the warning be l and x respectively. If the engineer runs to the exit of the tunnel, he will take three times as long as he would if he ran to the entrance. So the train takes three times as long to travel a distance $x + l$ as it does to travel a distance x. Hence $l = 2x$. The train, therefore, travels a distance x in the same time that the engineer would take to travel $\frac{1}{4}l$, that is to travel $\frac{1}{2}x$. So the speed of the train is twice that of the engineer.

20. D Adding all three equations: $x + [y] + \{z\} + y + [z] + \{x\} + z + [x] + \{y\} = 4.2 + 3.6 + 2.0 = 9.8$.
Now $[x] + \{x\} = x$, $[y] + \{y\} = y$, $[z] + \{z\} = z$, so $2x + 2y + 2z = 9.8$, that is $x + y + z = 4.9$.
Therefore: $x + y + z - (x + [y] + \{z\}) = 4.9 - 4.2$, that is $\{y\} + [z] = 0.7$. So $[z] = 0$, $\{y\} = 0.7$.
(*It is not necessary to find the values of x, y, z to solve this problem, but their values may be shown to be* 1.9, 2.7, 0.3 *respectively.*)

21. **B** The route of the ball is $A \to B \to C \to S$. The diagram also shows point D, the reflection of point A in PQ, and point E, the reflection of point S in QR. As the ball bounces off a side at the same angle at which it hits that side, points D, B, C, E lie in a straight line. Triangles DPB and DSE are similar since both are right-angled and they have a common angle at D. So $\frac{BP}{PD} = \frac{ES}{SD} = \frac{6}{7}$. Hence $BP = \frac{6}{7}$.

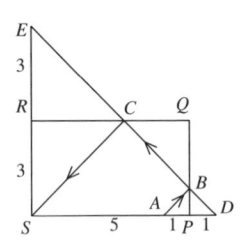

22. **A** The terms on the left-hand side of the equation form an arithmetic progression which has $n^3 - 5$ terms. So the sum of these terms is $\frac{n^3 - 5}{2}\left(\frac{3}{n^3} + \frac{n^3 - 3}{n^3}\right) = \frac{n^3 - 5}{2}$. Hence $n^3 - 5 = 120$, so $n = 5$.

23. **D** Let the vertices of the square be A, B, C, D and the centres of the circle and the two semicircles be P, Q, R, as shown. The midpoint of QR is S. By symmetry, P and S both lie on diagonal BD of square $ABCD$ and the whole figure is symmetrical about BD. As P is distance 1 from both AD and DC, the length of DP is $\sqrt{2}$. As the circles and semicircles are mutually tangent, PQR is an equilateral triangle of side 2, so the length of PS is $\sqrt{3}$. As angles QBS and BSQ are 45° and 90° respectively, triangle SBQ is isosceles, so $SB = SQ = 1$. Hence the length of BD is $\sqrt{2} + \sqrt{3} + 1$. Now the length of the side of the square is $BD \div \sqrt{2}$ so the perimeter of the square is $4 \times (BD \div \sqrt{2})$, that is $2\sqrt{2} \times BD$. So the perimeter is $2\sqrt{2}(\sqrt{2} + \sqrt{3} + 1)$, that is $4 + 2\sqrt{6} + 2\sqrt{2}$.

24. **A** Let O be the centre of the cube. Consider triangle ABO: from Pythagoras' Theorem, $OA = AB = BO = \sqrt{\left(\frac{1}{2}\right)^2 + \left(\frac{1}{2}\right)^2}$ cm $= \frac{1}{\sqrt{2}}$ cm. So triangle OAB is equilateral. A similar argument may be applied to triangles OBC, OCD etc. The area of each of these equilateral triangles is $\frac{1}{2} \times \frac{1}{\sqrt{2}} \times \frac{1}{\sqrt{2}} \times \sin 60°$ cm^2, that is $\frac{1}{8}\sqrt{3}$ cm^2. So the area of hexagon $ABCDEF$ is $6 \times \frac{\sqrt{3}}{8}$ cm^2. However, the total red area exposed by the cut is twice the area of this hexagon, that is $\frac{3\sqrt{3}}{2}$ cm^2.

25. **E** Let X consist of x digits, each of which is 1. So $X = \frac{10^x - 1}{9}$. Let $pX^2 + qX + r$ consist of y digits, each of which is 1. So $pX^2 + qX + r = \frac{10^y - 1}{9}$. Then $p\left(\frac{10^x - 1}{9}\right)^2 + q\left(\frac{10^x - 1}{9}\right) + r = \frac{10^y - 1}{9}$, that is $p(10^{2x} - 2 \times 10^x + 1) + 9q(10^x - 1) + 81r = 9(10^y - 1)$, that is (on dividing throughout by 10^{2x}) $p + (9q - 2p)10^{-x} + (p - 9q + 81r)10^{-2x} = 9 \times 10^{y-2x} - 9 \times 10^{-2x}$. We now let x tend to infinity (through integer values). The LHS of the above equation tends to p, and the second term on the right goes to 0. By continuity of the function $f(u) = 10^u = e^{u \log 10}$, we can deduce that $y - 2x$ must tend to a limit. Let this limit be L. Since $y - 2x$ is always an integer, it must actually equal L for all x sufficiently large. Passing to the limit, therefore, we obtain $p = 9 \times 10^L$. Since p is to be an integer, we must have that L (also an integer) is a non-negative integer. Substituting for p in the previous equation and simplifying leads to

$$9q - 18 \times 10^L + (9 \times 10^L - 9q + 81r)10^{-x} = -9 \times 10^{-x}.$$

Passing to the limit again leads to $q = 2 \times 10^L$ and the previous line then also gives $9 \times 10^L - 18 \times 10^L + 81r = -9$. So $r = \frac{10^L - 1}{9}$.

Possible values of (p, q, r) therefore are (9, 2, 0), (90, 20, 1), (900, 200, 11), etc. So of the values given in the question for q, only $q = 2$ is possible.

(*Observe that the three triples above correspond to* $L = 0, L = 1, L = 2$ *respectively and we note that increasing L by 1 corresponds to multiplying $pX^2 + qX + r$ by 10 and adding 1. As $pX^2 + qX + r$ consists only of* 1s, $10(pX^2 + qX + r) + 1$ *will also consist only of* 1s, *explaining why there is an infinite family of quadratics which satisfy the required condition.*)

Senior Challenge 2007 solutions

1. **C** $\dfrac{2007}{9} + \dfrac{7002}{9} = \dfrac{9009}{9} = 1001$.

2. **A** If Sam's birthday falls before 9 November, then the fact that she is aged 30 on 8 November means that she was born in 1977. However, if her birthday falls on 9 November or later then her 31st birthday will fall in 2007, which means that she was born in 1976.

3. **B** In general, $(n-1) \times (n+1) - n^2 = n^2 - 1 - n^2 = -1$. This applies with $n = 2007$.

4. **C** $\angle WPQ = 120°$ (interior angle of a regular hexagon), so $\angle WPS = (360 - 120 - 90)° = 150°$. Now $PW = PQ$ (sides of a regular hexagon) and $PS = PQ$ (sides of a square) so $PW = PS$. Therefore triangle PSW is isosceles and $\angle PSW = (180 - 150)° \div 2 = 15°$.

5. **E** $4^4 = (2^2)^4 = 2^8$; $8^{8/3} = (2^3)^{8/3} = 2^8$; $16^2 = (2^4)^2 = 2^8$. However, $32^{6/5} = (2^5)^{6/5} = 2^6$.

6. **A** Let the number of five-pence coins be x. Then $5x + 2(50 - x) = 181$, that is $3x = 81$, that is $x = 27$. So there are 27 five-pence coins and 23 two-pence coins.

7. **D** There are 1003 whole numbers between 1 and 2007 which are divisible by 2. Those which are also divisible by 7 are the multiples of 14, namely 14, 28, 42, ..., 2002. There are 143 of these, so the required number is $1003 - 143 = 860$.

8. **E** The distance travelled to Birmingham by the train was 300 km. The time taken to travel this distance at an average speed of 90 km/hr is $\tfrac{300}{90}$ hr = $3\tfrac{1}{3}$ hr = 3 hr 20 min. So the train was waiting for 20 minutes.

9. **E** Let the original cost price and original selling price of the dress be C and S respectively. Then $0.8 \times S = 1.04 \times C$. So $S = \tfrac{1.04}{0.8} \times C = 1.3 \times C$. Therefore the shopkeeper would have made a profit of 30% by selling the dress at its original price.

10. **B** The volume of water which fell at Sprinkling Tarn in 1954 is approximately equal to $(25\,000 \times 6)$ m³, that is 150 000 m³. Now 1 m³ = 10^6 cm³ = 10^6 ml = 1000 litres. So approximately 150 million litres of water fell on Sprinkling Tarn in 1954.

11. **D** Each of the original faces of the cube now has area $4 \times 4 - 2 \times 2$, that is 12. In addition, the drilling of the holes has created 24 rectangles, each measuring 2×1. So the required area is $6 \times 12 + 24 \times 2 = 120$.

12. **E** Let N be the two-digit number 'ab', that is $N = 10a + b$. So the sum of N and its 'reverse' is $10a + b + 10b + a = 11a + 11b = 11(a + b)$. As 11 is prime and a and b are both single digits, $11(a + b)$ is a square if, and only if, $a + b = 11$. So the possible values of N are 29, 38, 47, 56, 65, 74, 83, 92.

13. **B** The exact number of seconds in six complete weeks is $6 \times 7 \times 24 \times 60 \times 60 = 6 \times 7 \times (3 \times 8) \times (2 \times 5 \times 6) \times (3 \times 4 \times 5) = 1 \times 2 \times 3 \times 4 \times 5 \times 6 \times 7 \times 8 \times 9 \times 10 = 10!$.

14. **B** The shaded area is $\dfrac{x}{360}(\pi \times 4^2 - \pi \times 1^2) = \dfrac{15\pi x}{360} = \dfrac{\pi x}{24}$. So $\dfrac{\pi x}{24} = \dfrac{\pi \times 4^2}{6}$; thus $x = 64$.

15. **D** In the given diagram, there are four hexagons congruent to the hexagon in Figure (i), four hexagons congruent to the hexagon in Figure (ii) and eight hexagons congruent to the hexagon in Figure (iii).

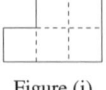

Senior Challenge 2007 solutions

16. A The smallest number of possible prime divisors of 457 that Damien needs to check is the number of prime numbers less than or equal to the square root of 457. Since $21^2 < 457 < 22^2$, he needs to check only primes less than 22. These primes are 2, 3, 5, 7, 11, 13, 17 and 19.

17. C Let the equal sides have length k. The height of the triangle on the left is $k \cos x°$ and its base is $2k \sin x°$, so its area is $k^2 \sin x° \cos x°$. The height of the triangle on the right is $k \sin x°$ and its base is k, so its area is $\frac{1}{2}k^2 \sin x°$. Hence $\cos x° = \frac{1}{2}$ and so $x = 60$.

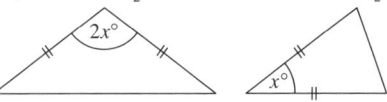

(*Alternatively, the formula* $\Delta = \frac{1}{2}ab \sin C$ *can be used to show that* $\sin x° = \sin 2x°$; *hence* $x + 2x = 180$.)

18. A There are 9 years of the form $123n$ as n may be any digit other than 4. Similarly, there are 9 years each of the forms $234n$, $345n$, $456n$, $567n$ and $678n$, but 10 years of the form $789n$ as, in this case, n may be *any* digit. There are also 9 years of the form $n012$ and 9 of the form $n123$, as in both cases n may be any digit other than 0. However, there are 8 years of the form $n234$ as in this case n cannot be 0 or 1. Similarly, there are 8 years each of the forms $n345$, $n456$, $n567$, $n678$ and $n789$.
So the total numbers of years is $1 \times 10 + 8 \times 9 + 6 \times 8 = 130$.

19. D By the Alternate Segment Theorem $\angle QUS = 55°$. Tangents to a circle from an exterior point are equal, so $QU = QS$ and hence $\angle QSU = \angle QUS = 55°$. So $\angle PQR = 180° - 2 \times 55° = 70°$.

20. C The diagram shows the original rectangle with the corner cut from it to form a pentagon. It may be deduced that the length of the original rectangle is 20 and that a, b, c, d are 8, 10, 13, 15 in some order.
By Pythagoras' Theorem $c^2 = (20 - b)^2 + (a - d)^2$. So c cannot be 8 as there is no right-angled triangle having integer sides and hypotenuse 8. If $c = 10$, then $(20 - b)$ and $(a - d)$ are 6 and 8 in some order, but this is not possible using values of 8, 13 and 15. Similarly, if $c = 15$, then $(20 - b)$ and $(a - d)$ are 9 and 12 in some order, but this is not possible using values of 8, 10 and 13. However, if $c = 13$, then $(20 - b)$ and $(a - d)$ are 5 and 12 in some order, which is true if and only if $a = 15, b = 8, d = 10$.
So the area of the pentagon is $20 \times 15 - \frac{1}{2} \times 5 \times 12 = 270$.

21. B In this solution, the notation $p / q / r / s / \ldots$ represents p beads of one colour, followed by q beads of the other colour, followed by r beads of the first colour, followed by s beads of the second colour etc.
Since the colours alternate, there must be an even number of these sections of beads. If there are just two sections, then the necklace is 4/4 and there is only one such necklace. If there are four, then each colour is split either 2, 2 or 3, 1. So the possibilities are 2/3/2/1 (which can occur in two ways, with the 3 being one colour or the other) or 2/2/2/2 (which can occur in one way) or 3/3/1/1(also one way). Note that 3/2/1/2 appears to be another possibility, but is the same as 2/3/2/1 rotated.
If there are six sections, then each colour must be split into 2, 1, 1 and the possibilities are 2/2/1/1/1/1 (one way)or 2/1/1/2/1/1 (one way). Finally, if there are eight, then the only possible necklace is 1/1/1/1/1/1/1/1. In total that gives 8 necklaces.

212   *Ten Further Years of Mathematical Challenges*

22. D   Let U be the point of intersection of QS and RT. As QS and RT are medians of the triangle, they intersect at a point which divides each in the ratio 2:1, so $QU = \frac{2}{3} \times 8 = \frac{16}{3}$. Therefore the area of triangle $QTR = \frac{1}{2} \times RT \times QU = \frac{1}{2} \times 12 \times \frac{16}{3} = 32$.

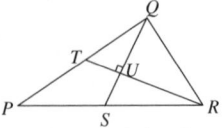

As a median of a triangle divides it into two triangles of equal area, the area of triangle PTR is equal to the area of triangle QTR, so the area of triangle PQR is 64.

23. E   Let the lengths of the sides of the cuboid, in cm, be a, b and c. So $4(a + b + c) = x$. Also, by Pythagoras' Theorem $a^2 + b^2 + c^2 = y^2$. Now the total surface area of the cuboid is

$$2ab + 2bc + 2ca = (a + b + c)^2 - (a^2 + b^2 + c^2) = \left(\frac{x}{4}\right)^2 - y^2 = \frac{x^2 - 16y^2}{16}.$$

24. D   The diameter of the sphere is $l - 2h$ where l is the length of a space diagonal of the cube and h is the perpendicular height of one of the tetrahedral corners when its base is an equilateral triangle.

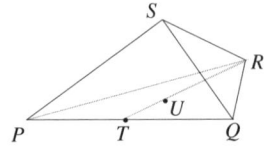

The diagram shows such a tetrahedron: S is a corner of the cube; the base of the tetrahedron, which is considered to lie in a horizontal plane, is an equilateral triangle, PQR, of side $\sqrt{2}$ units; T is the midpoint of PQ. Also U is the centroid of triangle PQR, so $RU : UT = 2 : 1$. As U is vertically below S, the perpendicular height of the tetrahedron is SU.

As RTP is a right angle, $RT^2 = RP^2 - TP^2 = (\sqrt{2})^2 - \left(\frac{\sqrt{2}}{2}\right)^2 = \frac{3}{2}$. Also, $RU = \frac{2}{3}RT$, so $RU^2 = \frac{4}{9}RT^2 = \frac{4}{9} \times \frac{3}{2} = \frac{2}{3}$.

So $SU^2 = SR^2 - RU^2 = 1 - \frac{2}{3} = \frac{1}{3}$. Therefore $h = \frac{1}{\sqrt{3}} = \frac{1}{3}\sqrt{3}$.

Now $l^2 = 2^2 + 2^2 + 2^2 = 12$, so $l = \sqrt{12} = 2\sqrt{3}$. Therefore the diameter of the sphere is $2\sqrt{3} - 2 \times \frac{\sqrt{3}}{3} = \frac{4\sqrt{3}}{3}$.

25. D   As the line $y = x$ is an axis of symmetry of the curve, if the point (a, b) lies on the curve, so too does the point (b, a). Hence the equation of the curve may also be written as $x = \dfrac{py + q}{ry + s}$.

Therefore, substituting for x in the original equation:

$$y = \frac{p\left(\dfrac{py + q}{ry + s}\right) + q}{r\left(\dfrac{py + q}{ry + s}\right) + s} = \frac{p(py + q) + q(ry + s)}{r(py + q) + s(ry + s)}.$$

Therefore $y(r(py + q) + s(ry + s)) = p(py + q) + q(ry + s)$,

that is $y^2 r(p + s) + y(qr + s^2 - p^2 - qr) - pq - qs = 0$,

that is $(p + s)(y^2 r + y(s - p) - q) = 0$.

Since r is non-zero, the expression in the second bracket is non-zero for all but at most two values of y. Hence $p + s = 0$.

Senior Challenge 2008 solutions

1. **C** $2 \times 2008 + 2008 \times 8 = 10 \times 2008 = 20080$.

2. **B**   The cost per pound is $£\frac{255}{1250} \approx £\frac{1}{5} = 20$ p.

3. **D** $\frac{1}{2^6} + \frac{1}{6^2} = \frac{3^2 + 2^4}{2^6 \times 3^2} = \frac{25}{2^6 \times 3^2} = \frac{5^2}{(2^3 \times 3)^2}$. Hence the answer is $\frac{5}{2^3 \times 3} = \frac{5}{24}$.

4. **C**   From the units column we see that $S = 0$. Then the tens column shows that $R = 9$, the hundreds column that $Q = 1$, and the thousands that $P = 6$. So $P + Q + R + S = 16$.

5. **E**   Since 1% of £400 = £4, the total VAT charged was £4 × 17.5 = £70, giving a total cost of £400 + £70 = £470. Therefore the minimum number of entries needed is 94.

6. **E**
```
6
4 5
1 2 3
```
We number the squares to identify them. The only line of symmetry possible is the diagonal through 1 and 5. For a symmetric shading, if 4 is shaded, then so too must be 2; so either both are shaded or neither. Likewise 3 and 6 go together and provide 2 more choices. Whether 1 is shaded or not will not affect a symmetry, and this gives a further 2 choices; and the same applies to 5. Overall, therefore, there are $2^4 = 16$ choices. However, one of these is the choice to shade no squares, which is excluded by the question.

7. **D**   In 1.8 miles there are 1.8×5280 feet $= 18 \times 528$ feet, while in 8 months there are roughly $8 \times 30 \times 24 \times 60$ minutes. Hence the time to 'run' one foot in minutes is roughly $\frac{10 \times 30 \times 20 \times 60}{20 \times 500} = 36$ minutes.

8. **A**   In triangle ACD, $\angle CAD = (180 - x - y)°$. As $AB = AF$, triangle ABF is isosceles hence $\angle ABF = \angle AFB = \frac{1}{2}(x + y)°$. Thus $\angle DFE = \angle AFB = \frac{1}{2}(x + y)°$ (vertically opposite angles). Now in triangle DFE, $\angle FDE = (180 - y)°$. Hence $z° = 180° - \angle DFE - \angle FDE = \frac{1}{2}(y - x)°$.

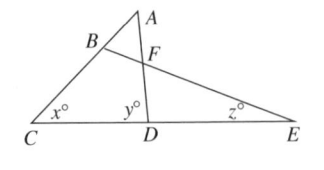

9. **D**   A number is divisible by 9 if, and only if, the sum of its digits is divisible by 9. The given number is $N + 2$, where $N = 222\ldots 220$ has 2007 2s. Since $2007 = 223 \times 9$, N is divisible by 9 and the required remainder is therefore 2.

10. **D**   By inspection
$$\frac{3}{4} = \frac{1}{2} + \frac{1}{4}; \quad \frac{3}{5} = \frac{1}{2} + \frac{1}{10}; \quad \frac{3}{6} = \frac{1}{3} + \frac{1}{6}; \quad \frac{3}{8} = \frac{1}{4} + \frac{1}{8}.$$
However $\frac{3}{7} \neq \frac{1}{m} + \frac{1}{n}$. [To see why, suppose that $\frac{3}{7} = \frac{1}{m} + \frac{1}{n}$ and note that $\frac{1}{m} > \frac{1}{n}$ or vice versa. We will suppose the former. Then $\frac{1}{m} \geq \frac{3}{14} > \frac{3}{15}$ and so $\frac{1}{m} > \frac{1}{5}$ and $m < 5$. Also $\frac{1}{m} < \frac{3}{7}$ and so $3m > 7$. Hence $m \geq 3$. So $m = 4$ or $m = 3$. However $\frac{3}{7} - \frac{1}{4} = \frac{5}{28}$ and $\frac{3}{7} - \frac{1}{3} = \frac{2}{21}$ neither of which has the form $\frac{1}{n}$.]

Senior Challenge 2008 solutions

11. B Let the six points where lines meet on the dot lattice be
A, B, C, D, E, F as shown and let the other two points of
intersection be P (where AC and BF meet) and Q (where CE
and DF meet).
Triangles APB and CPF are similar with base lengths in the ratio
3:5. Hence triangle CPF has height $\frac{5}{8} \times 2 = \frac{5}{4}$ units and base
length 5 units so that its area is $\frac{1}{2} \times \frac{5}{4} \times 5$ square units. Since
the same is true of triangle CQF, the required area is
$\frac{5}{4} \times 5 = 6\frac{1}{4}$ square units.

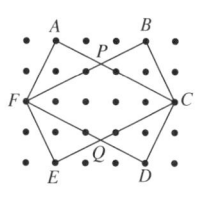

12. C There are 365 days in a normal year and 366 in a leap year. Apart from certain exceptions (none of which occurs in this period) a leap year occurs every 4 years. Now $365 = 7 \times 52 + 1$ and $366 = 7 \times 52 + 2$. Hence each date moves on by 5 days every 4 years. So in 60 years, it moves on 75 days. Since $75 = 7 \times 10 + 5$, that means it moves on to a Thursday.

13. C Since $1280 = 2^8 \times 5 = 2^8(2^0 + 2^2) = 2^8 + 2^{10}$, we may take $m=8$ and $n = 10$ (or vice versa) to get $m + n = 8 + 10 = 18$. It is easy to check that there are no other possibilities.

14. D The internal angle of a regular pentagon is $108°$. Let A be the centre of a touching circle, as shown. Since OA bisects $\angle RAQ$, $\angle OAQ = 54°$. Also, triangle OAQ is right-angled at Q (radius perpendicular to tangent). Since $AQ = 1$, $OQ = \tan 54°$.

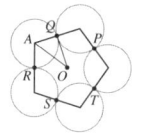

15. A The sequence proceeds as follows: $13, 40, 20, 10, 5, 16, 8, 4, 2, 1, 4, 2, 1 \ldots$. The block $4, 2, 1$ repeats *ad infinitum* starting after t_7. But $2008 - 7 = 2001$ and $2001 = 3 \times 667$. Hence t_{2008} is the third term in the 667th such block and is therefore 1.

16. A Adding the three given equations gives $4(x + y + z) = 3000$. Therefore $x + y + z = 750$. So the mean is $\frac{750}{3} = 250$.

17. E Let 'X' be a single digit. If $2008 - 200X = 2 + 0 + 0 + X$ then $8 - X = 2 + X$ so $X = 3$. So Alice (being the younger) could have been born in 2003. Next if $2008 - 199X = 1 + 9 + 9 + X$ then $18 - X = 19 + X$, which is impossible. Similarly if $2008 - 198X = 1 + 9 + 8 + X$ then $28 - X = 18 + X$, so $X = 5$. Thus Alice or Andy could have been born in 1985. Finally if $2008 - 19YX = 1 + 9 + X + Y$ for some digit $Y \leq 7$, then $108 - YX = 10 + Y + X$. Hence $98 = YX + Y + X$ which is impossible, since $YX + Y + X$ is at most $79 + 7 + 9 = 95$. Hence there are no more possible dates and so Andy was born in 1985 and Alice in 2003.

18. C Since $XY^2 = 18$, $YZ^2 = 32$ and $XZ^2 = 50$, we have $XZ^2 = XY^2 + YZ^2$. Hence by the converse of Pythagoras' Theorem, $\angle XYZ = 90°$. Since the angle in a semi-circle is $90°$ the segment XZ is the diameter of the specified circle. Hence the radius is $\frac{1}{2}\sqrt{50}$ and the area of the circle is $\frac{50\pi}{4} = \frac{25\pi}{2}$.

19. B Let $199p + 1 = X^2$. Then $199p = X^2 - 1 = (X + 1)(X - 1)$. Note that 197 is prime. If p is also to be prime then **either** $X + 1 = 199$, in which case $X - 1 = 197$, **or** $X - 1 = 199$, in which case $X + 1 = 201$ (and $201 = 3 \times 67$ is not prime). Note that $X - 1 = 1, X + 1 = 199p$ is impossible. Hence $p = 197$ is the only possibility.

20. B Let r_1, r_2 and r_3 be the radii of the shaded circle, semicircles and outer circle respectively. A right-angled triangle can be formed with sides $r_3, (r_1 + r_2)$ and r_2.
Hence, by Pythagoras' Theorem, $r_3^2 = (r_1 + r_2)^2 + r_2^2$.
Now $\pi r_1^2 = 4$, hence $r_1 = 2/\sqrt{\pi}$. Likewise $r_2 = 6/\sqrt{\pi}$.
Hence $r_2 = 3r_1$ so that $r_3^2 = (r_1 + 3r_1)^2 + (3r_1)^2 = 25r_1^2$. Thus the required area is $25 \times 4 = 100$.

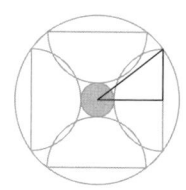

21. **B** Since $2008/1998$ lies between 1 and 2, $a = 1$. Subtracting 1 and inverting gives $b + 1/(c + 1/d) = 1998/10 = 199 + 4/5$ so that $b = 199$. Then $1/(c + 1/d) = 4/5$ so that $c + 1/d = 5/4$ and this gives $c = 1$ and $d = 4$.
{*Note : This is an example of a continued fraction.*}

22. **A** Let r be the length of a side of the equilateral triangle. Hence the width of the rectangle is $r\sin 60° + r + r\sin 60° = r(1 + 2\sin 60°) = r(1 + \sqrt{3})$ and its length is $3r + 2r\sin 60° = r(3 + \sqrt{3})$. So the ratio of the length to the width is
$$(3 + \sqrt{3}) : (1 + \sqrt{3}) = \sqrt{3}(1 + \sqrt{3}) : (1 + \sqrt{3}) = \sqrt{3} : 1.$$

23. **B** Let $X = x + 3$ and $Y = y - 3$. Then the given equation becomes $(X + Y)^2 = XY$. So $X^2 + XY + Y^2 = 0$. However X^2, Y^2 and $XY (= (X + Y)^2)$ are non-negative. Hence $X = Y = 0$; so $x = -3$ and $y = 3$ is the only solution.

24. **E** $1 + 3 + 5 + 7 + \ldots + (2n + 1) = (n + 1)^2$. The n in the three cases given is 12, $\frac{1}{2}(x - 1)$ and $\frac{1}{2}(y - 1)$. So, the triangle has sides of length $12 + 1, \frac{1}{2}(x - 1) + 1$ and $\frac{1}{2}(y - 1) + 1$. However the only right-angled triangle having sides of whole number length with hypotenuse 13 is the (5, 12, 13) triangle. So $x = 9$ and $y = 23$ (or vice versa). Hence $x + y = 32$.

25. **D** To work out the area of $||x| - 2| + ||y| - 2| \leq 4$, we first consider the region $|x| + |y| \leq 4$ which is shown in (a). This region is then translated to give $|x - 2| + |y - 2| \leq 4$ as shown in (b).
By properties of the modulus, if the point (x, y) lies in the polygon, then so do $(x, -y)$, $(-x, y)$ and $(-x, -y)$. Thus $||x| - 2| + ||y| - 2| \leq 4$ can be obtained from (b) by reflecting in the axes and the origin, as shown in (c).

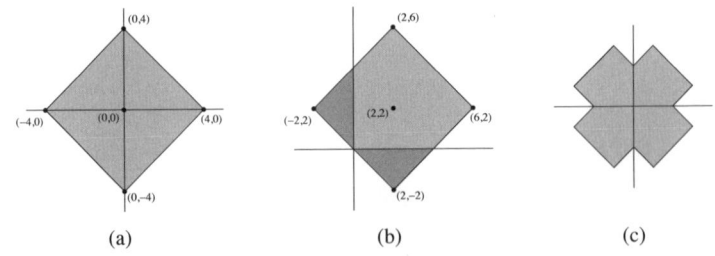

Hence the required area is 4 times the area in the first quadrant. From (b), the required area in the first quadrant is the area of a square of side $4\sqrt{2}$ minus two triangles (cut off by the axes) which, combined, make up a square of side $2\sqrt{2}$. So the area in the first quadrant is $(4\sqrt{2})^2 - (2\sqrt{2})^2 = 32 - 8 = 24$.
Hence the area of the polygon is $4 \times 24 = 96$ square units.

Senior Challenge 2009 solutions

1. **A** 20% of 30% = 0.2 × 0.3 = 0.06 = 6%.

2. **D** $\frac{785}{15} = 52\frac{1}{3}$ hence 785 is not a multiple of 15. But $\frac{135}{15} = 9, \frac{315}{15} = 21, \frac{555}{15} = 37, \frac{915}{15} = 61$.

3. **E** 1 − 32 + 81 − 64 + 25 − 6 = 5.

4. **E** Steve achieved $\frac{150}{10}$ × 4.5 miles per gallon which is 15 × 4.5 = 67.5 ≈ 70.

5. **A** As the ratio of the radii is 3 : 4 then the number of revolutions made by the larger wheel is 120000 × $\frac{3}{4}$ = 90000.

6. **C** If at most two marbles of each colour are chosen, the maximum number we can choose is 8, corresponding to 2 of each. Therefore, if 9 are chosen, we must have at least 3 of one colour, but this statement is not true if 9 is replaced by any number less than 9.

7. **B** The top left 2 by 2 outlined block must contain a 3 and a 4 and this can be done in two ways. For each choice there is only one way to complete the entire mini-sudoku.

8. **C** The increase in entries from 2007 to 2008 is 92 690 − 87 400 = 5290. Hence the percentage increase is $\frac{5290}{87400}$ × 100% = $\frac{5290}{874}$% ≈ $\frac{5400}{900}$% = 6%. (The exact value is $6\frac{1}{19}$.)

9. **D** As T is the midpoint of QR then $QT = \frac{1}{2}x$.
Since $\angle UQT = \angle SQR = 45°$ and $\angle QUT = 90°, \angle UTQ = 45°$.
Thus triangle QTU is isosceles with $UQ = UT$.
In triangle QTU, by Pythagoras' Theorem, $QT^2 = QU^2 + TU^2$.
Hence $(\frac{1}{2}x)^2 = 2TU^2$ so $TU^2 = \frac{1}{8}x^2$ giving $TU = \frac{x}{2\sqrt{2}}$.

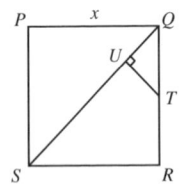

10. **B** A number is a multiple of 6 precisely when it is both a multiple of 2 and of 3. To be a multiple of 2, it will need to end with an even digit; i.e. 0 or 2. If it ends with 0, the sum of the other two digits must be a multiple of 3; and only 3 = 1 + 2 or 6 = 1 + 5 are possible. That gives the numbers 120, 210, 150, 510. If it ends with 2, the sum of the others must be 1 = 0 + 1 or 4 = 1 + 3. That gives 102, 132 and 312.

11. **C** $\sqrt{2} + \sqrt{2} + \sqrt{2} + \sqrt{2} = 4\sqrt{2} = 2^2 \times 2^{1/2} = 2^{2\frac{1}{2}}$. Hence $x = 2\frac{1}{2}$.

12. **E** cos 50° < sin 50° < 1. Hence $\frac{1}{\cos 50°} > \frac{1}{\sin 50°} > 1 > \sin 50° > \cos 50°$.
tan 50° = $\frac{\sin 50°}{\cos 50°} < \frac{1}{\cos 50°}$ hence $\frac{1}{\cos 50°}$ has the greatest value.

13. **C** $x - \frac{1}{x} = y - \frac{1}{y}$ hence $x^2y - y = xy^2 - x$. Thus $xy(y - x) + y - x = 0$.
Therefore $(y - x)(xy + 1) = 0$. As $x \neq y$ then $y - x \neq 0$.
Hence $xy + 1 = 0$ giving $xy = -1$.

Senior Challenge 2009 solutions

14. **D** Let the external angle of the regular polygon be $x°$.
Hence $\angle XQR = \angle XSR = x°$ and reflex angle
$\angle QRS = (180 + x)°$.
As the sum of the angles in the quadrilateral $QRSX$ is
$360°$ then $140 + x + x + 180 + x = 360$.
Hence $3x = 40$ and the polygon has $\dfrac{360}{40 \div 3} = 27$ sides.

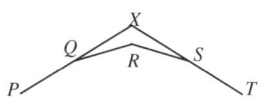

15. **D** Let $\dfrac{n}{100 - n} = x$ where x is an integer. Hence $n = 100x - nx$.
Hence $n(1 + x) = 100x$ giving $n = \dfrac{100x}{1 + x}$.
Now x and $1 + x$ can have no common factors. Therefore $1 + x$ must be a factor of 100 and can be any of them.
Hence $1 + x \in \{\pm 1, \pm 2, \pm 4, \pm 5, \pm 10, \pm 20, \pm 25, \pm 50, \pm 100\}$ thus the number of possible integers n is 18.

16. **B** Since $x^4 - y^4 = 2009$ it follows that $(x^2 + y^2)(x^2 - y^2) = 2009$.
But $x^2 + y^2 = 49$ hence $x^2 - y^2 = \dfrac{2009}{49} = 41$.
Subtracting gives $2y^2 = 8$ hence $y^2 = 4$. Since $y > 0, y = 2$.

17. **C** The greatest possible value of f is achieved by a rectangular cut through an edge of a cube and the furthest edge from it. If we take x as the side of the cube, by Pythagoras' Theorem the extra surface area formed by the cut is $2\sqrt{2}x^2$. Hence $f = \dfrac{2\sqrt{2}x^2}{6x^2} = \dfrac{\sqrt{2}}{3}$.

18. **A** We have $y^2 = x(2 - x)$. Now $y^2 \geq 0$ for all real y hence $x(2 - x) \geq 0$.
Hence $0 \leq x \leq 2$. In fact we can rewrite the equation as $(x - 1)^2 + y^2 = 1$; so this is a circle of radius 1 with centre $(1, 0)$.

19. **C** The distance cycled by Hamish between noon and 4 pm is $4x$.
The distance cycled by Ben between 2 pm and 4 pm is $2y$.
They meet at 4 pm hence $4x + 2y = 51$ or $2x + 2(x + y) = 51$ (*).
If they had both started at noon then they would have met at 2:50 pm and so $2\tfrac{5}{6}(x + y) = 51$.
Hence $x + y = 51 \times \dfrac{6}{17} = 18$. Hence from (*) $2x + 2 \times 18 = 51$.
Hence $2x = 15$ giving $x = 7\tfrac{1}{2}$. Thus $y = 10\tfrac{1}{2}$.

20. **E** If $\angle RPQ = 90°$ then P lies on a semicircle of diameter RQ.
Let x be the side-length of the square $QRST$.
Hence the area of the semicircle $RPQ = \tfrac{1}{2}\pi\left(\tfrac{1}{2}x\right)^2 = \tfrac{1}{8}\pi x^2$ and the area of square $QRST$ is x^2.
$\angle RPQ$ is acute when P is outside the semicircle RPQ.
Hence the probability that $\angle RPQ$ is acute is $\dfrac{x^2 - \tfrac{1}{8}\pi x^2}{x^2} = 1 - \dfrac{\pi}{8}$.

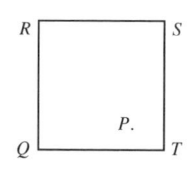

21. B Let r be the radius of the small cone and h the height.
Let l_1 and l_2 be the slant heights of the small and large cones respectively.
By Pythagoras' Theorem $l_2 = \sqrt{6^2 + 8^2} = 10$.
Using similar triangles, $\dfrac{l_1}{r} = \dfrac{10}{6}$ so $l_1 = \dfrac{5}{3}r$ and $\dfrac{h}{8} = \dfrac{r}{6}$ giving $h = \dfrac{4}{3}r$.
Thus the area of the curved surface of the frustum is

$$\pi \times 6 \times 10 - \pi \times r \times \dfrac{5}{3} \times r = \pi\left(60 - \dfrac{5r^2}{3}\right).$$

The sum of the areas of the two circles is $\pi \times 6^2 + \pi \times r^2 = \pi(36 + r^2)$.
Hence $\pi\left(60 - \dfrac{5r^2}{3}\right) = \pi(36 + r^2)$ and so $24 = \dfrac{8r^2}{3}$ giving $r = 3$, so $h = \dfrac{4}{3} \times 3 = 4$.
Therefore, in cms, the height of the frustum is $8 - 4 = 4$.

22. C Let the perpendicular distance between EH and FG be x cm and the area of the parallelogram $EFGH$ be y cm^2. Thus $y = FG \times x$.
The area of triangle EFN is $\tfrac{1}{2}FN \times x = \tfrac{1}{2} \times \tfrac{1}{2} \times FG \times x = \tfrac{1}{4}y$ cm^2.
Likewise the areas of triangles EHM and NGM are $\tfrac{1}{4}y$ cm^2 and $\tfrac{1}{8}y$ cm^2 respectively.
The area of triangle ENM is 12 cm^2, hence $y = 12 + \tfrac{5}{8}y$ and so $y = 32$. Hence the area of the parallelogram $EFGH$ is 32 cm^2.

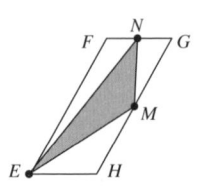

23. D Label the rows of the triangles from left to right as follows: $a_1, \ldots, a_5$; $b_1, \ldots, b_{10}$ and $c_1, \ldots, c_5$.
Now 1 cannot be at a_4, a_5, b_7, b_8 or c_4 hence 1 must be at c_3.
Hence b_4 and b_5 are 2 and 5 in either order. Hence a_3 is 1 or 4.
But 1 cannot be at a_4 or b_7 hence 1 must be at a_3.
4 cannot be at b_3 thus 4 is at a_2.
Hence the number on the face with the question mark must be 4.

24. B A shaded triangle is congruent to an unshaded triangle (ASA).
Hence the area of the dashed square is equal to the area of the cross and both are 5.
Thus the side-length of the dashed square is $\sqrt{5}$.
Hence the sides of a shaded triangle are: $\tfrac{1}{2}$, 1 and $\tfrac{1}{2}\sqrt{5}$.
Now the perpendicular distance between the squares is equal to the altitude, h, of the shaded triangle. The area of such a triangle is
$\tfrac{1}{2} \times \left(\tfrac{1}{2} \times 1\right) = \tfrac{1}{4}$ so that $\tfrac{1}{2} \times \left(\tfrac{1}{2}\sqrt{5} \times h\right) = \tfrac{1}{4}$ which gives $h = \dfrac{1}{\sqrt{5}}$.
Hence the length of the sides of the outer square are $\sqrt{5} + 2 \times \dfrac{1}{\sqrt{5}} = \dfrac{5}{\sqrt{5}} + \dfrac{2}{\sqrt{5}} = \dfrac{7}{\sqrt{5}}$.
Thus the area of the large square is $\left(\dfrac{7}{\sqrt{5}}\right)^2 = \dfrac{49}{5}$.

25. A The left-hand side of the equation can be written as

$$(a+1)(b+1)(c+1)(d+1) - 1.$$

Hence

$$(a+1)(b+1)(c+1)(d+1) = 2010.$$

Now expressing 2010 as a product of primes gives $2010 = 2 \times 3 \times 5 \times 67$ hence $a + b + c + d = 1 + 2 + 4 + 66 = 73$.

Senior Challenge 2010
solutions

1.	C	The only two-digit cubes are 27 and 64. As 1 *Down* is one less than a cube then 3 *Across* must start with 6 or 3 and so is 64. Thus $x = 4$.
2.	B	The smallest possible value is attained by using $p = 1, q = 2$ and $r = 3$. Therefore this value is $20 \times 1 + 10 \times 2 + 3 = 43$.
3.	C	The three internal angles of an equilateral triangle are all $60°$. As the sum of the angles on a straight line is $180°$ then the sum of the four marked angles is $2 \times (180 - 60)° = 2 \times 120° = 240°$.
4.	B	$2 + 0 + 1 + 1 = 4$. Multiples of 4 are even, hence 2011 is not valid and the same argument applies to 2013, 2015, 2017 and 2019. $2 + 0 + 1 + 2 = 5$. The units digit for multiples of 5 is 0 or 5, hence 2012 is not valid. $2 + 0 + 1 + 4 = 7$. But $\frac{2014}{7} = 287\frac{5}{7}$, hence 2014 is not valid. $2 + 0 + 1 + 6 = 9$. Since $2016 = 9 \times 224$, 2016 is valid. Hence we have to wait $2016 - 2010 (= 6)$ more years.
5.	D	If the statement is true then the capacity (in litres) of Morecambe Bay is approximately: $20 \times 10^6 \times 365 \times 24 \times 60 \times 6 = 10^8 \times (6 \times 365) \times (2 \times 24) \times 6$ $\approx 6 \times 10^8 \times 2000 \times 50 = 6 \times 10^{13}$.
6.	B	The length of the road is 8km. Hence the time taken to run down the mountain is $\frac{8}{12}$ hours $= \frac{8}{12} \times 60$ min $= 40$ min.
7.	C	There are 24 arrangements of the letters in the word ANGLE with A as the first letter. In alphabetical order AEGLN is first and ANLGE is last ie 24th. ANLEG is the 23rd and hence ANGLE is the 22nd.
8.	D	$(x + y + z)(x - y - z) = [x + (y + z)][x - (y + z)] = x^2 - (y + z)^2$.
9.	D	$(2 \diamond 3) \diamond 4 = (2^3 - 3^2) \diamond 4 = (-1) \diamond 4 = (-1)^4 - 4^{-1} = 1 - \frac{1}{4} = \frac{3}{4}$.
10.	E	Let the original square have sides of length y cm and the single square which is not 1×1 have sides of length x cm. Then $y^2 = 36 + x^2$, and so $y^2 - x^2 = 36$ and hence $(y + x)(y - x) = 36$. As $36 = 2^2 \times 3^2$ and $y + x > y - x$ the possible factors of 36 are:

$y + x$	$y - x$	y	x	
9	4	$6\frac{1}{2}$	$2\frac{1}{2}$	impossible
12	3	$7\frac{1}{2}$	$4\frac{1}{2}$	impossible
18	2	10	8	possible
36	1	$18\frac{1}{2}$	$17\frac{1}{2}$	impossible

We can check that $10^2 = 36 + 8^2 = 100$ and hence the length of the side of the *original* square is 10 cm.

11.	D	Squaring the numbers given allows us to see their order easily: $(9\sqrt{2})^2 = 81 \times 2 = 162 \qquad (3\sqrt{19})^2 = 9 \times 19 = 171 \qquad (4\sqrt{11})^2 = 16 \times 11 = 176$ $(5\sqrt{7})^2 = 25 \times 7 = 175 \qquad (6\sqrt{5})^2 = 36 \times 5 = 180$ As 175 is the middle one of these numbers, the answer is $5\sqrt{7}$.
12.	A	As the square has side length 1 its area is $1 \times 1 = 1$. Thus the area of each of the four rectangles is $\frac{1}{4}$. The length of the bottom rectangle is 1 hence its width is $\frac{1}{4}$. Thus the width of each of the two congruent rectangles is $\frac{1}{2}(1 - \frac{1}{4}) = \frac{3}{8}$. Hence the area of one of these congruent rectangles is $\frac{3}{8}x$. But we know this area is $\frac{1}{4}$, therefore $\frac{3}{8}x = \frac{1}{4}$ and hence $x = \frac{2}{3}$.

Senior Challenge 2010 solutions

13. A The lowest common multiple of 3 and 4 is 12. Hence both of the required conditions are satisfied only by numbers that are 2 less than multiples of 12 and also less than 100, ie: 10, 22, 34, 46, 58, 70, 82 and 94.
Therefore 8 two-digit numbers satisfy the conditions.

14. E Drop perpendiculars from the top vertices to the bottom line. The distance from the foot to the nearer base vertex is $\frac{1}{2}(2y - 2x) = y - x$. So the distance to the further base vertex is $2y - (y - x) = y + x$.
Hence $\cos\theta = \dfrac{x + y}{d}$ where d is the length of the diagonal.

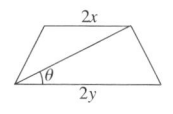

15. E The first eight prime numbers are: 2, 3, 5, 7, 11, 13, 17, 19.
If the sum of two prime numbers is prime, one of them must be 2.
If the sum of three different prime numbers is prime they must all be odd. The answer is therefore 19 as: $2 + 17 = 19$ and $3 + 5 + 11 = 19$.

16. E As PR is a diameter, $\angle PQR = \angle PSR = 90°$ (angles in a semicircle are 90°).
Since $PQ = 12 \times 5$ and $QR = 5 \times 5$, triangle PQR is an enlarged 5, 12, 13 triangle and so $PR = 13 \times 5 = 65$.
Since $PR = 5 \times 13$ and $SR = 4 \times 13$, triangle PRS is an enlarged 3, 4, 5 triangle and so $SP = 3 \times 13 = 39$.

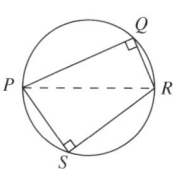

17. E $\sqrt{9^{16x^2}} = 9^{(16x^2)/2} = 9^{8x^2}$.

18. A Let x be the length of the shaded rectangle.
By Pythagoras' Theorem, $x^2 = 2^2 + 2^2$, hence $x = 2\sqrt{2}$.
The total surface area of the two prisms equals the surface area of the solid cube plus twice the surface area of that shaded rectangle, that is $6 \times 2 \times 2 + 2 \times 2 \times 2\sqrt{2} = 24 + 8\sqrt{2} = 8(3 + \sqrt{2})$.

19. B In the rhombus on the left, drawing vertical straight lines at distances of $1\frac{1}{2}$, 3 and $4\frac{1}{2}$ from the left edge of the square, and a horizontal straight line bisecting the square, creates 16 equivalent triangles. Of these, four are shaded giving a total shaded area of $\frac{1}{4} \times 6 \times 6 = 9$. 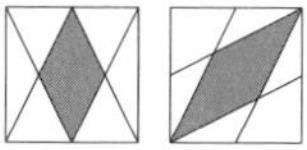
Draw in the diagonal from NW to SE in the rhombus on the right. The four unshaded triangles now above the shaded area are all equal in area (a say); and one can see that 3 of these together make up $\frac{1}{4}$ of the square. Hence $a = 3$. Thus the shaded area equals $36 - 3 \times 8 = 12$.
Therefore the difference between the shaded areas is $12 - 9 = 3$.

20. C Let the number of boys in the class be x. Hence $\dfrac{10}{10 + x} \times \dfrac{9}{9 + x} = \dfrac{3}{20}$.
Simplifying gives $1800 = 3(10 + x)(9 + x)$ and then $x^2 + 19x - 510 = 0$.
Factorising gives $(x + 34)(x - 15) = 0$ and, since $x \neq -34$, $x = 15$.

21. A The hypotenuse of one of the small right-angled triangles is parallel to the diagonal and hence makes angles of 45°. Since the hypotenuse has length 1, the other two sides have length $\frac{1}{\sqrt{2}}$, by Pythagoras' Theorem.
As the internal angle of a regular hexagon is 120°, drawing a diagonal from NW to SE forms two triangles, bottom right, each with angles 45°, 120° and 15°. (The sum of the angles in a triangle is 180°). 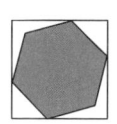
Let the square have length y units. Using the Sine Rule gives $\dfrac{y - \frac{1}{\sqrt{2}}}{\sin 120°} = \dfrac{1}{\sin 45°}$.
Hence $y - \dfrac{1}{\sqrt{2}} = \dfrac{\sqrt{3}}{2} \div \dfrac{1}{\sqrt{2}} = \dfrac{\sqrt{3}}{\sqrt{2}}$ and therefore $y = \dfrac{\sqrt{3} + 1}{\sqrt{2}}$.
Hence the area of the square is $y^2 = \left(\dfrac{\sqrt{3} + 1}{\sqrt{2}}\right)^2 = \dfrac{4 + 2\sqrt{3}}{2} = 2 + \sqrt{3}$.

22. B   Since $x^2 - px - q = 0$, it follows that $x^3 = px^2 + qx$.
But $x^2 = px + q$ and so $x^3 = p(px + q) + qx$, ie $x^3 = (p^2 + q)x + pq$.
The three possible values shown for pq are 3, 5 and 7.
If $pq = 3$, $p^2 + q = 1^2 + 3 = 4$ or $p^2 + q = 3^2 + 1 = 10$. Hence $4x + 3$ and $10x + 3$ could equal x^3.
If $pq = 7$, we may take $p = 1, q = 7$ to get $p^2 + q = 1^2 + 7 = 8$. Hence $8x + 7$ could equal x^3.
If $pq = 5$, we may take $p = 5, q = 1$ to get $p^2 + q = 5^2 + 1 = 26$. Hence $26x + 5$ could equal x^3.
However, the only other possibility, $p = 1, q = 5$ gives $p^2 + q = 6 \neq 8$. Therefore $8x + 5 \neq x^3$.

23. B   Let r_1 and r_2 represent the radii of the smaller and larger semicircles respectively. A vertical line through the common centre of the semicircles gives $r_1 + r_2 = 2 \ldots$ (1). Also, together with the diameter of the larger semicircle, this line forms a right-angled, isosceles triangle giving $\sin 45° = \dfrac{r_1}{r_2}$. Hence $r_2 = \sqrt{2}r_1 \ldots$ (2).
Substituting (2) into (1) gives $(1 + \sqrt{2})r_1 = 2$ so that $r_1 = 2(\sqrt{2} - 1)$.
Therefore $r_2 = 2\sqrt{2}(\sqrt{2} - 1)$.
Hence the total shaded area is $\frac{1}{2}\pi(r_1^2 + r_2^2) = \frac{1}{2}\pi[4(\sqrt{2}-1)^2 + 8(\sqrt{2}-1)^2] = 6\pi(3 - 2\sqrt{2})$.

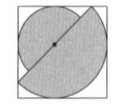

24. E   The volume of the three spheres is $3 \times \frac{4}{3}\pi \times 1^3 = 4\pi$.
Let r be the radius of the cross-sectional area of the cylinder.
Hence the volume of the cylinder is $2\pi r^2$.
Thus the required fraction is $\frac{2}{r^2}$.
The straight lines joining the centres of the three spheres form an equilateral triangle of side length 2.
Let x be the distance from the centre of a sphere to the midpoint of the triangle. Using the Sine Rule, $\dfrac{2}{\sin 120°} = \dfrac{x}{\sin 30°}$ hence $x = \dfrac{2}{\sqrt{3}}$.
As the sphere has radius 1, $r = x + 1$ and $r = 1 + \frac{2}{\sqrt{3}}$.
Thus $r^2 = \frac{1}{3}(2 + \sqrt{3})^2 = \frac{1}{3}(7 + 4\sqrt{3})$. Hence the required fraction is $\dfrac{6}{7 + 4\sqrt{3}}$.

25. D   The sum of 10 different digits is 45. As the sum of the digits in the question is 36 then digits adding to 9 are omitted.
The combinations of digits satisfying this are:

$$9; \ 1 + 8; \ 2 + 7; \ 3 + 6; \ 4 + 5; \ 1 + 2 + 6; \ 1 + 3 + 5; \ 2 + 3 + 4.$$

When '0' is not involved there are $(8! + 4 \times 7! + 3 \times 6!)$ numbers, whereas when '0' is used there are $(8 \times 8! + 4 \times 7 \times 7! + 3 \times 6 \times 6!)$.
This gives a total of $9 \times 8! + (4 + 28) \times 7! + (3 + 18) \times 6! = (72 + 32 + 3) \times 7! = 107 \times 7!$
Hence $N = 107$.

Senior Challenge 2011 solutions

1. **D** Every integer is divisible by 1; 2012 is divisible by 2 since it is even; 2013 is divisible by 3 since its digits total to a multiple of 3; and 2015 is divisible by 5 since its last digit is 5. However, 2014 is not divisible by 4 because 14 is not.

2. **D** After the first spill, $\frac{1}{3}$ of the water remains.
After the second spill, $\frac{2}{3} \times \frac{1}{3}$ of the water remains, hence $\frac{1}{3}$ of the pail had water left in it.

3. **A** After the nth step, *Lumber9* is at number: $\begin{cases} \frac{n+1}{2} & \text{for } n \text{ odd,} \\ \frac{-n}{2} & \text{for } n \text{ even.} \end{cases}$
Hence when $n = 2011$, *Lumber9* is at number $\frac{2011+1}{2} = 1006$.

4. **D** Since $3^1 = 3, 3^2 = 9, 3^3 = 27, 3^4 = 81, 3^5 = 243, \ldots$ we see that the final digits cycle through the four numbers 3, 9, 7, 1. As $2011 = 502 \times 4 + 3$, the last digit of 3^{2011} is 7.

5. **B** As the sum of the angles in a triangle is 180° and all four angles in a rectangle are 90°, the sum of the two marked angles in the triangle is $180° - 90° = 90°$.
Each interior angle of a regular hexagon is 120° and the sum of the angles in a quadrilateral is 360°; hence the sum of the two marked angles in the quadrilateral is $360° - 90° - (360° - 120°) = 30°$.
Hence the sum of the four marked angles is $90° + 30° = 120°$.

6. **C** Let Granny's age today be G and Gill's age today be g.
Therefore $G = 15g \ldots(1)$ and $G + 4 = (g + 4)^2 \ldots(2)$.
Substituting (1) into (2) gives $15g + 4 = g^2 + 8g + 16$, hence $g^2 - 7g + 12 = 0$.
Thus $(g - 3)(g - 4) = 0$, hence $g = 3$ or 4.
As G is even and $G = 15g$, g is also even. Thus $g = 4$ and $G = 15 \times 4 = 60$.
Hence today, Granny is 56 years older than Gill.

7. **D** In order to form a triangle, x must exceed the difference between 4 and 5 and x must be less than the sum of 4 and 5, i.e. $1 < x < 9$.
Hence $x = 2, 3, 4, 5, 6, 7$ or 8. So x can have 7 different values.

8. **C** The 1×2 rectangles can appear in two different ways: A ▭ or B ◫.
If, in the given shape, A forms the top 1×2 rectangle then the possible different ways to fill the remaining 2×4 rectangle are, from left to right:

    A, A, A, A;   A, A, B, B;   B, A, A, B;   B, B, A, A;   B, B, B, B.

If A does not form the top 1×2 rectangle, then the only possible way is to use 4B and an A. Hence there are 6 ways of dividing the given shape into 1×2 rectangles.

9. **B** Let the centre cube in the $3 \times 3 \times 3$ block be red. As no cubes of the same colour meet face-to-face then the 6 centre cubes on the outer faces must be yellow. All six outer faces are as shown alongside.
Thus 14 faces are yellow and 13 faces are red. If the centre cube is yellow then the situation is reversed. Hence the difference between the largest number of red cubes that Sam can use and the smallest number is 1.

Y	R	Y
R	Y	R
Y	R	Y

10. **C** The area of a triangle is $\frac{1}{2}ab \sin C$. The maximum area is attained when $\angle C = 90°$.
Hence, in order to maximise the area, the triangle must be right-angled with common side lengths equal to 5. Let x be the side length of the hypotenuse, so, by Pythagoras' Theorem, $x^2 = 5^2 + 5^2 = 50$. Thus $x = 5\sqrt{2}$ is the length that should be chosen.

Senior Challenge 2011 solutions

11. C Let x be the side length of the regular hexagon $PQRSTU$ and let $h = PT = QS$, the perpendicular height of triangle STV. Thus the area of triangle STV is $\frac{1}{2}xh$ and the areas of triangles PTV and QSV are both $\frac{1}{2}(\frac{1}{2}xh) = \frac{1}{4}xh$. The perpendicular heights of triangles PTU and QRS are
$$\frac{UR - PQ}{2} = \frac{2x - x}{2} = \frac{x}{2}.$$
Hence the area of each of triangles PTU and QRS is $\frac{1}{2}h \times \frac{1}{2}x = \frac{1}{4}hx$.
Therefore the area of triangle STV is one third of the area of $PQRSTU$.

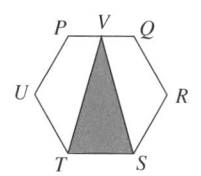

12. D The primorial of 7 is $2 \times 3 \times 5 \times 7 = 210$. As 8, 9 and 10 are not prime numbers, they also have a primorial of 210. The primorial of 11 is $2 \times 3 \times 5 \times 7 \times 11 = 2310$. Hence there are exactly four different whole numbers which have a primorial of 210.

13. D Let the centres of the starting and finishing squares in the maze have coordinates $(1,4)$ and $(4,1)$ respectively. Each path must pass through $(2,3)$ and $(3,2)$. There are two different routes from $(1,4)$ to $(2,3)$. The next visit is to $(3,3)$ or $(2,2)$.
When visiting $(3,3)$ the next visit has to be $(3,2)$ as $(3,4)$, $(4,3)$ and $(4,4)$ cannot be visited without subsequently revisiting a square. From $(2,2)$ the next valid visit is to $(1,2)$, $(2,1)$ or $(3,2)$. From each of these points there is only one route to $(3,2)$. Thus there are four ways of visiting $(3,2)$. Upon visiting $(3,2)$, the only valid route through the maze is $(4,2)$ then $(4,1)$.
Hence the number of different routes through the maze is $2 \times 4 = 8$.

14. C Let us define T_n to represent an equilateral triangle with side length n cm. Then an equilateral triangle of side length 4 cm can be divided into smaller equilateral triangles as follows:

$1 \times T_3$ and $7 \times T_1$ $4 \times T_2$ $3 \times T_2$ and $4 \times T_1$
$2 \times T_2$ and $8 \times T_1$ $1 \times T_2$ and $12 \times T_1$ $16 \times T_1$.

The number of triangles used are: 8, 4, 7, 10, 13 and 16. So it is not possible to dissect the original triangle into 12 triangles.

15. B If a, b are roots of $x^2 + ax + b = 0$ then $x^2 + ax + b = 0$ must be $(x - a)(x - b) = 0$. As $(x - a)(x - b) = x^2 + (-a - b)x + ab$ then $a = -a - b$ and $b = ab$. If $b = 0$ we see immediately that $a = 0$. But this is not possible as a and b are different. If $b \neq 0$ then $a = 1$ and $b = -2$. So there is just one solution pair.

16. E Let $QR = x$ and $RS = y$ in the rectangle $PQRS$. Hence the area of $PQRS$ is xy. The area of triangle QRT is $\frac{1}{2}RT \times x = \frac{1}{2}xy$, hence $RT = \frac{2}{3}y$. Thus $TS = RS - RT = \frac{1}{3}y$. The area of triangle TSU is $\frac{1}{2}SU \times \frac{1}{3}y = \frac{1}{8}xy$, hence $SU = \frac{5}{12}x$. Therefore the area of triangle PUQ is $\frac{1}{2} \times \frac{7}{12}xy = \frac{7}{24}xy$.
Hence, as a fraction of the area of rectangle $PQRS$, the area of triangle QTU is
$$\frac{xy(1 - \frac{1}{3} - \frac{1}{8} - \frac{7}{24})}{xy} = \frac{23}{60}.$$

17. A Let a, b, o and p represent the percentage of pupils liking apples, bananas, oranges and pears respectively.
As $a = 85$, there are 15% of pupils who do not like apples. As $b = 80$, $a \cap b$ is greater than or equal to $80 - (100 - 85) = 65$. As $o = 75$, $a \cap b \cap o$ is greater than or equal to $75 - (100 - 65) = 40$. Finally, as $p = 70$, $a \cap b \cap o \cap p$ is greater than or equal to $70 - (100 - 40) = 10$.
Hence the percentage of pupils who like all four fruits is at least 10%.

18. E Multiplying $\frac{1}{x} + \frac{1}{y} = \frac{1}{2}$ throughout by $2xy$ gives $2y + 2x = xy$. Hence $xy = 2(x + y) \ldots (1)$.
But since $x^2y + xy^2 = xy(x + y)$, we can use (1) to give $xy(x + y) = 2(x + y)(x + y)$.
But $x + y = 20$, hence $x^2y + xy^2 = 2 \times 20^2 = 800$.

19. B As each square has area 1 its side length must be 1.
The external angle of the small regular octagon is $\frac{1}{8} \times 360° = 45°$.
Hence, as the sum of the angles on a straight line is $180°$ and the sum of the angles in a kite is $360°$, the four angles in each of the eight kites (white) are: $90°$, $90°$, $135°$ and $45°$.
As the light grey kites and the white kites are similar, the interior angles are the same. Two of the sides of the grey kite have length 1. Let the other sides have length a. Using the Cosine Rule twice within a light grey kite, the square of the short diagonal is $1^2 + 1^2 - 2 \times 1 \times 1 \cos 135° = a^2 + a^2 - 2a \times a \cos 45°$. Hence $2 + 2 \times 1/\sqrt{2} = 2a^2 - 2a^2 \times 1/\sqrt{2}$.
Thus $a^2 = \dfrac{1 + \frac{1}{\sqrt{2}}}{1 - \frac{1}{\sqrt{2}}} = \dfrac{\sqrt{2}+1}{\sqrt{2}-1}$ and so $a = \sqrt{2}+1$.
But the area of one of the light grey kites is $2 \times \frac{1}{2}a \times 1 = a$.
Hence the area of one of the light grey kites is $\sqrt{2}+1$.

20. B Squaring the equation $\sqrt{x} - \sqrt{11} = \sqrt{y}$ gives $x - 2\sqrt{11x} + 11 = y$ ... (1). You see here that $2\sqrt{11x}$ is an integer. Thus $x = 11a^2$ for some integer a. Hence in (1), $y = 11a^2 - 22a + 11 = 11(a^2 - 2a + 1)$. Thus $\dfrac{x}{y} = \left(\dfrac{a}{a-1}\right)^2$ whose maximum value, for integer a, is easily seen to be $\left(\frac{2}{1}\right)^2 = 4$.

21. C At least one of d'Artagnan and Athos is lying. One of Porthos or Aramis is telling the truth and the other is lying. So the number of liars is either two (d'Artagnan and Porthos) or three (all except Porthos).

22. A As the sum of the angles in a triangle is $180°$, in triangle CBF, $\angle BFC = 90°$. As vertically opposite angles are equal $\angle DFE = \angle BFC = 90°$. As the sum of the angles on a straight line is $180°$, $\angle DFB = \angle EFC = 90°$. Hence in triangle EFD, $\tan \alpha = \frac{DE}{EF}$: in triangle DFB, $\tan 10° = \frac{DF}{FB}$: in triangle BFC, $\tan 20° = \frac{FB}{FC}$ and in triangle CEF, $\tan 50° = \frac{EF}{FC}$. Thus $\tan \alpha = \frac{DE}{EF} = \frac{\tan 10° FB}{EF} = \frac{\tan 10° \tan 20° FC}{EF} = \frac{\tan 10° \tan 20°}{\tan 50°}$.

23. B $x^2 + y^2 + 2xy + 6x + 6y + 4 = (x+y)^2 + 6(x+y) + 4 = [(x+y)+3][(x+y)+3] - 5 = (x+y+3)^2 - 5$. But $(x+y+3)^2 \geq 0$ for all values of x and y. As $x+y+3$ can be 0 for appropriate values of x, y the minimum value of $x^2 + y^2 + 2xy + 6x + 6y + 4$ is -5.

24. B Let the radii of the circles from smallest to largest be r_1, r_2 and r_3 respectively. Hence $16r_1 = r_3 + 2r_2 + r_1$, thus $r_3 = 15r_1 - 2r_2$... (1). Let $r_1 + x$ be the distance from Q to the centre of the smallest circle. By similar triangles,
$$\dfrac{r_1}{r_1+x} = \dfrac{r_2}{x+2r_1+r_2} = \dfrac{r_3}{16r_1+r_1+x} \ldots (2).$$
Thus $r_1(x+2r_1+r_2) = r_2(r_1+x)$. Hence $r_2 = \dfrac{r_1 x + 2r_1^2}{x}$ ... (3). From (1) and (2) $\dfrac{r_1 x}{r_1+x} = \dfrac{(15r_1-2r_2)x}{17r_1+x}$ hence $\dfrac{r_1 x}{r_1+x} = \dfrac{15r_1 x - 2(r_1 x + 2r_1^2)}{17r_1+x}$. Dividing throughout by r_1 and simplifying gives $12x^2 - 8r_1 x - 4r_1^2 = 0$. Hence $(3x + r_1)(x - r_1) = 0$ so, as $r_1 > 0$, $x = r_1$. Thus $\sin \dfrac{\angle PQR}{2} = \dfrac{r_1}{r_1+x} = \dfrac{r_1}{2r_1} = \dfrac{1}{2}$. Hence $\frac{1}{2} \angle PQR = 30°$ so $\angle PQR = 60°$.

25. C Three vertices of the smaller cube lie on edges of the larger cube, the same distance along each. Let this distance be x and let the distance between any two of these vertices be y. Hence, by Pythagoras' Theorem, $y^2 = x^2 + x^2$ and, as the side length of the smaller cube is 3, $y^2 = 3^2 + 3^2$. Thus $x = 3$ and $y = 3\sqrt{2}$.
The intersection of the cubes forms two congruent tetrahedra of base area equal to $\frac{1}{2}y^2 \sin 60° = \frac{1}{2}(3\sqrt{2})^2 \times \frac{\sqrt{3}}{2} = \frac{9\sqrt{3}}{2}$. Let h be the perpendicular height of the tetrahedra. Hence, using Pythagoras' Theorem twice gives $9 = h^2 + 6$, thus $h = \sqrt{3}$.
Thus the total volume of the sculpture is $4^3 + 3^3 - 2 \times \frac{1}{3} \times \frac{9\sqrt{3}}{2} \times \sqrt{3} = 91 - 9 = 82$.

Senior Challenge 2012 solutions

1. **E** If an odd number is written as the sum of two prime numbers then one of those primes is 2, since 2 is the only even prime. However, 9 is not prime so 11 cannot be written as the sum of two primes. Note that $5 = 2 + 3$; $7 = 2 + 5$; $9 = 2 + 7$; $10 = 3 + 7$, so 11 is the only alternative which is not the sum of two primes.

2. **B** The interior angles of an equilateral triangle, square, regular pentagon are $60°, 90°, 108°$ respectively. The sum of the angles at a point is $360°$. So $\theta = 360 - (60 + 90 + 108) = 102$.

3. **D** The cost now is $(70 + 4 \times 5 + 6 \times 2)\text{p} = £1.02$.

4. **B** One hundred thousand million is $10^2 \times 10^3 \times 10^6 = 10^{11}$. So the number of stars is $10^{11} \times 10^{11} = 10^{22}$.

5. **C** Let the required addition be 'ab' + 'cd' + 'ef', where a, b, c, d, e, f are single, distinct digits. To make this sum as large as possible, we need a, c, e (the tens digits) as large as possible; so they must be $7, 8, 9$ in some order. Then we need b, d, f as large as possible, so $4, 5, 6$ in some order. Hence the largest sum is $10(7 + 8 + 9) + (4 + 5 + 6) = 10 \times 24 + 15 = 255$.

6. **C** In order to be a multiple of 15, a number must be a multiple both of 3 and of 5. So its units digit must be 0 or 5. However, the units digit must also equal the thousands digit and this cannot be 0, so the required number is of the form '$5aa5$'. The largest such four-digit numbers are 5995, 5885, 5775. Their digit sums are 28, 26, 24 respectively. In order to be a multiple of 3, the digit sum of a number must also be a multiple of 3, so 5775 is the required number. The sum of its digits is 24.

7. **D** Add the first and third equations: $2x = 4$, so $x = 2$. Add the first two equations: $2x + 2y = 3$, so $y = -\frac{1}{2}$. Substitute for x and y in the first equation: $2 + \left(-\frac{1}{2}\right) + z = 1$ so $z = -\frac{1}{2}$. Therefore $xyz = 2 \times \left(-\frac{1}{2}\right) \times \left(-\frac{1}{2}\right) = \frac{1}{2}$.

8. **C** If an equilateral triangle is split into a number of smaller identical equilateral triangles then there must be one small triangle in the top row, three small triangles in the row below, five small triangles in the row below that and so on. So the total number of small triangles is 4 or 9 or 16 etc. These are all squares and it is left to the reader to prove that the sum of the first n odd numbers is n^2. So, for three copies of a given tile to form an equilateral triangle, the number of triangles which comprise the tile must be one third of a square number.
Only the tiles made up of three equilateral triangles and twelve equilateral triangles satisfy this condition. However, it is still necessary to show that three copies of these tiles can indeed make equilateral triangles. The diagrams above show how they can do this.

9. **C** If Pierre is telling the truth then Qadr is not telling the truth. However, this means that Ratna is telling the truth, so this leads to a contradiction as Pierre stated that just one person is telling the truth. So Pierre is not telling the truth, which means that Qadr is telling the truth, but Ratna is not telling the truth. This in turn means that Sven is telling the truth, but Tanya is not. So only Qadr and Sven are telling the truth.

10. **E** It can be deduced that N must consist of at least 224 digits since the largest 223-digit positive integer consists of 223 nines and has a digit sum of 2007. It is possible to find 224-digit positive integers which have a digit sum of 2012.
The largest of these is 99 999 ...999 995 and the smallest is 59 999 ...999 999.
So $N = 59\,999\ldots 999\,999$ and $N + 1 = 60\,000\ldots 000\,000$ (223 zeros).

11. **D** Let the radius of the circular piece of cardboard be r. The diagram shows a sector of the circle which would make one hat, with the minor arc shown becoming the circumference of the base of the hat. The circumference of the circle is $2\pi r$. Now $6r < 2\pi r < 7r$. This shows that we can cut out 6 hats in this fashion and also shows that the area of cardboard unused in cutting out *any* 6 hats is less than the area of a single hat. Hence there is no possibility that more than 6 hats could be cut out.

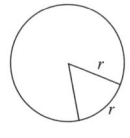

Senior Challenge 2012 solutions

12. E Two different ways of expressing 5 are 1 + 4 and 4 + 1. In the following list these are denoted as {1, 4: two ways}. The list of all possible ways is {5: one way}, {2, 3: two ways}, {1, 4: two ways}, {1, 2, 2: three ways}, {1, 1, 3: three ways}, {1, 1, 1, 2: four ways}, {1, 1, 1, 1, 1: one way}. So in total there are 16 ways.
{*Different expressions of a positive integer in the above form are known as 'partitions'. It may be shown that the number of distinct compositions of a positive integer n is 2^{n-1}.*}

13. B The table below shows the position of the face marked with paint when the base of the cube is on the 25 squares. Code: T - top, B - base; F - front; H - hidden (rear); L - left; R - right.

1	2	**3**	4	5	6	**7**	8	9	10	**11**	12	13	14	**15**	16	17	18	19	**20**	21	22	23	**24**	25
T	H	**B**	F	T	R	**B**	L	T	F	**B**	H	T	L	**B**	R	R	R	B	**B**	L	L	L	**B**	F

So the required sum is 3 + 7 + 11 + 15 + 20 + 24 = 80.

14. D Note that each student has a language in common with exactly four of the other five students. For instance, Jean-Pierre has a language in common with each of Ina, Karim, Lionel and Mary. Only Helga does not have a language in common with Jean-Pierre. So whichever two students are chosen, the probability that they have a language in common is 4/5.

15. A Let Professor Rosseforp's usual journey take t minutes at an average speed of v metres/minute. Then the distance to work is vt metres. On Thursday his speed increased by 10%, i.e. it was $11v/10$ metres/minute. The time taken was $(t - x)$ minutes. Therefore $11v/10 \times (t - x) = vt$. So $11(t - x) = 10t$, i.e. $t = 11x$.

16. A At points A and C, $x = 0$. So $y^2 - 4y = 12$, i.e. $(y - 6)(y + 2) = 0$, i.e. $y = 6$ or $y = -2$. So C is $(0, -2)$ and A is $(0, 6)$. At points B and D, $y = 0$. So $x^2 + x = 12$, i.e. $(x - 3)(x + 4) = 0$, i.e. $x = 3$ or $x = -4$. So D is $(-4, 0)$ and B is $(3, 0)$. Therefore the areas of triangles DAB and DBC are $\frac{1}{2} \times 7 \times 6 = 21$ and $\frac{1}{2} \times 7 \times 2 = 7$. So $ABCD$ has area 28. {*It is left to the reader to prove that area $ABCD = \frac{1}{2} BD \times AC$.*}

17. B In the diagram, B is the centre of the quarter-circle arc AC; D is the point where the central square touches arc AC; F is the point where the central square touches arc CE; O is the centre of the circle. As both the circle and arc AC have radius 1, $OABC$ is a square of side 1. By Pythagoras' Theorem: $OB^2 = 1^2 + 1^2$. So $OB = \sqrt{2}$. Therefore $OD = OB - DB = \sqrt{2} - 1$. By a similar argument, $OF = \sqrt{2} - 1$. Now $DF^2 = OD^2 + OF^2 = 2 \times OD^2$ since $OD = OF$. So the side of the square is $\sqrt{2} \times OD = \sqrt{2}(\sqrt{2} - 1) = 2 - \sqrt{2}$.

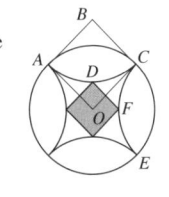

18. A In the diagram, D is the midpoint of AC. Triangle ABC is isosceles since $AB = BC = \frac{1}{2}$. Therefore, BD bisects $\angle ABC$ and BD is perpendicular to AC. The angles at a point total 360°, so $\angle ABC = 360° - 2 \times 90° - 2\alpha = 180° - 2\alpha$. Therefore $\angle ABD = \angle CBD = 90° - \alpha$. So $\angle BAD = \angle BCD = \alpha$. Therefore $x = AC = 2 \times AD = 2 \times AB \cos\alpha = 2 \times \frac{1}{2} \cos\alpha = \cos\alpha$.

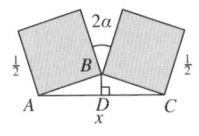

19. E Note that the number represented by x appears in both the horizontal row and the vertical column. Note also that $2 + 3 + 4 + 5 + 6 + 7 + 8 = 35$. Since the numbers in the row and those in the column have sum 21, we deduce that $x = 2 \times 21 - 35 = 7$. 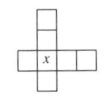
We now need two disjoint sets of three numbers chosen from 2, 3, 4, 5, 6, 8 so that the numbers in both sets total 14. The only possibilities are {2, 4, 8} and {3, 5, 6}. We have six choices of which number to put in the top space in the vertical line, then two for the next space down and one for the bottom space. That leaves three choices for the first space in the horizontal line, two for the next space and one for the final space. So the total number of ways is $6 \times 2 \times 1 \times 3 \times 2 \times 1 = 72$.

20. **E** The two tangents drawn from a point outside a circle to that circle are equal in length. This theorem has been used to mark four pairs of equal line segments on the diagram. In the circle the diameter, XY, has been marked. It is also a perpendicular height of the trapezium. We are given that $SR = PQ = 25$ cm so we can deduce that $(a + d) + (b + c) = 25 + 25 = 50$. The area of trapezium $PQRS = \frac{1}{2}(SP + QR) \times XY = 600$ cm^2. Therefore $\frac{1}{2}(a + b + c + d) \times 2r = 600$. So $\frac{1}{2} \times 50 \times 2r = 600$, i.e. $r = 12$.

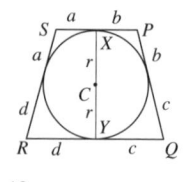

21. **D** $(x + y\sqrt{2})^2 = x^2 + 2xy\sqrt{2} + 2y^2$. Note that all of the alternatives given are of the form $a + 12\sqrt{2}$ so we need $xy = 6$. The only ordered pairs (x, y) of positive integers which satisfy this are $(1, 6), (2, 3), (3, 2), (6, 1)$. For these, the values of $x^2 + 2y^2$ are $73, 22, 17, 38$ respectively. So the required number is $54 + 12\sqrt{2}$.

22. **B** Let the perpendicular from Y meet UV at T and let $\angle ZXV = \alpha$. Note that $\angle VZX = 90°$ as a tangent to a circle is perpendicular to the radius at the point of contact. Therefore $\sin \alpha = \frac{r}{3r} = \frac{1}{3}$. Consider triangle YTX: $\sin \alpha = \frac{YT}{YX}$. So $YT = YX \sin \alpha = \frac{4r}{3}$. So the area of triangle $YVW = \frac{1}{2} \times VW \times YT = \frac{1}{2} \times r \times \frac{4r}{3} = \frac{2r^2}{3}$.

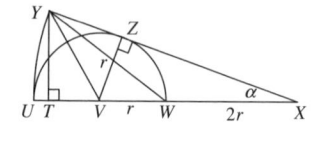

23. **C** Tom wins after one attempt each if he hits the target and Geri misses. The probability of this happening is $\frac{4}{5} \times \frac{1}{3} = \frac{4}{15}$. Similarly the probability that Geri wins after one attempt is $\frac{2}{3} \times \frac{1}{5} = \frac{2}{15}$. So the probability that both competitors will have at least one more attempt is $1 - \frac{4}{15} - \frac{2}{15} = \frac{3}{5}$.
Therefore the probability that Tom wins after two attempts each is $\frac{3}{5} \times \frac{4}{15}$. The probability that neither Tom nor Geri wins after two attempts each is $\frac{3}{5} \times \frac{3}{5}$. So the probability that Tom wins after three attempts each is $\left(\frac{3}{5}\right)^2 \times \frac{4}{15}$ and, more generally, the probability that he wins after n attempts each is $\left(\frac{3}{5}\right)^{n-1} \times \frac{4}{15}$.
Therefore the probability that Tom wins is $\frac{4}{15} + \left(\frac{3}{5}\right) \times \frac{4}{15} + \left(\frac{3}{5}\right)^2 \times \frac{4}{15} + \left(\frac{3}{5}\right)^3 \times \frac{4}{15} + \ldots$.
This is the sum to infinity of a geometric series with first term $\frac{4}{15}$ and common ratio $\frac{3}{5}$. Its value is $\frac{4}{15} \div \left(1 - \frac{3}{5}\right) = \frac{2}{3}$.

24. **B** The diagram shows one of the three quadrilaterals making up the tile, labelled and with a line BE inserted. Note that it is a trapezium. As three quadrilaterals fit together, it may be deduced that $\angle ABC = 360° \div 3 = 120°$, so $\angle BAD = 60°$. It may also be deduced that the length of AB is $1 + x$, where x is the length of BC. Now $\cos \angle BAD = \cos 60° = \frac{1}{2} = \frac{1-x}{1+x}$. So $1 + x = 2 - 2x$, i.e. $x = \frac{1}{3}$.
The area of $ABCD$ is $\frac{1}{2}(AD + BC) \times CD = \frac{1}{2}\left(1 + \frac{1}{3}\right) \times \frac{4}{3} \sin 60°$ $= \frac{2}{3} \times \frac{4}{3} \times \frac{\sqrt{3}}{2} = \frac{4\sqrt{3}}{9}$. So the area of the tile is $3 \times \frac{4\sqrt{3}}{9} = \frac{4\sqrt{3}}{3}$.

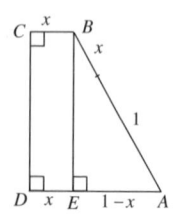

25. **B** Starting with $(x + y)^2 = (x + 4)(y - 4)$ and expanding both sides gives $x^2 + 2xy + y^2 = xy - 4x + 4y - 16$, i.e. $x^2 + (y + 4)x + y^2 - 4y + 16 = 0$.
To eliminate the xy term we let $z = x + \frac{1}{2}y$ and then replace x by $z - \frac{1}{2}y$. The equation above becomes $z^2 + 4\left(z - \frac{1}{2}y\right) + \frac{3}{4}y^2 - 4y + 16 = 0$. However,

$$z^2 + 4\left(z - \tfrac{1}{2}y\right) + \tfrac{3}{4}y^2 - 4y + 16 = (z + 2)^2 + \tfrac{3}{4}y^2 - 6y + 12$$

$$= (z + 2)^2 + \tfrac{3}{4}(y^2 - 8y + 16) = (z + 2)^2 + \tfrac{3}{4}(y + 4)^2.$$

So the only real solution is when $z = -2$ and $y = 4$; i.e. $x = -4$ and $y = 4$.

Senior Challenge 2013 solutions

234 Ten Further Years of Mathematical Challenges

1. **A** Calculating the value of each option gives $2 + 0 + 1 + 3 = 6, 2 \times 0 + 1 + 3 = 4$, $2 + 0 \times 1 + 3 = 5, 2 + 0 + 1 \times 3 = 5$ and $2 \times 0 \times 1 \times 3 = 0$ so $2 + 0 + 1 + 3$ is the largest.

2. **C** In metres, the height 2m 8cm and 3mm is $2 + 8 \times 0.01 + 3 \times 0.001 = 2 + 0.08 + 0.003 = 2.083$ m.

3. **D** Factorising $2013^2 - 2013$ gives $2013(2013 - 1)$ which equals 2013×2012. So the tens digit is 5 as $13 \times 12 = 156$ and only this part of the product contributes to the tens digit of the answer.

4. **C** In order to pass through each square exactly once, a route must pass in and out of both unlabelled corner squares and also pass through the middle. Passing in and out of a corner involves three squares, coloured grey, white and grey in that order. Passing in and out of the two unlabelled corners therefore accounts for six unlabelled squares, leaving only the middle square which must be in the middle of any possible route. So, there are two possible routes as shown.

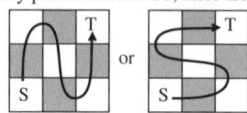

5. **E** Since $x(y + 2) = 100$ and $y(x + 2) = 60$ then $xy + 2x = 100$ and $xy + 2y = 60$. Subtracting gives $2x - 2y = 40$ and therefore $x - y = 20$.

6. **E** Let d be the number of lengths that Rebecca intended to swim. Then $6 = \dfrac{d}{4} - \dfrac{d}{5} = \dfrac{d}{20}$ and therefore $d = 6 \times 20 = 120$.

7. **B** The first item that Susanna buys makes her bill a number of pounds and 99 pence. Each extra item she buys after that decreases by one the number of pence in her total bill. Let n be the number of items bought. To be charged £65.76, $1 + 99 - n = 76$ so $n = 100 - 76 = 24$. Alternatives of 124 items or more are infeasible as they would each give a total greater than £65.76.

8. **B** The area of the shaded square is equal to the area of the large square minus the area of the four triangles. Thus the area of the shaded square is $(4x)^2 - 4 \times \frac{1}{2} \times 4x \times x = 16x^2 - 8x^2 = 8x^2$. So the side-length is $\sqrt{8x^2} = 2\sqrt{2}x$.

9. **A** When a square loses a quarter of its area, thereby becoming a smaller square, three quarters of its area remains. Therefore the lengths of the sides of the original square have been multiplied by $\sqrt{\frac{3}{4}} = \frac{1}{2}\sqrt{3} \approx 0.866$. This means a reduction of $(100 - 86.6)\%$ which is approximately 13%.

10. **B** The median is 10. Therefore the mode must be 11 and there must be two 11s in Frank's list. The mean is 9, so the total of the five numbers is 45. This means that the total of the two smallest integers is $45 - (10 + 2 \times 11) = 13$. The maximum size of the second largest integer is 9 so the smallest integer that Frank could include in his list is $13 - 9 = 4$.

11. **A** Let the radius of the circle be r. Then its area is πr^2. The height of the triangle is r and its area is $\frac{1}{2} \times PQ \times r$. So $\frac{1}{2} \times PQ \times r = \pi r^2$ and therefore $PQ = 2\pi r$, which is also the circumference of the circle. Therefore the ratio of the length of PQ to the circumference of the circle is 1 : 1.

12. **B** There are three options for Sammy's first choice and then two options for each subsequent choice. Therefore the number of possible ways is $3 \times 2 \times 2 \times 2 \times 2 = 48$.

13. **D** Angus completes the course in 40 minutes, so he spends 20 minutes (which is $\frac{1}{3}$ of an hour) walking and the same time running. By using distance = speed × time, the length of the course is $3 \times \frac{1}{3} + 6 \times \frac{1}{3} = 1 + 2 = 3$ miles.
Bruce completes the course by walking for $1\frac{1}{2}$ miles and running for $1\frac{1}{2}$ miles. So, by using time = $\dfrac{\text{distance}}{\text{speed}}$, Bruce's total time in hours is $\dfrac{1\frac{1}{2}}{3} + \dfrac{1\frac{1}{2}}{6} = \dfrac{1}{2} + \dfrac{1}{4} = \dfrac{3}{4}$ of an hour. So Bruce takes 45 minutes to complete the course.

Senior Challenge 2013 solutions

14. **D** Triangle RST is similar to triangle RPS as their corresponding angles are equal. Using Pythagoras' Theorem, the ratio of RS to RP is $1 : \sqrt{5}$. So the ratio of RT to RS is also $1 : \sqrt{5}$. Therefore the ratio of the area of the triangle RST to the area of triangle RPS is $1 : 5$. Triangle RPS is half the rectangle $PQRS$, so the ratio of the area of triangle RST to the area of rectangle $PQRS$ is $1 : 10$.

15. **B** A prime number has exactly two factors, one of which is 1. The expression $4^n - 1$ can be factorised as $4^n - 1 = (2^n + 1)(2^n - 1)$. For $4^n - 1$ to be prime, the smaller of the factors, $2^n - 1$, must equal 1.
If $2^n - 1 = 1$ then $2^n = 2$ giving $n = 1$. So there is exactly one value of n for which $4^n - 1$ is prime and this value is 1.

16. **D** By the Fundamental Theorem of Arithmetic, every positive integer greater than 1 is either prime or a product of two or more primes. A number that is the product of two or more primes is called a *composite* number.
We are looking to choose, from the options provided, a composite number which is of the form $8n + 3$ but does not have a prime factor of the form $8n + 3$.
Option A is prime, so is not possible. Options B and C are not of the form $8n + 3$.
Option E is $8 \times 12 + 3 = 99$. The number 99, when expressed as a product of its prime factors, is $3 \times 3 \times 11$ and the factor 11 is of the required form as $11 = 8 \times 1 + 3$.
However, option D is of the form $8n + 3$ as $8 \times 11 + 3 = 91$ but neither of the prime factors of 91, which are 7 and 13, are of the form $8n + 3$.

17. **A** Triangle PQR is equilateral so $\angle QPU = \angle UPT = \angle TPR = 20°$. Triangle PUT is isosceles, so $\angle PUT = 80°$. Let X be the midpoint of PQ and Y be the midpoint of UT.
Considering the right-angled triangle PXU gives $\cos 20° = \dfrac{PX}{PU} = \dfrac{\frac{1}{2}}{PU}$, so $PU = \dfrac{1}{2\cos 20°}$.
Considering the right-angled triangle PUY gives $\cos 80° = \dfrac{UY}{PU}$, so $UY = PU \cos 80° = \dfrac{\cos 80°}{2\cos 20°}$. Therefore $UT = 2UY = \dfrac{2\cos 80°}{2\cos 20°} = \dfrac{\cos 80°}{\cos 20°}$.
{*Note that triangle UTS is a Morley triangle, named after the mathematician Frank Morley. His 1899 trisector theorem states that in any triangle, the three points of intersection of the adjacent angle trisectors form an equilateral triangle, in this case, triangle UTS.*}

18. **C** The product of all the numbers in the list is $2 \times 3 \times 12 \times 14 \times 15 \times 20 \times 21$ which, when expressed in terms of prime factors is $2 \times 3 \times 2 \times 2 \times 3 \times 2 \times 7 \times 3 \times 5 \times 2 \times 2 \times 5 \times 3 \times 7$ which is equal to $2^6 \times 3^4 \times 5^2 \times 7^2 = (2^3 \times 3^2 \times 5 \times 7)^2 = 2520^2$. The answer 2520 is expressible as both $2 \times 3 \times 20 \times 21$ and $12 \times 14 \times 15$.

19. **C** There are 25 vertices in the diagram. Each vertex is part of a row of 5 vertices and a column of 5 vertices. Each vertex is therefore an integer number of units away from the 4 other vertices in its row and from the other 4 vertices in its column. This appears to give $25 \times (4 + 4) = 200$ pairs. However, counting in this manner includes each pair twice so there are 100 different pairs.
By using the Pythagorean triple 3, 4, 5, each corner vertex is five units away from two other non-corner vertices, giving another 8 pairs. No other Pythagorean triples include small enough numbers to yield pairs of vertices on this grid.
Thus the total number of pairs is 108.

20. **E** Let the two positive numbers be x and y with $x > y$. The sum of the numbers is greater than their difference, so the two ratios which are equal are $x : y$ and $x + y : x - y$. Therefore $\dfrac{x}{y} = \dfrac{x+y}{x-y}$. By dividing the top and bottom of the right-hand side by y we obtain $\dfrac{x}{y} = \dfrac{\frac{x}{y}+1}{\frac{x}{y}-1}$.
Letting $k = \frac{x}{y}$ gives $k = \frac{k+1}{k-1}$ which gives the quadratic $k^2 - 2k - 1 = 0$. Completing the square gives $(k-1)^2 = 2$ whence $k = 1 \pm \sqrt{2}$. However, as x and y are both positive, $k \neq 1 - \sqrt{2}$. As the ratio $\frac{x}{y} = 1 + \sqrt{2}$, the ratio $x : y$ is $1 + \sqrt{2} : 1$.

21. **B** Let the top vertex of the square be A and the midpoints of the two lines that meet at A be B and C. The line BC is of length $\frac{1}{2}$ and is perpendicular to the diagonal of the square through A. Let the point of intersection of these two lines be D. Let the end of the uppermost arc, above B, be E. Then $ADBE$ is a rhombus, made from four radii of the arcs, AD, DB, BE and EA, each of length $\frac{1}{4}$. As $\angle ADB = 90°$, this rhombus is a square.
It then follows that the four arcs whose centres are the vertices of the original square are all semi-circles. The remaining four touching arcs are each $\frac{3}{4}$ of a circle.
In total, the length of the border is $4 \times \frac{1}{2} + 4 \times \frac{3}{4}$ times the circumference of a circle with the same radius, so is $5 \times 2\pi \times \frac{1}{4} = \frac{5}{2}\pi$.

22. **C** The numbers in the sequence $11, 21, 31, 41, \ldots, 981, 991$ are of the form $10n + 1$ for $n = 1$ to 99. There are therefore 99 numbers in this sequence.
Twelve terms of this sequence can be expressed using factors of the form $10k + 1$. In this form, these terms are $11 \times 11, 11 \times 21, 11 \times 31, \ldots, 11 \times 81$ and 21×21, $21 \times 31, 21 \times 41$ and 31×31. All other pairings give products that are too large. Hence, there are $99 - 12 = 87$ 'grime' numbers.

23. **A** The pentagon $RTWVU$ is the remainder when triangles SUV and WTQ are removed from the bottom right half of the square. Draw in the diagonal PR and consider the triangle PRS. The medians of triangle PRS join each vertex P, R and S to the midpoint of its opposite side, i.e. P to U and S to the middle of the square. The medians intersect at V and therefore the height of V above SR is $\frac{1}{3}$ of PS.
The area of triangle SUV is therefore $\frac{1}{2} \times \frac{1}{2}SR \times \frac{1}{3}PS = \frac{1}{12}$ of the area of the square. By symmetry, this is also the area of triangle WTQ. The area of the pentagon $RTWVU$ is then $\frac{1}{2} - \left(\frac{1}{12} + \frac{1}{12}\right) = \frac{1}{3}$ of the area of the square $PQRS$.

24. **E** As they are vertically opposite, $\angle POQ = \angle SOR$. Let α denote the size of each of these. Applying the cosine rule to triangle SOR gives $8^2 = 4^2 + 5^2 - 2 \times 4 \times 5 \cos\alpha$, therefore $40 \cos\alpha = -23$.
Similarly, from triangle POQ we obtain $x^2 = 4^2 + 10^2 - 2 \times 4 \times 10 \cos\alpha$. So $x^2 = 16 + 100 - 2 \times (-23) = 162$.
Hence $x = \sqrt{162} = \sqrt{81 \times 2} = 9\sqrt{2}$.

25. **D** Jessica must travel alternately on lines which are connected to station X (i.e. s, t or u), and connected to station Y (i.e. p, q or r). In order to depart from X and end her journey at Y, she must travel along an even number of lines. This can be 2, 4 or 6 lines, making 1, 3 or 5 changes respectively.
Case A, 2 lines: Jessica leaves station X along one of the lines s, t or u, makes one change onto one of lines p, q or r and reaches station Y. Here there are 3×3 possibilities.
Case B, 4 lines: Jessica leaves station X along one of the lines s, t or u and makes her first change onto one of lines p, q or r. She then makes her second change onto either of the two lines s, t or u on which she has not previously travelled and her third change onto either of the two lines p, q or r on which she has not previously travelled and reaches station Y. Here there are $3 \times 3 \times 2 \times 2$ possibilities.
Case C, 6 lines: Her journey is as described in Case B but her fourth change is onto the last of the lines s, t or u on which she has not previously travelled and her fifth change is onto the last of the lines p, q or r on which she has not previously travelled. Here there are $3 \times 3 \times 2 \times 2 \times 1 \times 1$ possibilities.
So in total Jessica can choose $9 + 36 + 36 = 81$ different routes.

Senior Challenge 2014 solutions

238   *Ten Further Years of Mathematical Challenges*

1. **C** $98 \times 102 = (100 - 2)(100 + 2) = 10000 - 4 = 9996$.

2. **B**   There are points on the diagram, such as A, where the edges of three regions meet, so three or more different colours are required. A colouring with three colours is possible as shown, so the smallest number of colours required is three.

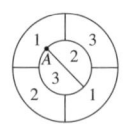

3. **D**   The year 1997 was not a leap year so had $365 = 52 \times 7 + 1$ days. Hence, starting from 1st January, 1997 had 52 complete weeks, each starting with the same day as 1st January, followed by 31st December. As 31st December was a Wednesday, so too were all the first days of the 52 complete weeks. So there were 53 Wednesdays in 1997.

4. **A**   Let the original amount of money be x (in pounds). If I spend $\frac{1}{5}$ then $\frac{4}{5}$ remains. When I spend $\frac{1}{4}$ of that, $\frac{3}{4}$ of it remains. So $\frac{4}{5} \times \frac{3}{4}$ is what is left and that is £15. As $\frac{4}{5} \times \frac{3}{4} = \frac{3}{5}$, we have $x = \frac{5}{3} \times 15 = 25$. So the original amount of money is £25.

5. **C**   The prime factorisations of 20 and 14 are $20 = 2 \times 2 \times 5$ and $14 = 2 \times 7$. The lowest common multiple of 20 and 14 is 140 as $140 = 2 \times 2 \times 5 \times 7$. For a number to be a multiple of 20 and 14 it must be a multiple of 140. As $2014 \div 140 = 14$ remainder 54, there are 14 integers in the required range. Note: The integer 0, which is also a multiple of 20 and of 14 is excluded as we are considering numbers *between* 1 and 2014.

6. **B**   Working from right to left, the units column shows that $S = 2$ or 7. If $S = 2$, then $I + I = 1$ or 11, neither of which is possible. Hence $S = 7$ and it follows that $I + I = 0$ or 10. However, as the digits are non-zero, $I = 5$. The hundreds column then shows that $H = 9$ and so $T = 1$. This gives $T + H + I + S = 1 + 9 + 5 + 7 = 22$.

7. **B**   Since $36.8 \div 86$ is approximately $40 \div 100 = 0.4$, the sea level rises by roughly 0.4 cm, which is 4 mm, per year.

8. **C**   The intersections occur in six groups and the total number of points is $2 \times 3 + 2 \times 4 + 2 \times 5 + 3 \times 4 + 3 \times 5 + 4 \times 5$ which is $6 + 8 + 10 + 12 + 15 + 20 = 71$.

9. **D**   A number is divisible by 9 if and only if its digit sum is divisible by 9. The number 10^{2014} can be written as a 1 followed by 2014 zeros, so this part has a digit sum of 1. Of all the options given, only adding on 8 to this will make a digit sum of 9, so $10^{2014} + 8$ is the required answer.

10. **C**   Let the length of the rectangle be x cm and its width be y cm. The area is given as 120 cm^2 so $xy = 120$. The perimeter is 46 cm, so $46 = 2x + 2y$ and therefore $23 = x + y$. Using Pythagoras' Theorem, the length of the diagonal is $\sqrt{x^2 + y^2}$. As $x^2 + y^2 = (x + y)^2 - 2xy, \sqrt{x^2 + y^2} = \sqrt{23^2 - 2 \times 120} = \sqrt{529 - 240} = \sqrt{289} = 17$. So the diagonal has length 17 cm.

11. **E**   First note that the exponent in each of the five options is prime, so we need to see which of the five numbers is not prime. By direct calculation the numbers are 3, 7, 31, 127 and 2047. Only the last number is not prime, as $2047 = 23 \times 89$.

12. **D**   Let Lionel have x cherries. Michael then has $(x + 7)$ cherries. Karen's number of cherries is described in two ways. She has $3x$ cherries and also $2(x + 7)$ cherries. So $3x = 2x + 14$ and therefore $x = 14$. Lionel has 14 cherries, Michael 21 cherries and Karen 42 cherries giving a total of $14 + 21 + 42 = 77$ cherries.

13. **E**   Each of P, Q, R, S and T when folded to form a cube consists of a ▟ shape of three black faces and an interlocking ▛ shape of three white faces, so they are all nets of the same cube.

14. **E**   Rearranging the equation $\dfrac{3x + y}{x - 3y} = -1$ gives $3x + y = -x + 3y$. So $4x = 2y$ and therefore $y = 2x$. Hence $\dfrac{x + 3y}{3x - y} = \dfrac{x + 3 \times 2x}{3x - 2x} = \dfrac{7x}{x} = 7$.

Senior Challenge 2014 solutions

15. **C**

A		
B	C	D
E	F	G

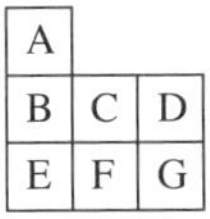

Label the squares as shown. Possible pairs to be shaded which include A are AD, AE, AF and AG. Pairs excluding A are BD, BG, DE, EG. Triples must include A and there are two possibilities, ADE and AEG. This gives 10 ways of shading the grid,

16. **A** The diameter of the circle is the same length as the longest sides of the rectangle, so the radius of the circle is 6. The perpendicular distance from the centre of the circle to the longest sides of the rectangle is half of the length of the shortest sides which is 3.

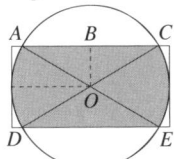

Drawing two diameters AE and DC as shown splits the shaded area into two sectors and two isosceles triangles. As OA is 6 and OB is 3, $\angle AOB = 60°$ and, by Pythagoras' Theorem, $AB = 3\sqrt{3}$. Thus $\angle AOD = 180° - 2 \times 60° = 60°$. So the shaded area is

$$2 \times \frac{60}{360} \times \pi \times 6^2 + 2 \times \frac{1}{2} \times 2 \times 3\sqrt{3} \times 3 = 12\pi + 18\sqrt{3}.$$

17. **C** The tanker and the cruise liner are travelling in parallel and opposite directions, each making an angle of 45° with the line joining their starting positions. The shortest distance between the ships is d, the perpendicular distance between the parallel lines. This is independent of the speeds of the ships.

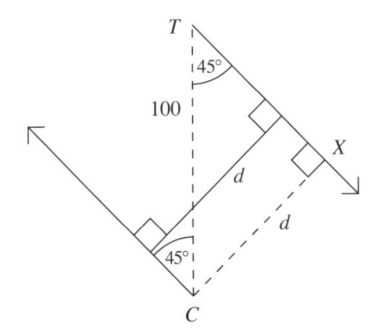

Considering triangle TCX gives $\sin 45° = \dfrac{d}{100}$

so $d = \dfrac{1}{\sqrt{2}} \times 100 = 50\sqrt{2}.$

18. **D** To draw the longest unbroken line Beatrix must be able to draw her design on the net of a cube without taking her pen off the paper. She must minimise the number of lines of length $\sqrt{2}$ and maximise the number of lines of length 2. If no lines of length $\sqrt{2}$ are used, the maximum number of lines of length 2 is four, forming a loop and leaving two faces blank. Thus the longest possible unbroken line would have four lines of length 2 and two lines of length $\sqrt{2}$. A possible configuration to achieve this is shown in the diagram. The length of Beatrix's line is then $8 + 2\sqrt{2}$. Note: This path is not a loop but it is not required to be.

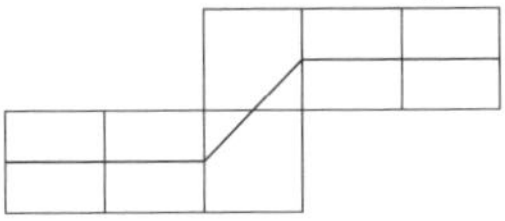

19. **E** Let the centre of the quadrant be O, the centre of the larger semicircle be A and the centre of the smaller semicircle be B. Let the radius of the smaller semicircle be r. It is given that $OA = 1$. The common tangent to the two semicircles at the point of contact makes an angle of 90° with the radius of each semicircle. Therefore the line AB passes through the point of contact, as $2 \times 90° = 180°$ and angles on a straight line sum to 180°. So the line AB has length $r + 1$. This is the hypotenuse of the right-angled triangle OAB in which $OA = 1$ and $OB = 2 - r$. By Pythagoras' Theorem $(2 - r)^2 + 1^2 = (r + 1)^2$, so $4 - 4r + r^2 + 1 = r^2 + 2r + 1$ and therefore $4 = 6r$ and so $r = \frac{2}{3}$.

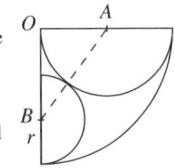

20. **A** It is always possible to draw a circle through three points which are not on a straight line. The smallest circle containing all six squares must pass through (at least) three of the eight vertices of the diagram. Of all such circles, the smallest passes through S, V and Z and has its centre at X. The radius is then $\sqrt{4^2 + 2^2} = \sqrt{16 + 4} = \sqrt{20} = 2\sqrt{5}$.

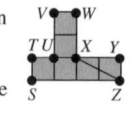

21. **B** The diagram shows that it is possible to draw a square whose edges go through P, Q, R and S. By drawing lines through P and S each making an angle of $60°$ with QR, we can construct an equilateral triangle, as shown, whose edges pass through P, Q, R and S. However there is no circle through these four points. The centre of such a circle would be equidistant from Q and R, and hence would lie on the perpendicular bisector of QR. Similarly it would lie on the perpendicular bisector of PS, but these perpendicular bisectors are parallel lines which don't meet.

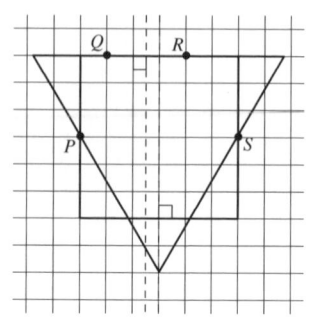

22. **A** The probability that the second marble is blue equals P(2nd marble is blue given that the 1st marble is blue) + P(2nd marble is blue given that the 1st marble is yellow), which is
$$\frac{m}{m+n} \times \frac{m+k}{m+n+k} + \frac{n}{m+n} \times \frac{m}{m+n+k} = \frac{m^2 + mk + mn}{(m+n)(m+n+k)} = \frac{m(m+k+n)}{(m+n)(m+n+k)} = \frac{m}{m+n}.$$
Note: this expression is independent of k.

23. **E** If the graphs of $y = 2x$, $y = 2^x$ and $y = x^2$ are sketched on the same axes it can be seen that case (i) holds for $2 < x < 4$, case (ii) holds for $0 < x < 1$, case (iv) holds for $1 < x < 2$ and case (vi) holds for $x > 4$.
There are no real solutions for case (iii). Consider $x^2 < 2x$, which is true for $0 < x < 2$. However for $0 < x < 2$ it can be seen that $2^x > x^2$ rather than $2^x < x^2$ as stated.
There are no real solutions for case (v). Consider $2x < x^2$, which is true for $x < 0$ or $x > 2$. However, when $x < 0$ we have $2^x > 2x$ as 2^x is positive and $2x$ is negative, rather than $2^x < 2x$ as stated. Also, when $x = 2$ we have $2^x = 2x$, but for $x > 2$, $2^x > 2x$ rather than $2^x < 2x$ as stated.

24. **A** Each of the five expressions can be written in the form $\sqrt{x} - \sqrt{x-1}$, where x is in turn 100, 64, 25, 81 and 49. As $(\sqrt{x} - \sqrt{x-1})(\sqrt{x} + \sqrt{x-1}) = x - (x-1) = 1$, we can write $(\sqrt{x} - \sqrt{x-1}) = \dfrac{1}{(\sqrt{x} + \sqrt{x-1})}$. Since $(\sqrt{x} + \sqrt{x-1})$ increases with x, then $(\sqrt{x} - \sqrt{x-1})$ must decrease with x. Therefore, of the given expressions, the one corresponding to the largest value of x is the smallest. This is $\sqrt{100} - \sqrt{99}$ which is $10 - 3\sqrt{11}$.

25. **B** Let the supplementary angle to α be β. Let tile 1 on the outside of the star polygon be horizontal. Counting anti-clockwise around the star polygon, tile 3 has an angle of elevation from the horizontal of
$\beta - \alpha = 96\frac{2}{3}° - 83\frac{1}{3}° = 13\frac{1}{3}°$. As $360° \div 13\frac{1}{3}° = 27$, we need 27 pairs of tiles to complete one revolution. So there are 54 tiles in the complete pattern.

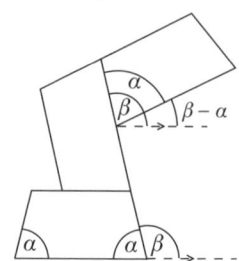

Senior Challenge 2015 solutions

1. **D** The expression $2015^2 - 2016 \times 2014$ can be written as $2015^2 - (2015+1)(2015-1)$ which simplifies, using the difference of two squares, to $2015^2 - (2015^2 - 1) = 1$.

2. **A** Rearranging $6x = \dfrac{150}{x}$ gives $x^2 = \dfrac{150}{6}$, so $x^2 = 25$. This has two solutions, $x = 5$ and $x = -5$. Therefore the sum of the solutions is $5 + (-5) = 0$.

3. **B** When 50 litres of petrol cost £40, 1 litre cost $\dfrac{£40}{50}$ which is 80 pence. More recently, 1 litre cost $\dfrac{£50}{40} = 125$ pence. The percentage increase is then $\dfrac{\text{actual increase}}{\text{original price}} \times 100$ which is $\dfrac{45}{80} \times 100 = \dfrac{450}{8} = 56.25$. So the approximate increase is 56%.

4. **B** Let the radius of the smaller circle be r and so the radius of the larger circle is $2r$. The area of the smaller circle is then πr^2 and the area of the larger circle is $\pi \times (2r)^2$ which is $4\pi r^2$. The fraction of the larger circle which is outside the smaller circle is then $\dfrac{4\pi r^2 - \pi r^2}{4\pi r^2} = \dfrac{3\pi r^2}{4\pi r^2} = \dfrac{3}{4}$.

5. **A** The mean of 17, 23 and $2n$ is given to be n, so $\dfrac{17 + 23 + 2n}{3} = n$ which gives $40 + 2n = 3n$. As n is then 40, the sum of the digits of n is 4.

6. **E** The prime numbers which are the sums of pairs of numbers in touching circles are all odd as they are greater than 2. This means that any two adjacent circles in the diagram must be filled with one odd number and one even number. The number 10 may not be placed on either side of 5, since $10 + 5 = 15 = 3 \times 5$. So either side of the 5 must be 6 and 8. Below 6 and 8 must be 7 and 9 respectively leaving 10 to be placed in the shaded circle at the bottom.

7. **B** Evaluating each option gives

   A $\dfrac{\left(\frac{1}{2}\right)}{\left(\frac{3}{4}\right)} = \dfrac{1}{2} \times \dfrac{4}{3} = \dfrac{2}{3}$ B $\dfrac{1}{\left(\frac{2}{12}\right)} = \dfrac{1}{\left(\frac{1}{2}\right)} = \dfrac{12}{2} = 6$ C $\dfrac{\left(\frac{1}{2}\right)}{4} = \dfrac{\left(\frac{1}{6}\right)}{4} = \dfrac{1}{24}$

   D $\dfrac{1}{\left(\frac{2}{4}\right)} = \dfrac{1}{\left(\frac{8}{3}\right)} = \dfrac{3}{8}$ E $\dfrac{\left(\frac{1}{\left(\frac{1}{3}\right)}\right)}{4} = \dfrac{\left(\frac{3}{2}\right)}{4} = \dfrac{3}{8}$.

   So B has the largest answer.

8. **D** Let the squares in the diagram be labelled as shown. Each of the nets formed from six squares must contain all of R, S and T. The net must also include one of P and Q (but not both as they will fold into the same position), and any two of U, V and W. This therefore gives $2 \times 3 = 6$ different ways.

9. **B** Possible configurations of four different straight lines drawn in a plane are shown here to give 1, 3, 4 and 5 points of intersection respectively. In order to have exactly 2 points of intersection, two of the straight lines would need to lie in the same position and so would not be 'different'.

10. **D** The total of the numbers from 1 to 20 is $\frac{1}{2} \times 20 \times (20 + 1) = 210$. If Milly and Billy have totals which are equal, their totals must each be 105. Milly's total, of the numbers from 1 to n, is $\frac{1}{2}n(n+1)$ so $\frac{1}{2}n(n+1) = 105$ which gives $n^2 + n = 210$. Therefore $n^2 + n - 210 = 0$ which factorises to give $(n + 15)(n - 14) = 0$. As n is a positive integer, $n = 14$.

Senior Challenge 2015 solutions   243

11. C There are several different ways to count systematically the number of towers that Rahid can build. Here is one way.

	All blocks the same size			Exactly two blocks the same size					All blocks of different sizes
	10	6	4	4	6	4	10	6	10	4
	10	6	4	10	10	6	6	4	4	6
	10	6	4	10	10	6	6	4	4	10
Total height	30	18	12	24	26	16	22	14	18	20

So there are nine different heights of tower (as the height of 18cm can be made from $6 + 6 + 6$ or $10 + 4 + 4$).

12. A Each of the three sides of triangle PQR is a tangent to the circle. Two tangents to a circle which meet at a point are of equal length. So QU and QS are of equal length. Similarly $RT = RS$. This means that $\angle QUS = \angle QSU = \frac{1}{2}(180 - \alpha)$ and also $\angle RTS = \angle RST = \frac{1}{2}(180 - \beta)$. At S we can consider the sum of the three angles, so $\frac{1}{2}(180 - \alpha) + \gamma + \frac{1}{2}(180 - \beta) = 180$. Simplifying gives $90 - \frac{1}{2}\alpha + \gamma + 90 - \frac{1}{2}\beta = 180$ and so $\gamma = \frac{1}{2}(\alpha + \beta)$.

13. E

Knave of	Mon	Tue	Wed	Thu	Fri	Sat	Sun	Mon
Hearts	T	T	T	T	L	L	L	T
Diamonds	T	L	L	L	T	T	T	T

When a knave says "Yesterday I told lies" it could be that today he is telling the truth and he did indeed tell lies yesterday. In the table, this is a T preceded by an L.
It could also be that today he is lying, in which case he was in fact telling the truth yesterday. In the table, this is an L preceded by a T. The only day when one or the other of these options applies to each knave is Friday.

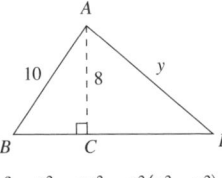

14. E Let the vertices of the triangle be labelled A, B and D as shown. Let the point where the perpendicular from A meets BD be labelled C. The area of triangle ABD is given as 88. As BD is 22, AC must be 8. Considering triangle ABC and using Pythagoras' Theorem gives $BC = 6$. The remainder of the base CD is then $22 - 6 = 16$. Considering triangle ACD and using Pythagoras' Theorem again gives $y^2 = 8^2 + 16^2 = 8^2(1^2 + 2^2) = 8^2 \times 5$. So $y = 8\sqrt{5}$.

15. C Let the original water level in the larger vase be h cm. The volume of water at the start is then $\pi \times 10^2 \times h$ cm^3. The volume of water completely within the vase is constant, but when the smaller vase is pushed down, some of the water moves into it. In the end the depth of the water in the larger vase is the same as the height of the smaller vase itself, which is 16 cm. We are given that the final depth of water in the smaller vase is 8 cm. So the total volume of water is then $\pi \times 10^2 \times 16$ cm^3 less the gap in the top half of the smaller vase. So $\pi \times 10^2 \times h = \pi \times 10^2 \times 16 - \pi \times 5^2 \times 8$, giving $100\pi h = 1600\pi - 200\pi$ and therefore $h = 14$.

16. A Let the six Fnargs in their final positions be denoted by $F_1 F_2 F_3 F_4 F_5 F_6$. There are six choices for F_1. Once this Fnarg is chosen, the colours of the Fnargs must alternate all along the line and so we need only consider the number of heads. There are $3 - 1 = 2$ choices for F_2 as the number of heads for $F_2 \neq$ the number of heads for F_1. There is only one choice for F_3 as F_3 cannot have the same number of heads as F_2 or F_1 (F_3 and F_1 are the same colour and so have different numbers of heads). There is only one choice for F_4 as it is completely determined by F_3 and F_2, just as F_3 was completely determined by F_2 and F_1. There is only one choice for each of F_5 and F_6 as they are the last of each colour of Fnargs. The total number of ways of lining up the Fnargs is $6 \times 2 \times 1 \times 1 \times 1 \times 1$ which is 12.

17. C Let the radius of each of the smaller circles be r and let the centres of the circles be A, B, C and D in order. We are given that $ABCD$ is a square. When two circles touch externally, the distance between their centres equals the sum of their radii. Hence AB and BC have length $r + 1$ and AC has length $1 + 1 = 2$. By Pythagoras' Theorem $(r + 1)^2 + (r + 1)^2 = 2^2$, so $2(r + 1)^2 = 2^2 = 4$ and therefore $(r + 1)^2 = 2$. Square rooting both sides gives $r + 1 = \sqrt{2}$, as we must take the positive root, and so $r = \sqrt{2} - 1$.

18. D Expressed as a product of its prime factors, 10! is
$2 \times 5 \times 3 \times 3 \times 2 \times 2 \times 2 \times 7 \times 2 \times 3 \times 5 \times 2 \times 2 \times 3 \times 2$ which is $2^8 \times 3^4 \times 5^2 \times 7$. This can be written as $(2^4 \times 3^2 \times 5)^2 \times 7$ so the largest integer k such that k^2 is a factor of 10! is $2^4 \times 3^2 \times 5$ which is 720.

19. A Let the length of the side of the smallest square be x cm. So the three squares have sides of lengths x cm, $(x + 8)$ cm and 50 cm respectively. The gradient of PQ is then $\frac{8}{x}$ and the gradient of PR is $\frac{50 - x}{x + x + 8}$. As P, Q and R lie on a straight line, $\frac{8}{x} = \frac{50 - x}{2x + 8}$ so $8(2x + 8) = x(50 - x)$. Expanding gives $16x + 64 = 50x - x^2$ and therefore $x^2 - 34x + 64 = 0$, giving $x = 2$ or 32.

20. E Let the corner of the square about which it is rotated be O and the opposite vertex of the square be A. As the circle is rotated through 180° about O, the vertex A travels along a semicircle whose centre is O. The area coloured black by the ink is then formed from two half squares and a semicircle. The square has side-length 1, so $OA = \sqrt{2}$. The total area of the two half squares and the semicircle is $2 \times (\frac{1}{2} \times 1 \times 1) + \frac{1}{2} \times \pi \times (\sqrt{2})^2$ which is $1 + \pi$.

21. C All of the triangles in the diagram are similar as they contain the same angles. The sides of each triangle are therefore in the ratio 2 : 3 : 4. First consider triangle APM. Let $AP = x$, so that $AM = 2x$. Now considering triangle TBM, as $BT = x$, $BM = \frac{4x}{3}$. The quadrilateral $AMSX$ is a parallelogram as AM is parallel to XS and MS is parallel to AX. So $AM = XS = 2x$. Similarly $QZ = BM = \frac{4x}{3}$. Considering the base of triangle XYZ, $XS + SQ + QZ = 4$. So $2x + x + \frac{4x}{3} = 4$ and therefore $x = \frac{12}{13}$.

22. B $f(x) = x + \sqrt{x^2 + 1} + \dfrac{1}{x - \sqrt{x^2 + 1}} = \dfrac{(x + \sqrt{x^2 + 1})(x - \sqrt{x^2 + 1}) + 1}{x - \sqrt{x^2 + 1}}$. The numerator is $x^2 - (\sqrt{x^2 + 1})^2 + 1 = -1 + 1 = 0$. So $f(x) = 0$. Hence $f(2015) = 0$.

23. D Let a four-digit positive integer be expressed as $1000a + 100b + 10c + d$ where a, b, c and d are all different. In the 24 possible permutations of a, b, c and d, each of the four letters appears in each position six times. Adding all 24 numbers together gives $1000(6a + 6b + 6c + 6d) + 100(6a + 6b + 6c + 6d) + 10(6a + 6b + 6c + 6d) + 6a + 6b + 6c + 6d$. The total is therefore $1111 \times 6(a + b + c + d)$ which factorises to $2 \times 3 \times 11 \times 101(a + b + c + d)$. As $a + b + c + d < 101$, the largest prime factor of the sum is 101.

24. C There are five cards in Peter's set that are printed with an integer that has no prime factors in common with any other number from 1 to 25. The five numbers are 1 (which has no prime factors) and the primes 13, 17, 19 and 23. These cards cannot be placed anywhere in the row of N cards. One possible row is: 11, 22, 18, 16, 12, 10, 8, 6, 4, 2, 24, 3, 9, 21, 7, 14, 20, 25, 15, 5. So the longest row is of 20 cards.

25. C Repeatedly using the rule that $f(xy) = f(x) + f(y)$ allows us to write $f(500)$ as $f(2 \times 2 \times 5 \times 5 \times 5) = f(2) + f(2) + f(5) + f(5) + f(5) = 2f(2) + 3f(5)$. We are given values for $f(40)$ and $f(10)$ and from them we need to calculate the values of $f(2)$ and $f(5)$. Now $f(40)$ can be written as $f(2) + f(2) + f(10)$ so $20 = 2f(2) + 14$ and therefore $f(2) = 3$. Similarly $f(10) = f(2) + f(5)$ so $14 = 3 + f(5)$ giving $f(5) = 11$. So $f(500) = 2f(2) + 3f(5) = 2 \times 3 + 3 \times 11 = 39$.